ISBN 978-0-265-90151-9
PIBN 10906960

FB &c Ltd, Dalton House, 60 Windsor Avenue, London, SW19 2RR.
Company number 08720141. Registered in England and Wales.

0

HISTORICAL RECORDS

OF THE

FIFTY-SEVENTH,

OR,

WEST MIDDLESEX REGIMENT OF FOOT,

COMPILED FROM OFFICIAL AND PRIVATE SOURCES, FROM THE DATE OF ITS FORMATION IN

1755,

TO THE PRESENT TIME,

1878.

With PREFACE and EPITOME, together with the Services of the Honorary Colonels and Lieutenant-Colonels Commanding, and APPENDIX by the EDITOR.

EDITED BY

LIEUT.-GEN. H. J. WARRE, C.B.,

Late Lieut.-Col. Commanding 57th Regt.

WITH PLATES.

LONDON:

W. MITCHELL & CO., 39, CHARING CROSS, S.W.

1878.

ERRATA.

Page 5, line 10, omit '*to*' me.
„ 5, line 18, insert '*to*.'
„ 25, foot-note line 2, insert '*of*' our, &c.
„ 31, line 6, should be North or Hudson.
„ 34, line 8, 'Lieutenant-Colonel Hay McDowal' should be '*McDowall*.'
„ 35, line 2 from bottom, full stop after commotion. While all, &c.
„ 36, line 27, for 'laying,' read '*lying*.'
„ 38, line 9, for '*on*,' read '*upon*.'
„ 41, line 2, after 'of,' insert '*the*.'
„ 42, line 21, after '*and*,' insert '*had*.'
„ 42, line 24, for 'Expediti*ons*,' read 'Expediti*ous*.'
„ 43, line 21, for 'Nimequen,' read '*Nimeguen*.'
„ 45, line 11, read 'amongst.'
„ 45, line 25, read 'bes*ie*ged.'
„ 48, omit parenthesis after D.A.G. and before July.
„ 50, side-date 1811 omitted.
„ 50, lines 7, 13, 21, 24, for 'Houghton,' read '*Hoghton*.'
„ 52, lines 14, 18, for 'Houghton,' read '*Hoghton*.'
„ 53, line 11, for 'suffered,' read '*suffering*.'
„ 56, line 22, for 'Carncross,' read '*Cairncross*.'
„ 59, lines 20, 21, for 'Guadaraina,' read '*Guadarama*.'
„ 59, line 29, for 'Arapileo,' read '*Arapiles*.'
„ 60, line 19, for 'Carncross,' read '*Cairncross*.'
„ 63, line 10, for 'Roncevalles,' read '*Roncesvalles*.'
„ 63, line 25, for 'Pampaluna,' read '*Pampeluna*.'
„ 63, line 29, for 'Zubini,' read '*Zubiri*.'
„ 73, line 19, omit '*the*' before 'Male Convicts.'
„ 81, line 26, 'Henry Townsend Gahan,' should be one name.

Page 81, line 27, for 'Timbra,' read '*Timbrell.*'

„ 93, line 9, for 'Pool,' read '*Poole.*'

„ 110, line 1, for 'Munro,' read '*Monro.*'

„ 114, line 26, for 'Conyer's,' read '*Conyers*'.

„ 131, line 33, for 'Hazatch,' read '*Kazatch.*'

„ 133, lines 26, 27, for 'Hazatch,' read '*Kazatch.*'

„ 136, line 17, for 'Eveliegh,' read '*Evelegh.*'

„ 143, line 18, for 'Major R. D. Logan,' read 'Major R. A. Logan.'

„ 163, line 14, for 'Douglas,' read '*Douglass.*'

„ 210, lines 16, 21, for 'Kenny,' read '*Renny.*'

„ 211, line 24, for 'Fnfield,' read '*Enfield.*'

„ 213, line 22, 'greatly' deleted.

„ 215, line 23, for 'Eyer,' read '*Eyre.*'

„ 233, line 11, for 'Canon Wigley,' read 'Canon *Gregory.*'

„ 234, line 33, for 'Canon Wigley,' read 'Canon *Gregory.*'

„ 263, line 6, for 1855, read 1854.

„ 263, line 24, omit apostrophe and 's after Queen, and read 'the Queen, Apartments at, &c.'

„ 287, line 24, for 'Stagpole,' read 'Stagpool.'

THE FIFTY-SEVENTH,

OR

THE WEST MIDDLESEX

REGIMENT OF FOOT.

CONTENTS.

THE FIFTY-SEVENTH,

OR

WEST MIDDLESEX REGIMENT,

BEARS ON THE REGIMENTAL COLOUR THE FOLLOWING HONOURABLE DISTINCTIONS FOR GOOD SERVICE AND VALOUR DISPLAYED BY THE REGIMENT

IN THE PENINSULA AT

Albuhera,
Vittoria,
Nivelle,
Nive,
Pyrenees,

Crimea,
Inkerman,
Sevastopol,

New Zealand.

As a mark of Her Most Gracious Majesty's special favour, the Queen has ordered that the word "Albuhera" with the "Laurel Wreath," shall be worn on the forage caps and shoulder straps under authority, dated Horse Guards, 3rd October, 1873.

This honourable distinction was originally granted by His Royal Highness, The Prince Regent, on behalf of His (late) Majesty King George III., in 1816.

GOD SAVE THE QUEEN.

SUCCESSION OF COLONELS

OF

THE FIFTY-SEVENTH,

OR

WEST MIDDLESEX REGIMENT.

1743 John Price
1743 The Hon. Thomas Murray
1755 John Arabin
1757 Sir David Cunninghame, Bart.
1765 Sir John Irvine, K.B.
1780 John Campbell
1806 The Rt. Hon. Lord Hutchison
1819 Sir Hew Dalrymple, Bart.
1830 Sir William Inglis, K.C.B.
1835 The Rt. Hon. Sir Frederick Adam, G.C.B.
1843 The Rt. Hon. Viscount Hardinge, G.C.B.
1856 Sir Frederick Love, K.C.B.
1865 Charles R. Fox
1873 Freeman Murray, C.B.
1875 Sir Edward Allen Holdich, K.C.B.

SUCCESSION OF LIEUTENANT-COLONELS

COMMANDING THE

FIFTY-SEVENTH REGIMENT.

1755	
1757	
1758	Lieutenant-Colonel McLeroth
1782	,, Brownlow
1796	Hay McDowall
1796	Balfour
1796	Gledstanes (2nd Batt.)
1797	Picton
1804	William Inglis
1804	MacDonald (2nd Batt.)
1804	MacDonald (1st. Batt.)
1804	Spring (2nd. Batt.)
1804	Thomas Arbuthnot
1809	Octavius Carey
1826	James Allan
1830	Thomas Shadforth
1832	Hartley
1835	Jones, K.H.
1847	H. Shakespear Phillips, C.B.
1848	T. Leigh Goldie, C.B.
1854	Thomas Shadforth
1855	Henry James Warre, C.B.
1867	Edward Bowen
1872	Robert Abraham Logan, C.B.
1877	James Stewart
1878	Chas. Mansfield Clarke

GENERAL ORDERS.

HORSE-GUARDS,
1st January, 1836.

HIS MAJESTY has been pleased to command that, with the view of doing the fullest justice to Regiments, as well as to Individuals who have distinguished themselves by their Bravery in Action with the Enemy, an Account of the Services of every Regiment in the British Army shall be published under the superintendence and direction of the Adjutant-General; and that this Account shall contain the following particulars, viz:—

——The Period and Circumstances of the Original Formation of the Regiment; The Stations at which it has been from time to time employed; The Battles, Sieges, and other Military Operations in which it has been engaged, particularly specifying any Achievement it may have performed, and the Colours, Trophies, &c., it may have captured from the Enemy.

——The names of the Officers, and the number of Non-Commissioned Officers and Privates Killed or Wounded by the Enemy, specifying the place and Date of the Action.

——The Names of those Officers who, in consideration of their Gallant Services and Meritorious Conduct in Engagements with the Enemy, have been distinguished with Titles, Medals, or other Marks of His Majesty's gracious favour.

——The Names of all such Officers, Non-Commissioned

Officers, and Privates, as may have specially signalised themselves in Action.

And,

——The Badges and Devices which the Regiment may have been permitted to bear, and the Causes on account of which such Badges or Devices, or any other Marks of Distinction, have been granted.

By Command of the Right Honourable
GENERAL LORD HILL,
Commanding-in-Chief

JOHN MACDONALD,
Adjutant-General.

PREFACE.

At the special desire of Lieutenant-Colonel James Stewart and the Officers, I have undertaken to superintend the publication of the Records of the Fifty-seventh or "West Middlesex" Regiment.

Having passed some twenty years of my soldier's life in the Fifty-seventh Regiment, and during twelve eventful years—in the Crimea, in India, and in New Zealand—had the honour of commanding it, I feel that although there may be others better fitted for the task, I can yield to none in my love for the Corps, nor in my desire to do full justice to the deeds of the gallant "Die Hards."

" Scattered as is the British Army from India to the " " Pole and from the Pillars of Hercules to the Eastern " " extremity of the earth," the publication of Regimental Records is peculiarly desirable ; first, for their preservation in a compact form; second, that the substance of the voluminous originals, to which few have access, may be made available for the instruction and benefit of all. No argument will better serve to illustrate the necessity of reducing the Records to a portable form than the following detail of movements during the last tour of Foreign Service, viz.—

In 1853 the Regiment left Cork for Corfu.

In 1854 the Regiment left Corfu for the Crimea.

In 1855 on the termination of the Siege of Sevastopol, the Regiment took part in the Expedition to Fort Kinburn at the mouth of the Dnieper River.

In 1856 the Regiment left the Crimea for Malta.

In 1857, 200 Officers and men were sent, viâ Egypt, to Aden.

In 1858 the Regiment left Malta, viâ Egypt, &c., for India.

In 1859 and 1860, the Regiment was employed in India on Field Service, and stationed at five different and distant Garrisons.

In 1860 the Regiment left Bombay for New Zealand, where it arrived early in 1861; and continued to be employed, chiefly on Active Service, until 1867, when it returned to England. During its tour of fifteen years consecutive Foreign Service, it had encircled the world, and been actively employed in seven different countries covering the greater part of the Eastern hemisphere.

In all quarters of the globe the Fifty-seventh has proved that the British soldier "knows not how to yield." His courage and endurance under difficulties and privations, foreign to his nature, have made him worthy of his prototypes; and we may claim for our British Infantry a share in Merivale's admirable tribute to the Roman Legions under the Cæsars, whom he describes as "Brave, patient, resolute and faithful soldiers." " Men deeply impressed with a sense of duty, superior " " to vanity, despisers of boasting, content to toil in " " obscurity, and shed their blood on the frontiers of the " " Empire; unrepining at the cold mistrust of their " " masters—not clamorous for the honours so sparingly " " awarded—but satisfied in the daily work of their hands," " and full of faith in the national destiny which they " " were daily accomplishing."

For the sake of uniformity I have adopted the form of publication initiated by the late Mr. Richard Cannon, Chief Clerk in the Adjutant-General's Office, who was originally appointed under the General Order, dated Horse Guards, 1st January, 1836, to compile the Records of every Regiment in the British Army. This excellent intention, originating with His late

Majesty King William IV., motives of economy have since caused to be abandoned. I have, however, reprinted Mr. Cannon's Introduction to Infantry, and am greatly indebted to him for much valuable information; and, although the present work does not bear the stamp of official recognition, it is published with the concurrence of the Military Authorities, to whom I render my thanks for the interest they have taken in its progress.

To my late brother officers I am also greatly indebted for the kind assistance they have given to me, and more especially have I to thank my old friend Major-General William Inglis, C.B., who served with me in the Regiment, and whose name, as also that of his father, has been associated with the Fifty-seventh for nearly a century. The late Lieut.-General Sir W. Inglis, K.C.B., entered the Regiment in 1780: the particulars of his service, as well as that of his son, will be found in the Records, being far too voluminous and interesting be inserted in a Preface.

In the hope that the publication of the records of the Fifty-seventh will excite a spirit of emulation, and maintain that "*esprit de corps*" so essential to the well-being and discipline of a Regiment, I offer this humble tribute of admiration for the zeal and gallantry of the "Die Hards," to the kind and favourable consideration of my late comrades—believing that by following the example of their predecessors the Colours of the Fifty-seventh will always be unfurled to victory, and—

"Each soldier's name"
"Shall shine untarnish'd on the roll of fame,"
"And stand th' example of each distant age,"
"And add new lustre to th' historic page."

H. J. WARRE,
Lieut.-General.

London,
1*st January*, 1878.

INTRODUCTION AND EPITOME

OF THE OFFICIAL

HISTORICAL RECORDS.

The reduction of the Army in 1748 after the ratification of the treaty of Aix-la-Chapelle caused an alteration in the numbers of the existing Regiments.

Ten Marine Regiments were disbanded, numbered from the 44th to the 53rd inclusive.

Seven lower numbered Regiments, viz.: 54th to 60th (raised in 1741,) took the numbers of the ten Marine Regiments; and on the further reduction of two other Regiments, which had been raised exclusively for service in North America, the old Fifty-seventh became the Forty-sixth.

On the renewal of hostilities in 1755, Colonel John Arabin was commissioned to raise a Regiment of Foot in the counties of Somerset and Gloucester, and the Fifty-seventh permanently became a Regiment of British Infantry.

There is no record to show by what county title it was then called, but in 1782, when county titles were conferred on Infantry Regiments, the Fifty-seventh became, and has since continued to be designated, the "West Middlesex" Regiment.

For two years the Regiment continued on Home Service; it was then embarked on board the ships comprising the British Fleet, and saw sea-service before being landed at Gibraltar. where it continued in garrison, until the treaty of 1763 restored the Island of Minorca to the protection of the British Flag. The Fifty-seventh formed part of that island's defensive force.

Returning to Ireland in 1767, the Regiment was not again actively employed until 1776, when it took part in the indecisive actions in North America, which were terminated in 1782, by England's recognition of the "Independence of the United States."

In 1790 the Fifty-seventh returned to England and remained on home duty until the disasters which befel the Duke of York's Army in 1793-4, enabled the Regiment again to share with Lord Moira's Army "the honourable dangers of active service."

After a short stay in England the Regiment, in 1796, embarked for the West Indies, was present at the attack on and surrender of the Island of St. Lucia, and suffered severely from the effects of that deleterious climate.

In 1803 the Head-quarters (reduced to a mere skeleton by sickness, and the drafts given to other Regiments) landed at Portsmouth.

The disturbed state of Europe rendering an increase necessary to the British Army, Second Battalions were added to many Regiments, and Lieutenant-Colonel W. Inglis was directed to raise a second Battalion for the Fifty-seventh.

From this Battalion, which was never employed on active service, and was eventually disbanded in 1816, the First Battalion was at once completed to its proper strength, and was made ready for further foreign service.

Gibraltar was again the foreign station of the Fifty-seventh, where during 1804 and 1805 the Regiment suffered terribly from the malady and epidemic which decimated the civil population of that fortress.

In 1809 the Regiment landed at Lisbon, and became part of the Army of the Peninsular.

The noble deeds of the Fifty-seventh Regiment are duly recorded in the Official Records, and in the History of the War. The Regiment distinguished itself whenever it came into collision with the enemy; was specially mentioned in Marshal Beresford's dispatches, and brought under the immediate notice of the Duke of Wellington at "Albuhera"; and at the passage of the River "Bidassoa."

On the cessation of hostilities and the restoration of the Bourbons in 1814, the Fifty-seventh was sent to Canada, from whence, in the following year, it was hastily recalled, unfortunately it arrived too late to share in the crowning triumph at Waterloo.

Landing at Ostend in June, 1815, the Fifty-seventh marched to Paris, and during two years formed part of the Army of Occupation in France.

In 1817 the regiment returned to England, and for seven years (ending 1824) it occupied country quarters, chiefly in Ireland.

In 1824 and 1825 the Fifty-seventh embarked by detachments for colonial service in New South Wales.

No event of importance occurred during its six years service in the then penal colony, of which Sydney is now the populous and thriving capital.

In 1830 the Regiment again embarked by detachments for India, and continued to serve in the Madras Presidency until 1846, when, after twenty-two years of consecutive colonial and Indian service, it returned once more to England.

It is worthy of notice, that, as stated in the Regimental Orders of the day, "in order to fortify discipline," "and diminish crime, by giving the Non-Commissioned" "Officers and men an opportunity not only of saving" "their money, but of profitably investing their Indian" "pay and allowances," a Regimental Savings Bank was established in 1832 with most gratifying and important results.

The Regiment in peace, as in war, maintained its high standard of excellence, and was most warmly commended for its appearance under arms, as well as its interior economy and discipline, at all its periodical Inspections.

Before leaving India the last Inspection Order (dated 27th May, 1845) expressed " the Major-General's entire " " approbation of the zealous co-operation of the Officers " " and Non-Commissioned Officers, and his entire assur- " " ance, that should opportunity offer, the Fifty-seventh " " would not fail to add fresh laurels to the already well " " worn and unfading wreath of the 'Die Hards.' "

On its first inspection in England by that gallant and distinguished disciplinarian, the late Adjutant-General, Sir George Brown, G.C.B., the above high eulogium was confirmed. Sir G. Brown considered the Regiment in a " higher state of order and discipline, than any other he " had inspected on arriving from India."

After two years service in England the Regiment was removed to Ireland, where it earned the commendation of the authorities (even of the then Commander in Chief of the Army the late Duke of Wellington) ; and the thanks of the inhabitants on four different occasions, more especially at Enniskillen during a fearful conflagration, which, but for the timely aid, and excellent conduct of the men of the Fifty-seventh, had threatened the destruction of the town.

In 1852, the tour of home service was brought to a close. Prior to the embarkation of the Regiment at Cork early in 1853, New Colours (the gift of Viscount Hardinge, Colonel of the Regiment, and General Commanding in Chief of the Army) were presented by Colonel Thomas Leigh Goldie, its Commanding Officer, who, in a spirited address, reminded the Regiment of its past deeds of glory, and little anticipating the early renewal of hostilities, expressed a hope that the New Colours, "if "not to be adorned with fresh victories, would be kept as "free from taint as those which were now claimed by the "gallant General, whose early fame the Regiment con-"tributed to win."

During 1853, and part of 1854, the Fifty-seventh was quartered in the Ionian Islands.

On the 13th July, 1854, orders were received for the embarkation of the Regiment to join the Army of the East. It was, however, some weeks before transport could be provided, and delays arose from stress of weather and want of coals at Constantinople. In consequence of these unforeseen circumstances, the Fifty-seventh was deprived of the privilege of sharing in the first great victory at the "Alma." It landed on the 25th September, at the Katcha River, joined the Fourth Division under Lieut.-General the Hon. Sir George Cathcart, K.C.B., and marching with the rest of the Army round the head of the harbour, took up its position (on what became known as Cathcart's Hill) on the heights before Sebastopol.

Here the Regiment remained encamped for nearly eighteen months, suffering from the exceptional cold of the winter of 1854, and taking its part in every action and sortie during the long protracted siege.

Its share in the Battle of Balaklava was confined to the support of the Divisional Artillery, on the plains of Kadikoi, where its casualties were not large; but at Inkerman, considering the number of men employed, its return of killed and wounded shows how gallantly the Second Division, in conjunction with small bands from other Regiments similar to that supplied by the Fifty-seventh, resisted the attempt of enormous masses of

Russians to turn the flank of the Allied Army, and force the position, by the dogged maintenance of which, England and France at length drove the enemy from his stronghold in Sebastopol, and terminated the war.

On the 18th June, 1855, four hundred men of the Fifty-seventh were selected to lead the storming party of the English left attack, on the right flank of the Redan; the death of Lieutenant-Colonel Shadforth at the head of his Regiment, and the fact that nine Officers, and 105 Non-Commissioned Officers and men of that "Forlorn Hope," were placed *hors-de-combat*, on the glacis of the work, proves the pluck with which the attempt was made, although from causes beyond Infantry control the attack was unsuccessful; as were also the several attempts made by the French, until on the 8th September, the town became no longer tenable, and was abandoned by the enemy, who blew up his fortresses, and destroyed his works, which had protracted for so long a period this ever memorable seige.

In October, following the evacuation of Sebastopol, the Regiment joined the force of Infantry under the command of Major-General the Hon. Sir Augustus Spencer, K.C.B., and was present at the bombardment and surrender of Fort Kinburn, at the mouth of the Dnieper River, having remained for several days on board the ships of the Allied Fleet of France and England, before Odessa.

The official records give the number of casualties, showing the Regiment's loss in Officers and men during the eighteen months it was employed with the Army of the Crimea. Sickness and overwork in the trenches, where Officers and men were exposed to all the vicissitudes of climate, as well as to the bullets of the enemy, helped to reduce the ranks, nevertheless, the Fifty-seventh embarked for Malta on the 28th May, 1856, with 29

Officers and 751 Non-Commissioned Officers and men, in excellent physique and admirable order, having added the words "Inkerman" and "Sebastopol" to the colors which but three years before Colonel Goldie had presented to the Regiment at Cork.

In the words of the then Secretary of State for War, (in his despatch to the General Commanding) the Fifty-seventh had, with the rest of the Army, "triumphed" "in engagements in which heavy odds were on the" "enemy's side, and carried on under difficulties almost" "incredible, a siege of unprecedented duration, during" "which the trying duties of the trenches, privations" "from straightened supplies, and the fearful diminution" "of its numbers by disease, neither shook its courage" "nor impaired its discipline."

On the termination of the Crimean War (1856), the Fifty-seventh was sent to Malta and remained in that garrison, under the command of the Hero of Inkerman, Lieutenant-General Sir J. L. Penefather, K.C.B., for about two years.

When in 1857 the Mutiny in India so severely taxed the strength of the Army in that country, two Companies of the Fifty-seventh Regiment, under the command of Major Logan, were sent to Aden, in order to release the Indian Troops there quartered, who joined their comrades in India.

As these two Companies were the first British Troops that had passed through Egypt, by what is now so well known as the "Overland Route," it was thought necessary to dress them like civilians, and pack their arms in cases, lest our Allies should take exception to the passage of our Troops through that country. This idea proving fallacious, several Regiments followed in quick succession, but it was not until May 1858, that the Head-quarters of Fifty-seventh under the command of

Colonel Warre, C.B., received the orders, they had been so long expecting, and proceeded by the same route to Bombay.

The two Companies remained at Aden about two years before they joined the Regiment in India. They saw some wild fighting against the Arab Tribes of the surrounding country, who frequently endeavoured to cut off the supply of water, brought from a considerable distance, before Aden was rendered independent by obtaining water by condensation.

The neck of the Indian Mutiny was broken before the arrival of the Fifty-seventh at Bombay; but scattered bands of rebels still harassed the country, causing anxiety to local authorities. As soon as summer clothing could be provided the Regiment was sent to guard the frontier of Kandiesh from the incursion of the Rebel Natives. Here in conjunction with the Poona horse and Bheel Rifles it formed a small brigade, under Colonel Warre's command, encamped upon the banks of the Taptee River, and co-operated with the Central Indian Field Force, under the direction of Lieutenant-General Sir Hugh Rose, K.C.B., who had just completed his splendid march through Central India, during the course of which, he not only dispersed the rebels, but attacked and stormed the strong Forts of Gwalior and Jhansi.

During 1859 and 1860 the Regiment occupied no less than five different stations in the Bombay Presidency. Being re-assembled at last at Poona, in the expectation of returning soon to England, it was suddenly ordered to proceed at once to New Zealand, where reinforcements were urgently required to put down a rising of the Natives.

The Regiment proceeded to New Zealand under command of Major Logan, Colonel Warre having been appointed in the first instance to the command of the

Brigade at Mhow; and, on its reduction, having availed himself of Sir Hugh Rose's kind offer to accompany His Excellency, as Acting Military Secretary, to Bengal; a responsible position, which, on his Regiment being ordered on active service to New Zealand, Colonel Warre immediately resigned.

In New Zealand the Fifty-seventh was employed chiefly on the West and South-West Coasts of the Northern Island.

Arriving at Taranaki (New Zealand) in 1861 in time to witness the closing scenes of a long protracted attempt to drive the rebel natives from their fastnesses on the Waitara River, it found the English settlers unable to cultivate their farms, or live unmolested upon their land. Their homesteads and farms having been destroyed and burnt by the rebel Maories, the families of the settlers were crowded into the small town of New Plymouth.

With the cessation of hostilities in 1861, the troops were reduced, and the Province of Taranaki (under martial law) was left to the protection of the Fifty-seventh Regiment.

Between 1861 and 1863, great political changes took place. The late Governor, Colonel Gore Browne, C.B., was replaced by Sir George Grey, from whose influence with the natives, acquired during a former term of office, great expectations were raised, but on His Excellency attempting, early in 1863, to replace the settlers on their land, a fresh war broke out. Settlers and soldiers fell into "Maori" ambuscades, and were brutally murdered; but, although the Regiment suffered heavily in this savage warfare, where the enemy was seldom visible, it gallantly, during the two following years, drove the Rebels from their strongholds, and rendered the country comparatively safe for occupation.

In 1861, Lieutenant-General Sir Duncan Cameron succeeded Lieutenant-General Sir Thomas Pratt in command of the troops, and in 1865 Sir Duncan Cameron was succeeded by Major-General Sir Trevor Chute, but other disturbed parts of New Zealand claimed their attention; and although Taranaki originated the war, it spread over the Waikato District in the Auckland Province, and extended to Wanganui on the South, and Napier on the East Coast, where some of the most serious fighting occurred.

The Fifty-seventh continued to guard the West and South-west Coasts, gaining much commendation for its gallantry and discipline, but losing both Officers and men in a war of extermination, as lamentable for the Maories as it was demoralising for the settlers and troops employed.

In 1867 the Regiment returned to England, from whence it had been absent since 1853, during nearly the whole of which period it had been employed, more or less, on active service. Prior to leaving New Zealand, the Regiment erected at New Plymouth a Monument to the memory of the Officers and men who had been killed in action with the Maories, or who had died of disease during its term of service in that country.

On its arrival at Liverpool (August, 1867) the Regiment was sent to Manchester, where it helped to preserve the tranquillity of that great emporium during the Fenian disturbances, which culminated in the murder of Police-Serjeant Brett, and the execution of his murderers.

During its stay at Manchester, New Colours to replace those given to the Regiment in 1853, by its late Colonel, Viscount Hardinge, G.C.B., were presented by Lieutenant-General Sir John Garvock, K.C.B., commanding the Northern district.

The old Colours have subsequently been hung in St. Paul's Cathedral, where a beautiful mural marble Tablet has been erected, with brass inscriptions, &c., to the memory of those Officers and men who have fallen in action, during the 15 years that the Regiment was employed on its last tour of duty abroad.

Prior to the removal from Manchester, Colonel Warre, C.B., retired upon half-pay, after twelve years tenure of office in command.

Having served its allotted time in England and Ireland, in 1873 the Fifty-seventh Regiment again proceeded on foreign service, and is now maintaining in Ceylon that high standard of excellence which betokens good discipline, whether in the field or in quarters, ever mindful of Lord Beresford's stirring words, of which it is so justly proud, and with an extract from whose dispatch this short epitome of a Regiment's career during upwards of a century's service may be concluded.

"It is impossible by any description to do justice to" "the distinguished gallantry of the troops, but every" "individual most nobly did his duty, which will be" "proved by the great loss we have suffered through" "repulsing the enemy."

"It was observed that our dead, particularly the" "Fifty-seventh Regiment, were lying as they had" "fought in ranks, and every wound was in front."

"FAMA SEMPER VIVET."

INTRODUCTION

TO

THE INFANTRY.*

THE natives of Britain have, at all periods, been celebrated for innate courage and unshaken firmness, and the national superiority of the British troops over those of other countries has been evinced in the midst of the most imminent perils. History contains so many proofs of extraordinary acts of bravery, that no doubts can be raised upon the facts which are recorded. It must therefore be admitted, that the distinguishing feature of the British soldier is INTREPIDITY. This quality was evinced by the inhabitants of England when their country was invaded by Julius Cæsar with a Roman army, on which occasion the undaunted Britons rushed into the sea to attack the Roman soldiers as they descended from their ships; and, although their discipline and arms were inferior to those of their adversaries, yet their fierce and dauntless bearing intimidated the flower of the Roman troops, including Cæsar's favourite tenth legion. Their arms consisted of spears, short swords, and other weapons of rude construction. They had chariots, to the axles of which were fastened sharp pieces of iron, resembling scythe-blades, and infantry in long chariots resembling waggons, who alighted and fought on foot, and for change of ground, pursuit or retreat, sprang into the

* Introduction to the Infantry, taken from Mr. Cannon's Historical Records of British Army.

chariot and drove off with the speed of cavalry. These inventions were, however, unavailing against Cæsar's legions: in the course of time a military system, with discipline and subordination, was introduced, and British courage, being thus regulated, was exerted to the greatest advantage; a full development of the national character followed, and it shone forth in all its native brilliancy.

The military force of the Anglo-Saxons consisted principally of infantry: Thanes, and other men of property, however, fought on horseback. The infantry were of two classes, heavy and light. The former carried large shields armed with spikes, long broad swords and spears; and the latter were armed with swords or spears only. They had also men armed with clubs, others with battle-axes and javelins.

The feudal troops established by William the Conqueror consisted (as already stated in the Introduction to the Cavalry) almost entirely of horse; but when the warlike barons and knights, with their trains of tenants and vassals, took the field, a proportion of men appeared on foot, and, although these were of inferior degree, they proved stouthearted Britons of staunch fidelity. When stipendiary troops were employed, infantry always constituted a considerable portion of the military force; and this *arme* has since acquired, in every quarter of the globe, a celebrity never exceeded by the armies of any nation at any period.

The weapons carried by the infantry, during the several reigns succeeding the Conquest, were bows and arrows, half-pikes, lances, halberds, various kinds of battle-axes, swords, and daggers. Armour was worn on the head and body, and in course of time the practice became general for military men to be so completely cased in steel, that it was almost impossible to slay them.

The introduction of the use of gunpowder in the

destructive purposes of war, in the early part of the fourteenth century, produced a change in the arms and equipment of the infantry soldier. Bows and arrows gave place to various kinds of fire-arms, but British archers continued formidable adversaries; and, owing to the inconvenient construction and imperfect bore of the fire-arms when first introduced, a body of men, well trained in the use of the bow from their youth, was considered a valuable acquisition to every army, even as late as the sixteenth century.

During a great part of the reign of Queen Elizabeth each company of infantry usually consisted of men armed five different ways; in every hundred men forty were "*men-at-arms*," and sixty "*shot*;" the "men-at-arms" were ten halberdiers, or battleaxe men, and thirty pikemen; and the "shot" were twenty archers, twenty musketeers, and twenty harquebusiers, and each man carried, besides his principal weapon, a sword and dagger.

Companies of infantry varied at this period in numbers from 150 to 300 men; each company had a colour or ensign, and the mode of formation recommended by an English military writer (Sir John Smithe) in 1590 was:—the colour in the centre of the company guarded by the halberdiers; the pikemen in equal proportions, on each flank of the halberdiers: half the musketeers on each flank of the pikes; half the archers on each flank of the musketeers, and the harquebusiers (whose arms were much lighter than the muskets then in use) in equal proportions on each flank of the company for skirmishing.* It was customary to unite a number of companies

* A company of 200 men would appear thus:—

20	20	20	30	20	30	20	20	20
Harquebuses.	Archers.	Muskets.	Pikes	Halberds.	Pikes.	Muskets.	Archers.	Harquebuses.

into one body, called a REGIMENT, which frequently amounted to three thousand men: but each company continued to carry a colour. Numerous improvements were eventually introduced in the construction of fire-arms, and, it having been found impossible to make armour proof against the muskets then in use (which carried a very heavy ball) without its being too weighty for the soldier, armour was gradually laid aside by the infantry, in the seventeenth century: bows and arrows also fell into disuse, and the infantry were reduced to two classes, viz: *musketeers*, armed with matchlock muskets, swords, and daggers; and *pikemen*, armed with pikes from fourteen to eighteen feet long, and swords.

In the early part of the seventeenth century Gustavus Adolphus, King of Sweden, reduced the strength of regiments to 1000 men. He caused the gunpowder, which had heretofore been carried in flasks, or in small wooden bandoliers, each containing a charge, to be made up into cartridges, and carried in pouches; and he formed each regiment into two wings of musketeers, and a centre division of pikemen. He also adopted the practice of forming four regiments into a brigade; and the number of colours was afterwards reduced to three in each regiment. He formed his columns so compactly that his infantry could resist the charge of the celebrated Polish horsemen and Austrian cuirassiers; and his armies became the admiration of other nations. His mode of formation was copied by the English, French, and other European states; but so great was the prejudice in favour of ancient customs, that all his improvements were not adopted until near a century afterwards.

In 1664 King Charles II. raised a corps for sea-service, styled the Admiral's Regiment. In 1678 each company of 100 men usually consisted of 30 pikemen, 60 musketeers, and 10 men armed with light firelocks.

In this year the King added a company of men armed with hand grenades to each of the old British regiments, which was designated the "grenadier company." Daggers were so contrived as to fit in the muzzles of the muskets, and bayonets, similar to those at present in use were adopted about twenty years afterwards.

An Ordnance regiment was raised in 1685, by order of King James II., to guard the artillery, and was designated the Royal Fusiliers (now 7th Foot). This corps, and the companies of grenadiers, did not carry pikes.

King William III. incorporated the Admiral's regiment in the second Foot Guards, and raised two Marine regiments for sea-service. During the war in this reign, each company of infantry (excepting the fusiliers and grenadiers) consisted of 14 pikemen and 46 musketeers; the captains carried pikes; lieutenants, partisans; ensigns, half-pikes; and serjeants, halberds. After the peace in 1697 the Marine regiments were disbanded, but were again formed on the breaking out of the war in 1702.*

During the reign of Queen Anne the pikes were laid aside, and every infantry soldier was armed with a musket, bayonet, and sword; the grenadiers ceased, about the same period, to carry hand grenades; and the regiments were directed to lay aside their third colour: the corps of Royal Artillery was first added to the Army in this reign.

About the year 1745, the men of the battalion companies of infantry ceased to carry swords; during the

---

The 30th, 31st, and 32nd Regiments were formed as Marine corps in 1702, and were employed as such during the wars in the reign of Queen Anne. The Marine corps were embarked in the Fleet under Admiral Sir George Rooke, and were at the taking of Gibraltar, and in its subsequent defence in 1704; they were afterwards employed at the siege of Barcelona in 1705.

reign of George II. Light Companies were added to infantry regiments; and in 1764 a Board of General Officers recommended that the Grenadiers should lay aside their swords, as that weapon had never been used during the Seven Years' War. Since that period the arms of the infantry soldier have been limited to the musket and bayonet.

The arms and equipment of the British Troops have seldom differed materially, since the Conquest, from those of other European states; and in some respects the arming has, at certain periods, been allowed to be inferior to that of the nations with whom they have had to contend; yet, under this disadvantage, the bravery and superiority of the British infantry have been evinced on very many and trying occasions, and splendid victories have been gained over very superior numbers.

Great Britain has produced a race of lion-like champions who have dared to confront a host of foes, and have proved themselves valiant with any arms. At *Crecy*, King Edward III., at the head of about 30,000 men defeated, on the 26th of August, 1346, Philip King of France, whose army is said to have amounted to 100,000 men; here British valour encountered veterans of renown:—the King of Bohemia, the King of Majorca, and many princes and nobles were slain, and the French army was routed and cut to pieces. Ten years afterwards, Edward Prince of Wales, who was designated the Black Prince, defeated, at *Poictiers*, with 14,000 men, a French army of 60,000 horse, besides infantry, and took John I., King of France, and his son Philip prisoners. On the 25th of October, 1415, King Henry V., with an army of about 13,000 men, although greatly exhausted by marches, privations, and sickness, defeated at *Agincourt*, the Constable of France, at the head of the flower of the French nobility and an army said to amount to 60,000 men, and gained a complete victory.

During the seventy years' war between the United Provinces of the Netherlands and the Spanish monarchy, which commenced in 1578 and terminated in 1648, the British infantry in the service of the States-General were celebrated for their unconquerable spirit and firmness;* and in the thirty years' war between the Protestant Princes and the Emperor of Germany, the British Troops in the service of Sweden and other states were celebrated for deeds of heroism.† In the wars of Queen Anne, the fame of the British Army under the great MARLBOROUGH was spread throughout the world; and if we glance at the achievements performed within the memory of persons now living, there is abundant proof that the Britons of the present age are not inferior to their ancestors in the qualities which constitute good soldiers. Witness the deeds of the brave men, of whom there are many now surviving, who fought in Egypt in 1801, under the brave Abercromby, and compelled the French army, which had been vainly styled *Invincible*, to evacuate that country; also the services of the gallant Troops during the arduous campaigns in the Peninsula, under the immortal WELLINGTON; and the determined stand made by the British Army at Waterloo, where Napoleon Bonaparte, who had long been the inveterate enemy of Great Britain, and had sought and planned her destruction by every means he could devise, was compelled

---

* The brave Sir Roger Williams, in his discourse on War, printed in 1590, observes:—"I persuade myself ten thousand our nation would beat thirty thousand of theirs (the Spaniards) out of the field, let them be chosen where they list." Yet at this time the Spanish infantry was allowed to be the best disciplined in Europe. For instances of valour displayed by the British Infantry during the Seventy Years' War, see the Historical Record of the Third Foot, or Buffs.

† *Vide* the Historical Record of the First, or Royal Regiment of Foot.

to leave his vanquished legions to their fate, and to place himself at the disposal of the British Government. These achievements, with others of recent dates, in the distant climes of India, prove that the same valour and constancy which glowed in the breasts of the heroes of Crecy, Poictiers, Agincourt, Blenheim, and Ramilies, continue to animate the Britons of the nineteenth century.

The British Soldier is distinguished for a robust and muscular frame,—intrepidity which no danger can appal, —unconquerable spirit and resolution—patience in fatigue and privation, and cheerful obedience to his superiors. These qualities, united with an excellent system of order and discipline to regulate and give a skilful direction to the energies and adventurous spirit of the hero, and a wise selection of officers of superior talent to command, whose presence inspires confidence,—have been the leading causes of the splendid victories gained by the British arms.* The fame of the deeds of the past and present generations in the various battle-fields where the robust sons of Albion have fought and conquered, surrounds the British arms with a halo of glory; these achievements will live in the page of history to the end of time.

---

* "Under the blessing of Divine Providence, His Majesty ascribes the successes which have attended the exertions of his troops in Egypt to that determined bravery which is inherent in Britons; but His Majesty desires it may be most solemnly and forcibly impressed on the consideration of every part of the Army, that it has been a strict observance of order, discipline, and military system, which has given the full energy to the native valour of the troops, and has enabled them proudly to assert the superiority of the national military character, in situations uncommonly arduous, and under circumstances of peculiar difficulty."—*General Orders in* 1801.

In the General Orders issued by Lieut-General Sir John Hope (afterwards Lord Hopetoun), congratulating the army upon the successful result of the Battle of Corunna, on the 16th of January, 1809, it is stated:—"On no occasion has the undaunted valor of British troops ever been more manifest. At the termination of a severe and harassing march, rendered necessary by the superiority which the enemy had acquired, and which had materially impaired the efficiency of the troops, many disadvantages were to be encountered. These have all been surmounted by the conduct of the troops themselves: and the enemy has been taught, that whatever advantages of position or of numbers he may possess, there is inherent in the British officers and soldiers a bravery that knows not how to yield,—that no circumstances can appal,—and that will ensure victory, when it is to be obtained by the exertion of any human means."

HISTORICAL RECORDS

OF

THE FIFTY-SEVENTH,

OR

WEST MIDDLESEX REGIMENT.

On the termination of the Scotch Rebellion, and the conclusion of Peace by the Treaty of Aix-la-Chapelle (1748), ten regiments, which had chiefly been employed as marines on board the British Fleet, were reduced, and the numerical rotation of the Regiments that still held their place in the British Army, was re-arranged.

The old Fifty-seventh under this new arrangement became the Forty-sixth, and for the time the Fifty-seventh ceased to exist.

When France determined to assist the Canadians to resist the attempt of England to make Canada a British Colony, and the Continent of Europe became again disturbed by the preparations for the continued struggle for power, afterwards known as the "Seven Years War," it became necessary to increase the British Army, and the Fifty-seventh became permanently one of the Regular Regiments of Infantry of the Line.

1755 In 1755 Colonel John Arabin was commissioned to form the Regiment in the Counties of Somerset and Gloucester, and as soon as its numbers were complete the Regiment appears to have been embarked on board the ships forming the British Squadron in the Mediterranean, continuing to serve as marines until 1757, when the Regiment was landed at Gibraltar, where Colonel Arabin died, and was succeeded in command by Major-General Sir David Cunningham, Baronet.

1763 The Regiment continued in that Garrison till the year 1763, when it removed to Minorca, and in 1767 from that Garrison to Ireland.

Sir John Irvine succeeded Sir David Cunningham (deceased 4th November 1765), in command of the Regiment.

1775 In December 1775, the Regiment embarked at Cork, under the command of Lieutenant-Colonel John Campbell. Two companies of the Royal Artillery, the fifteenth, twenty-eighth, thirty-third, thirty-seventh, fifty-fourth, and eight companies of the forty-sixth Regiment, under the command of Major-General Lord Cornwallis, also joined the fleet under Admiral Sir Peter Parker.

1776 On the 12th February 1776, the fleet sailed on an expedition against Charlestown, South Carolina; but having failed in the attack upon Charlestown, the troops being again embarked, sailed for New York, landed on Staten Island where they remained a short time, and embarked on the 26th of August in flat bottomed boats for Long Island. The Battle of Brooklyn was fought on that morning.

After the battle, the Fifty-seventh Regiment was ordered, in the flat boats, to storm Redbank. On its advance the enemy retreated to New York.

The Regiment remained some days at Redbank, was then ordered to embark to take York Island, which was carried with some loss, immediately after this, Colonel Campbell with the Fifty-seventh Regiment, was ordered to attack Powell's Hook, and embarked in flat boats; two frigates covering the landing.

The moment the Regiment was formed on the beach,

it attacked the works; but the enemy had retreated across a swamp to the Jerseys.

1777 In 1777 the Fifty-seventh, with several other Regiments, embarked on board transports, and landed at Crown Point, only eight miles from Fort Montgomery, having sailed up the north or Hudson's River. The enemy having cut down the trees to impede their march, the Force was from eight in the morning to six in the evening marching the eight miles. The Fifty-second and the Fifty-seventh stormed the fort in gallant style. Colonel Mungo Campbell of the Fifty-second Regiment was killed, and Captains Brownlow and Lord Berriedale of the Fifty-seventh were wounded, the loss of Non-Commissioned Officers and men was very great. After destroying the fort and works, the expedition returned to New York.

1778 In 1778 the Regiment was in an expedition against a fort called Britain's Defiance, which failed, and the Regiment returned to New York.

1779 In 1779 a detachment of the Regiment under Major Brownlow was ordered on board the flat boats to land on the Jerseys, in order to attack the Court House at Newark, the enemy having a strong detachment there. At daybreak the troops arrived at the Court House, and executed the duty they were sent upon, retreating to the boats without losing officers or men.

The Regiment was employed on another expedition, with the Seventeenth, Fortieth, Forty-fourth and Colonel Emerick's Corps, to Horse Neck, 30 miles from Kingsbridge, York Island, to destroy the Salt Works there, which duty was completed, but the enemy on their return treated them very roughly.

Major-General Sir John Irvine, K.B., being appointed to the command of a Regiment of Cavalry on the 2nd of November, was succeeded by the Lieutenant-Colonel of the Regiment, Colonel John Campbell; and Major McLeroth was appointed to the Lieutenant-Colonelcy.

The flank companies were formed into separate Battalions.

The light company of the Fifty-seventh was in the 2nd Light Battalion, commanded by Lieutenant-Colonel Abercromby.

1781 This Battalion served the campaign under Lord Cornwallis in Virginia, and were taken prisoners with his Lordship at York Town in October, 1781.

This Battalion wore red feathers, and the light company of the Fifty-seventh continued to wear them, until His Majesty's order for the whole Light Infantry to wear green.*

1782 In 1782 Lieutenant-Colonel McLeroth sold out, the succession going in the Regiment; Major Brownlow to be Lieutenant-Colonel; Captain George Nugent, Major; Lieutenant Charles Irvine, Captain; Ensign William Inglis, Lieutenant.

The promotion appeared in an after General Order by Sir Henry Clinton, dated New York, May 3rd.

The Regiment was then commanded by Major Nugent,

* After the Battle of Brandywine, in 1777, General Washington planted ambuscades to harass and annoy the soldiers of the Royal Army. The Commander of the Forces, General Sir William Howe, having received intelligence that a considerable body of American troops, under General Wayne, was concealed in a wood a short distance from the British Camp, sent Major-General Charles (afterwards Earl) Grey to drive it from its position. At midnight on the 20th September the enemy's bivouack was surprised and assailed. Three hundred American soldiers were killed or wounded, and a considerable number made prisoners, the darkness of the night alone saving the few that escaped. The Americans, enraged at their comrades having fallen into their own trap, declared they would give no quarter to the troops of the Light Battalion. To prevent others not engaged in this night attack from suffering on their account, the soldiers of the Light Companies composing this Battalion dyed their plumes *red*, as a distinguishing mark for the enemy, and as a memorial of the signal success of the expedition. This practice was continued by the Light Companies of the Regiments engaged until they were ordered to wear green.

Lieutenant-Colonel Brownlow being in command of a Battalion of Grenadiers, which on the preliminary Articles of Peace being signed in 1783 was broken up by Sir Guy Carlton, who had succeeded Sir Henry Clinton in the command of the Army; and the companies were sent to rejoin their respective Regiments.

1783 Colonel Brownlow took the command for a short time, when he returned to England on leave of absence.

Major Nugent resuming the command, remained until the Regiment was ordered to Nova Scotia in the end of October, when Captain Thompson took the command.

The Regiment, with several others, embarked and sailed for Halifax, in Nova Scotia; after a boisterous passage of eleven days, it landed and immediately marched to Annapolis Royal, two companies crossing the Bay of Fundy to garrison Fort Howe on St. John's River. One of these companies was afterwards detached to assist in forming Frederick Town, the new capital of New Brunswick, which at that time was separated from Nova Scotia and formed into a New province.

Captain Thompson succeeded to the Majority of the Regiment by purchase, Major Nugent being promoted to the Lieutenant-Colonelcy of another Regiment, date 22nd September, 1783.

1785 In 1785 the Regiment was relieved from the outposts and quartered in the town of Halifax until its embarkation for England; Three companies were detached to Windsor for about a year.

1790 On the 1st of November, 1790, the Regiment sailed for England on board two 44-gun ships, fitted up for troops, head-quarters on board the "*Assurance*," Captain Shortlands, and the "*Argo*," Captain Tatham. The *Assurance* struck sounding on the ninth day, the Head-quarter Companies landed on the fourteenth day, and marched to Hilsea Barracks. The *Argo* passed her port and was a week beating between the French Coast and Beachey Head before she arrived at Spithead.

1791 From Hilsea Barracks, in the Spring of 1791, the Regiment marched to Chesterfield (riots being expected at Sheffield,) the Regiment still under the command of Major Thompson.

After remaining a few weeks, it continued its march to Tynemouth Barracks, where Lieut.-Colonel Hay McDowal, from the Seventy-third Regiment, joined, having succeeded to the Lieutenant-Colonelcy of the Regiment, vice Brownlow, who sold out. It remained there during the winter, and was inspected by General Grant, after having had an independant company drafted into it.

1792 In the Spring of 1792, the Regiment marched to Edinburgh Castle, and received another independant company.

1793 The Regiment after being inspected by the Commander-in-Chief, Lord Adam Gordon, embarked at Leith for Portsmouth, and put into the Downs. While lying there, windbound, the *Brilliant* frigate, Captain Mark Robinson, hove in sight and signalled the retreat of His Royal Highness the Duke of York from before Dunkirk, and his want of assistance. The signal for the transports to weigh was immediately made, and after a short run they entered Ostend Harbour. On the 15th September the Regiment landed and marched, with the Sixteenth Infantry, and a Detachment of the Forty-second, under the command of General Coates, of the Nineteenth Infantry, to join the Duke of York at Tourhout.

On the following morning the whole army marched to Menin, where the Regiment was brigaded with the Nineteenth, Twenty-seventh and Twenty-eighth Regiments, commanded by Major-General Steward of the Buffs, General Coates having been removed to Ostend.

After remaining some weeks in camp with the Army,

the Brigade marched by Ypres and Dixmude to Ostend, and embarked to return to England. The troops were detained some time on board the transports, the enemy having besieged Nieuport.

Sir Charles Grey, who had embarked part of the troops, composing his expedition to the West Indies, at Spithead, sailed for the relief of Nieuport. On his arrival off that port he ordered the light companies from the Regiments embarked at Ostend, with the Forty-second Regiment, to reinforce the Garrison; landing part of his own force, with the intention of attacking the enemy in their camp, at day-break the following morning. The enemy however retreated in confusion during the night.

Nieuport being relieved, the troops returned to their transports, sailed for Portsmouth, and were ordered to join the army forming under Lord Moira, who was appointed Commander of a Force intended to co-operate with the Royalists in Brittany. This expedition shortly afterwards sailed for the French Coast (Admiral McBride having the naval command;) but the frigate sent to reconnoitre the coast being fired upon by the batteries, the expedition returned to Spithead, and the Fifty-seventh Regiment remained for some time on board ship at East Cowes, Isle of Wight. In consequence of the long confinement on board crowded transports, a malignant fever broke out and the whole of the troops were landed. The Fifty-seventh was quartered at West Cowes and
1794 afterwards at Newport. In the spring the whole expedition was collected and encamped at Netley, on the Southampton River, the transports remaining in attendance.

About midnight of the 20th of June, a violent thunder storm, with torrents of rain, put the whole camp in commotion, while all were busily employed in keeping their blankets, &c., from the flood, the account of the

Duke of York's retreat, and that he wanted assistance, was communicated to Lord Moira, who ordered the troops instantly to embark, and in a few hours the whole expedition sailed through Lord Howe's Fleet, lying at anchor at Spithead, and showing evident marks of the severe conflict of the 1st June, from which engagement Lord Howe had just returned, victorious.

1794 On the 26th of June, 1794, after a short run, Lord Moira arrived at Ostend, with 7,000 men, consisting of the Nineteenth, Twenty-seventh, Twenty-eighth, Fortieth, Forty-second, Fifty-fourth, Fifty-seventh, Fifty-ninth, Eighty-seventh, and Eighty-ninth Regiments, which were encamped on the Sand Hills.

The General Officers employed were Major-General William Crosbie, Brigadier-Generals Charles Graham, Lord Cathcart, and Peter Hunter.

The Fifty-seventh was in Hunter's Brigade, with the Fortieth and Fifty-ninth Regiments.

On the evening of the 28th Lord Moira gave orders to the troops to stand to their arms, marched them through the town, crossed the ferry, and halted within two miles of Ostend; the officers leaving their clothing and camp equipage behind, expecting to be encamped the following day.

About two o'clock the next morning the Army was on its march, passing through Bruges to the Camp de Malle. The troops halted that night, laying in their ranks, expecting momentarily to be attacked, knowing the enemy to be in force close to them. The presence of mind of Major-General W. Ellis Doyle was the cause of their not being attacked. In making requisitions, as Quartermaster General, he thought the Burgomaster of Bruges was very anxious to learn the strength of the force under Lord Moira's command.

General Doyle therefore ordered the Burgomaster to

prepare rations for 15,000 men for that evening, and to be ready with 15,000 more, for the men who were being disembarked at Ostend, who would arrive at Bruges on the following morning. This information was communicated and credited by General Vandamme, who refrained from interfering with so large a force.

On the 30th the Force marched by Ecloo to Ostaker, within three miles of Ghent, whence they joined General Walmoden, and remained for three days in very inclement weather, without tents, or even the ordinary requirements for the Officers.

On the 3rd July, Lord Moira left Ostaker, and on the 6th arrived at Alort. Here Colonel Doyle was wounded, a patrol of the enemy's cavalry, having been mistaken for the cavalry of Hesse Darmstadt. About 40 of the 8th Light Dragoons drove the enemy from the market-place, where they had penetrated before their identity was discovered.

On the 7th, the Duke of York met Lord Moira's column at Malines. After the Duke had passed it crossed the Neith, and encamped at Kouticq.

The Army under Lord Moira had undergone unusual fatigue: neither officers nor men having been in either tent or house from the time of their landing, on the 26th June.

On the 12th July, in the afternoon, the enemy attacked all the outposts occupied by the advanced corps in front of the canal leading from Brussels to Antwerp; and being greatly superior in numbers, drove them into Malines, upon which they fired, but on a reinforcement coming up under the Earl of Moira, the enemy retired with some loss.

On the 13th July they renewed the attack and succeeded in obliging the posts on the left of Malines to abandon the canal and retire from the dyke; Lieut.-

General Dalwich with the hussars fell back on Walheim, where he took up a position to cover that part of the river; Lord Moira was posted at the village of Duffil, while General Walmoden was detached to Lierre. There was constant skirmishing.

On the 15th July, at daybreak, an attack was made on the left of Malines; at the same time the enemy advanced another column to attack Lord Moira's Army, on which he detached a Regiment of Infantry, with the Eighth, Fifteenth, and Sixteenth Light Dragoons, who compelled it to retire with great loss. The force was commanded by Colonel Churchill, who met the French Colonel and cut him down.

On the 16th July, constant skirmishing at the outposts.

On the 20th July, Lord Moira's Army was informed by the following order that he had been ordered home, to be succeeded by Lieutenant-General Abercromby.

Never did an Army part with a Commander, nor a Commander with an Army, with greater regret. Lord Moira issued the following Order:—

"Lord Moira cannot surrender his command without "entreating the Officers, Non-Commissioned Officers and "men of the Corps which accompanied him from Ostend, "to accept his warmest and most grateful thanks for the "kind and cheerful acquiescence he has experienced from "them in the severe fatigues to which he was obliged to "subject them.

"He has the assurance that he is still to have their "support in the service for which they were originally "destined, and that hope lessens his reluctance at ceasing "for the present to share the honourable dangers of "service.

"He trusts they will believe that no light considera- "tion would have obliged him to quit them; for he "persuades himself they are sensible of his having "endeavoured to repay the generous attachment they "have shown to him by the most lively interest for their "welfare. For the present he bids them farewell, and "with the most fervent prayers for their honour and "prosperity."

As a great majority of Lord Moira's Army could not be acquainted with the cause of the extraordinary fatigues they had undergone, and as it appears that his Lordship wished to give them every information on that head, the following address was circulated in his Army after his departure.

"Lord Moira is so solicitous to possess the good "opinion of the professional Officers whom he has had "extraordinary reason to esteem, that he must beg leave "to explain some circumstances relative to the march of "his corps from Ostend.

"From the well-known situation of the place, it "appeared that protection could not be ensured by "any reinforcement of the garrison, but must be effected "by measures which would probably entail battle.

"That he might share the danger of such a contest "with troops to whom he is so fervently attached, Lord "Moira resolved to embark, notwithstanding that he "had before told His Majesty's Ministers that any orders "for his serving in Flanders must occasion his immediate "resignation.

"Ostend seemed secured by the debarkation of the "troops, and the object of his mission was completed, "had events proved favourable in other parts. The day, "however, after the landing, Lord Moira heard so much "respecting the state of affairs in the country, that he "thought he could not honestly confine his attention to "the service exactly assigned to him. He, therefore, took "upon himself to write to General Clairfait, and to

" General Walmoden, proposing a junction of their " forces, in order that they might act from Bruges to " Thielt, upon the left wing of the French.

" This measure would have covered Ostend, at the " same time that the consequence of it as to lightening " the pressure on the Duke of York, could not but be " very important.

" General Clairfait eagerly adopted the idea, but " made it a condition that Lord Moira should singly " possess himself of the City of Bruges, before he " (General Clairfait) should move.

" The condition was nice, as Lord Moira had " not time to land any heavy cannon, and the move " would be impracticable, were it not made before the " French in that neighbourhood received the reinforce- " ment they hourly expected, so that the corps at " Wingham (which had only six miles to march to " Bruges, whilst Lord Moira had twelve) might, by " throwing a thousand men into the town, defeat the " attempt of seizing it, and would thereby oblige Lord " Moira to form the junction with the Austrians by Sluys " or Sas-de-Gand, or return to Ostend, leaving the rest " of Flanders to its fate.

" The enterprise was, however, undertaken.

" On the road to Bruges Lord Moira received by an " Estafette a letter from the Duke of York, which had " come by Sluys, desiring that Lord Moira would embark " his whole force, and join His Royal Highness by way " of Antwerp. The other project was too far advanced " to leave room for obedience to this order. Bruges was " luckily secured; but at the very gates of it Lord " Moira was overtaken by Captain Clinton, who came " by way of Sluys, Blankenburg, and Ostend, from " the Duke of York and General Clairfait. The " message from the Duke was to know whether

" Lord Moira could not undertake to march by Sluys " and Sas-de-Gand (the other road appearing out of " question to His Royal Highness), so as to join the " Duke's army more rapidly than the passage by sea " would allow.

" From Clairfait there was a declaration that, on " account of Coburg's defeat, he could not fulfil any " engagement with Lord Moira, and that he expected to " leave Ghent in a few hours. From General Walmoden " there was not any letter or information.

" Lord Moira, from the urgent tenor of the Duke of " York's message, and from the apprehension of possible " difficulties to His Royal Highness's army, should " General Clairfait be ordered by Prince Coburg to " retire, resolved to push forward by the route of Ecloo " and Ghent, notwithstanding that he had no longer " the appearance of co-operation, in an attempt to pass " through Bruges to the Camp-de-Malle.

"This variation from the original purpose discon- " concerted all the plans which had been arranged for " the support and convenience of the Corps, for it had " been settled with Colonel Vyse that the baggage should " be forwarded by the canal from Ostend to Bruges, the " latter being destined to be made the store and magazine " for the Army as long as it should be in the direction " intended.

" The case seemed to leave no room for hesitation " under all the inconvenience impending from privation " of baggage, and the obvious danger from the want " of reserve ammunition, but the embarrassment which " threatened the Duke of York, demanded that an " immediate junction should be attempted.

" The evacuation of Ostend and the transmission of " baggage through Sas-de-Gand was therefore im- " mediately determined upon.

"From Malle, Lord Moira sent to apprise General "Walmoden that he should continue his march next "day to Ecloo, requesting such movements on the part "of that General as could be made without hazard, to "impress the enemy with a suspicion of a projected "attack, and he took every possible measure to circulate "an exaggerated account of his own force and to obtain "accurate intelligence of the approach of the enemy.

"The exertion of General Walmoden upon this "occasion cannot be too gratefully acknowledged, as he "was not in any manner pledged to give the assistance "he furnished.

"The march was undertaken without any confidence "of such support. Lord Moira was greatly encouraged "to run the risk by the consideration that should he find "himself overpowered, Sluys would still be open to him "to retire upon when he had reached Maldegbrem.

"The rapidity of the march fortunately exposed "nothing to chance, though he has since been informed "that the enemy's Generals had orders to strike at the "Corps at all events, and taken every preliminary measure "for the purpose.

"Whether any service was rendered to the Army of "the Duke of York by the movement and expeditions "junction is not here the consideration, Lord Moira's "sole object being to explain the circumstances under "which the Corps suffered in that march, so that "it may not appear that it was lightly or unnecessarily "imposed."

1794 On the 22nd July, the Army marched towards Bergen-op-Zoom, they passed close by Antwerp which was evacuated in the evening, when a vast quantity of stores was destroyed to prevent their falling into the hands of the enemy. The British Troops encamped on the 24th on the plain near Rosendale, where they remained until the 4th of August, when the Duke of York's Army marched to the plain of Breda, Head-quarters at Osterhout.

Here Lord Moira's Troops received their Tents, of which they had been deprived since their landing at Ostend, on the 26th June. Nevertheless, the men were as healthy as any part of the British Force.

On the 28th of August the enemy attacked the British outposts in great force and drove them in, on which the Duke of York held a Council of War, and that evening retreated, and took up a position within four miles of Bois-le-Duc, where the Army remained unmolested until the 14th of September, when the enemy again drove in the outposts; on the 15th the Duke of York retreated, and on the following day crossed the Meuse.

The Fifty-seventh was brigaded, under Major-General De Burgh, with the Eighth, the King's, Forty-fourth, and Eighty-eighth.

1795 The 57th continued to serve in Flanders and Holland till May 1795, during which time the Regiment formed part of the Garrison of Nimequen during the siege; its post was the covered way, both fires passing closely over the men's heads; but the loss was only one man killed by a dead shell.

The Army was obliged to evacuate Nimequen, the bridge of boats across the Lack being nearly destroyed by the enemy's fire, and took up its winter quarters on the opposite bank, to defend the passage of the river.

The Duke of York in a general order informed the Army that there was to be a winter campaign, and directed the commanding Officers of Regiments to provide warm clothing for the comfort and health of the men, deviating from His Majesty's Regulations for clothing as might be necessary. Captains Balfour and Inglis, with the Quarter-Master, proceeded to Rotterdam, and provided blue cloth trousers and gaiters, with warm stockings and a supply of shoes, these precautions being taken, the 57th bore the winter campaign, as well as the hazardous and calamitous retreat through Holland and Westphalia, without any loss; and embarked at Bremerlee for Portsmouth, where it rejoined Lord Moira's Army, and in the summer it embarked and sailed with the expedition for Quiberon, with two Brigades commanded by Major-Generals Charles Graham and Alexander Campbell. The 57th was brigaded with the 12th and 28th in Campbell's Brigade. Having been obliged to put into Plymouth by adverse winds, His Majesty's ship *Anson*, Captain Durham, brought the melancholy account of the disaster that had befallen the Royalists, the two Brigades in consequence relanded, and were encamped with the Army, which was collected at Nutshaling, near Southampton.

The object of Lord Moira's expedition being now at an end, he gave up the Command to Sir Ralph Abercromby, who was preparing an expedition for the West Indies; previous to its embarkation the 101st Regiment was drafted into the 57th, which made it up to nearly 1,000 strong.

Before Sir Ralph assumed the command, the Army was reviewed by the Prince of Wales, attended by His Royal Highness the Duke of York.

1795 In October, 1795, the Fifty-seventh Regiment embarked on board H. M.'s ship the *Commerce-de-Marseilles,* Captain Child, and after being detained for some weeks at St. Helen's by contrary winds, sailed and encountered the dreadful and destructive gales which Admiral Sir H. C. Christian's Fleet experienced, and was compelled to bear up for Portsmouth. The ship not being considered seaworthy, the Regiment was moved from the *Commerce-de-Marseilles* into three

44-gun ships, the *Adventure*, Captain W. Rutherford, Lieutenant-Colonel William Balfour, commanding the Regiment; *Ulysses*, Lieutenant . . . . Lieutenant-Colonel Gledstanes; and, the *Charon*, Captain Stevenson, Major Inglis. A second time the Regiment sailed for the West Indies.

The Fleet was again unfortunate, being dispersed in a severe gale, which lasted without intermission for six weeks; many vessels were obliged to put back in distress, while others made good their passage out, amougst the latter was the *Charon*, with three Companies of the Fifty-seventh, under the command of Major Inglis.

The *Adventure* and *Ulysses*, with the remainder of the Regiment, after a fruitless struggle, returned to Portsmouth, and this part of the Regiment was landed at East Cowes, Isle of Wight, where during its stay it had about 200 men of the Eighth Regiment drafted into it.

1796 The Regiment embarked again in May, under the command of Lieutenant-Colonel Gledstanes, Colonel Balfour being left behind, sick. Head-Quarters on board the *Ulysses*, and Major Frederick Buller on board the *Highland Lass*, sailed a third time, and after a pleasant passage of six weeks, arrived at Barbadoes, and proceeded to Saint Lucia, then beseiged by Sir Ralph Abercromby, and joined Major Inglis, who with his detachment, and one of the Sixty-third Regiment, was under the command of Brigadier-General John Moore.*

The Light Company, on one occasion, was detached under Brigadier General John Hope, who expressed himself highly pleased with its gallant conduct.

After the surrender of St. Lucia, the Regiment proceeded to Grenada, then in a state of insurrection;

* Afterwards Lieut.-General Sir John Moore, who was killed at Corunna, 1809.

it remained till tranquillity was restored, and received the thanks of Brigadier General Moore for its steady conduct, and his regret at losing it from under his command.

The Regiment received drafts from the 8th and 10th Regiments, which made its strength 1,131 men.

After getting into settled quarters in the Town of Gouyave or Charlotte Town, it suffered dreadfully from the epidemic of the country, and in nine months lost many officers and upwards of 700 men.

1797 In 1797 the Regiment proceeded to Trinidad, where the 2nd (Queen's) Regiment was drafted into it, and remained stationary for six years under the command of Colonel Picton.*

1803 In 1803 the Regiment was drafted, and the skeleton, with that of the Fourteenth Infantry, embarked on board H.M. Ship the *Excellent*, Captain Nash. After a most expeditious passage the Regiment landed at Gosport, and marched to Winchester Barracks; and in June following to Silver Hill, Sussex, where it was brigaded with the Fourteenth, Thirty-ninth, and Eighty-eighth Regiments, under Major-General McKenzie Fraser.

On the war breaking out again the Army of Reserve was raised, and a second Battalion added to the Regiment.

The 57th marched to Ashford to receive the men. The Second Battalion was formed by Brevet Lieutenant-Colonel Inglis, who, after that duty was performed, gave over the command to Brevet Lieutenant-Colonel Ross (Major-General half-pay 62nd Regiment) and re-joined the 1st Battalion.

1804 The 1st Battalion, being completed with unlimited service men, embarked on the 1st April, 1804, at Ramsgate for Guernsey, three Companies being detached

* Afterwards Lieutenant-General Sir Thomas Picton, K.C.B.

to Alderney, under Lieutenant-Colonel Inglis, which re-joined the Regiment in June.

Lieutenant-Colonels Balfour and Gledstanes were promoted to the rank of Colonel, and employed on the staff in 1803.

Brevet Lieutenant-Colonel Inglis succeeded Colonel Balfour in the Regimental Lieutenant-Colonelcy on the 16th August, with the command of the First Battalion, and Lieutenant-Colonel McDonald from the half-pay of the Fifteenth Infantry, succeeded Colonel Gledstanes in the command of the Second Battalion.

1805 On the 13th of October, 1805, the Second Battalion embarked at Ramsgate for Jersey, and landed on the 13th November following, where it remained until the 16th August, 1811, landed at Gosport on the 23rd of the same month, and remained quartered in England till its disbandment in 1816.

In October, 1804, the First Battalion embarked for Gibraltar; the transports being overcrowded the Regiment was landed on the Isle of Wight, and was detained there on account of the dreadful fever which was raging at Gibraltar. In November the Regiment, under Lieutenant Colonel Inglis, sailed for its destination, but it did not land until the 22nd January, 1805, when the sickness had somewhat abated. The Regiment remained for four years at Gibraltar, with little variation except the usual changes of quarters.

1806 Major General Lord Hutchinson, Colonel vice Campbell deceased, 8th September, 1806.

1809 On the 9th of July 1809, the Regiment embarked for the Peninsula.

The First Battallion of the Fifty-seventh Regiment, under the command of Lieutenant-Colonel Inglis, landed at Lisbon on the 17th July, and encamped at Alcantara.

The following five Regiments were placed under the orders of Brevet-General Catlin Crawford:—Second Battalion Twenty-eighth, Lieutenant-Colonel the Honourable A. Abercromby; Second Battalion Thirty-fourth, Lieutenant-Colonel Maister; Second Battalion Thirty-ninth, Lieutenant-Colonel Nilson; Second Battalion Forty-second, Lieutenant-Colonel Lord Blantyre; First Battalion Fifty-seventh, Lieutenant-Colonel Inglis; attached to which were about 500 men from the Hospital at Belem to join their respective Regiments.

On the 29th the Fifty-seventh Regiment embarked in boats and sailed up the Tagus as far as Vellada, marched from thence to Santarem, and on the 2nd reached Abrantes, where the several Regiments united.

It was the Brigadier's intention that the whole should go by water to Abrantes, to save the long march, but the want of water in the Tagus prevented its execution.

From Abrantes the division marched for the Spanish Frontier by the following route, Grivao, on August 5th (on the march the division was joined by Captain F. Cockburn, D.A.G.), who had just left the Army, and gave the information of the battle of Talavera (July 27th and 28th), Nisa on the 6th, crossed the Tagus at Villa-Velha on the 10th, Castello-Branco on the 11th, Bivouac Lodociro on the 12th, Zibriera on the 13th, Salvaterra on the 13th, Sarza La Mayor on the 14th.

The Brigadier having received information that Soult had been detached with a strong force, against him on the 15th, retrograded with great speed on Nisa, which he reached on the 20th August, took post, and remained until the Army got into cantonments.

On the 7th of September the division marched to Elvas by the following route, Alpalpas, Portalegre, Arronches, and on the 10th arrived at Elvas, from which place, on the following morning, the five Regiments marched to join the Brigades to which they were appointed. The Fifty-seventh to the Second Brigade, Brigadier-General Richard Stewart, at Puebla-de-la-Calcada, in Spanish Estremadura, consisting of the Twenty-ninth Regiment and the First Battalion Forty-eighth, in the Second Division, under Major-General Hill.

On the 14th December the Army retired into Portugal. The Second Division was quartered in Portalegre, remaining there for some months, the cavalry in cantonments, during which time the movements of the enemy occasioned the division many marches and counter-marches.

1810 The Fifty-seventh afterwards was cantoned in the villages of Montalvas and Arinonira, Major-General Richard Stewart being with the Twenty-ninth and Forty-eighth at Punhete.

On the 2nd of August the division took up its ground at the village of Sarcedes.

On the 7th Major-General the Honourable William Stewart was appointed to the command of the Second Division under General Hill.

On the 13th Colonel Inglis took the command of the Brigade in consequence of the illness of Major-General Richard Stewart.

On the 16th of September the Division marched from Sarcedes, and on the Twenty-third took up a position on the left bank of the Mondego, near Pena-Cova, on the 26th crossed the Mondego, and joined the main body of the Army under Lord Wellington. On the next morning (27th September,) the Battle of Busaco was fought.

On the following day the enemy was observed to be in motion on the road over the mountain towards the Vouga on the Oporto road.

Lord Wellington, therefore, re-crossed the Mondego, and retreated to the Lines (of Torres Vedras) he had ordered to be constructed in front of Lisbon, having his right on the Tagus at Alhandra, and his left on the sea.

The Second Brigade took post at the Village of Sobral Piquins, on 10th of October, where Major-General Houghton took the command, being appointed in the room of General Stewart, deceased.

The Brigade then became the Third.

On the 11th the Army formed in the lines of Torres Vedras, and the Regiments were made acquainted with their alarm posts.

On the 16th General Houghton's Brigade marched from the lines to Carregado, and on the 18th to Valado, where it crossed the Tagus to Mugem, on the 19th to Chamusca, where it remained in cantonments till the retreat of the enemy from Santarem and our pursuit.

1811 During the night of the 5th of March Marshal Massena retreated from his position at Santarem, pursued by Lord Wellington, when Colonel Inglis again commanded the Brigade (General Houghton having been appointed to a corps consisting of his own Brigade and a Brigade of Portuguese, under Lieutenant-Colonel Collins). Major-General Houghton followed in pursuit of the enemy as far as Condexia, when he was ordered to recross the Tagus, and join the Corps placed under the orders of Marshal Beresford.

The Marshal advanced against Campo Mayor, and found the enemy's corps, consisting of four Regiments of Cavalry, three Battalions of Infantry, and some Horse Artillery, drawn up on the outside of the Town. Two Squadrons of the Thirteenth Dragoons, and two Squadrons of Portuguese charged the French Cavalry, who were broken and pursued to Badajos; the Infantry effected their retreat in a solid body, although with considerable loss, and recovered sixteen pieces of cannon, which had been taken by the Allied Cavalry.

On the 4th April the Second Division marched by Villa Viciosa and Borba, and encamped on the Ribeira de Mores, about one and a-half miles from Jeramenha.

About two o'clock p.m. the Bridge of Casks over the Guadiana being completed, the Second Division commenced crossing the river, and took up a position upon the heights near Villa Real, where, on the 8th, the whole of the Marshal's Corps were united.

The Second Division continued its movements, and on the 9th encamped near Olivença; on the 10th, Valverde; 12th, Albuhera; 15th, Santa Martha; 16th, Los Santos (where an affair of Cavalry took place) and Zapa.

Major-General Cole, with the Fourth Division, remained before Olivença, which surrendered at discretion on the 15th.

The Second Division remained about Zapa a few days in cantonments, and on the 20th marched to Almendrajo, where they remained till the 6th of May, when it moved towards Badajos for the purpose of besieging that Fortress.

On the 7th May, Marshal Beresford invested that place, and on the following day the batteries were opened on Fort St. Christoval, and a very brisk fire was returned from the Garrison.

On the 12th May, the Marshal received intelligence that Marshal Soult was advancing from Seville, joined by the Corps under General Latour Maubourg, to attack the Allied Army, with the intention of relieving Badajos.

General Beresford immediately suspended his operations, sending his heavy artillery and stores to Elvas, and with his whole Corps marched to meet the enemy, taking up a position near the Village of Albuhera on the 15th.

The battle of Albuhera was fought on the 16th May.

At 8 o'clock in the morning some skirmishing and cannonading commenced, and at about 9 a heavy French column advanced upon the Bridge, and Village of Albuhera, whilst another crossed the river and made an impetuous attack on the Spaniards, who were compelled to retire after a brave resistance.

The 2nd Division Major-General the Hon. William Stewart, was ordered up to their support, and formed the Second Line.

On this occasion the Fifty-seventh made part of the Central Brigade under Major-General Houghton.

This Brigade consisted of the Twenty-ninth; First Battalion, Forty-eighth; and First Battalion, Fifty-seventh; the latter Regiment being in the centre.

The Spaniards in the First Line were at this time warmly engaged.

Although occasionally disparaging the genius of Marshal Beresford as a Commander, Sir W. Napier in his history of the war, gives him full credit for zealous activity and courage in the field and does the fullest justice to the British Infantry who, against heavy odds, so bravely stood their ground.

The Spaniards in the first line had been very hotly engaged and were being forced back, when General Stewart's Division, of which Houghton's Brigade formed part, was ordered by Colonel Hardinge to hold the crest of the hill. General Houghton was killed early in the day, and the command of the Brigade devolved upon Lieut.-Colonel Inglis of the Fifty-seventh. The astonishing firmness with which the position was held succeeded in checking the French columns, and the arrival of General Coles' Division and Abercrombie's Brigade secured the victory. The casualties on both sides were enormous, but although "the streams flowed with blood" (the rain descending heavily during the latter part of the engagement) the victory was won, and "fifteen hundred "unwounded men, the remnant of six thousand uncon-"querable British soldiers, stood triumphant on that fatal "hill."

Colonel Inglis, 22 officers and more than 400 men, out of 570 that had gone into action, were placed *hors de combat* in the Fifty-seventh alone, the other Regiments suffered nearly as heavily. The remains of the Fifty-seventh Regiment were marched off the field of battle, under the command of Lieutenant and Adjutant Mann, who at the commencement of the action was the fourteenth officer in rank. Early in the day the staff of the King's colour was broken and received 17 shots, and the Regimental colour was pierced by 21 shots during the action. Ensign Jackson, carrying the King's colours, being wounded in three places, was relieved by Lieutenant Veitch. Jackson finding his wounds not very severe, returned to his colours, but Veitch would not part with them without express orders, although he had received two wounds.

Amongst the many instances of personal gallantry that distinguished the troops at Albuhera, and obtained for the Fifty-seventh the *Sobriquet* of the "Die Hards," the *sang froid* of Captain Ralph Fawcett as an example of devotion to duty is worthy of record. Although only 23 years of age, Captain Fawcett had already distinguished himself in previous actions. Being severely wounded on the 16th May, he desired his men, who were carrying him off the field, to place him on some high sloping ground close to his company, from whence he continued to give orders, especially urging his men to "*fire low*" and not to waste their ammunition.

On the 19th May, General William Stewart, spoke in the highest terms of the conduct of the Fifty-seventh Regiment, and said "that the situation on which the" "Fifty-seventh Regiment fought was the key of the" "position, and that their gallant conduct was the chief" "means of maintaining that key, and ensuring the" "Victory of Albuhera."

NAMES OF OFFICERS KILLED.

Major Scott. Captain Fawcett.

WOUNDED.

Lieut.-Col. Inglis, severely.
Major Spring, slightly.
Capt. Shadforth, severely.
„ McGibbon, severely.
„ Jermyn, died.
„ Stainforth, severely.
„ Kirby, died.
„ Hely, slightly.
Lieut. Evatt, severely.
„ Baxter, severely.
Lieut. M'Farlane, severely.
„ Sheridan, died.
„ Hughes, severely.
„ Dix, severely.
„ Patterson, severely.
„ Macdougall, slightly.
„ Myers, severely.
„ Torrens, severely.
„ Veitch, severely.
Ensign Jackson, severely.
Lieut. M'Lachlan.

The effective remaining Officers after the action were Lieutenant and Adjutant W. Mann, V. Y. Donaldson, A. Sankey R. Ross, G. M'Farlane, P. Macdougall, slightly wounded, B. Hobhouse, Staff-Paymaster Shapter, Quartermaster Moore, Surgeon Wood, Assistant Humphries.

Extract from Lieutenant-General Beresford's Orders after the Action of Albuhera.

"It is impossible by any description to do justice to" "the distinguished gallantry of the troops, but every"

" individual most nobly 'did his duty,' as will be proved " " by the great loss we suffered through repulsing the " " enemy. And it was observed that our dead, particu- " " larly the Fifty-seventh Regiment were lying as they " " fought in ranks and every wound was in front."

In speaking of individuals who distinguised themselves, the Lieutenant-General says, " and nothing could " " exceed the conduct and gallantry of Colonel Inglis at " " the head of his Regiment."

The Regiment has since been permitted by His Royal Highness the Prince Regent, to bear on its colours and appointments the word "Albuhera" which was notified to General Sir Hew Dalrymple, the Colonel, in a letter from the Adjutant-General, of which the following is a copy:

HORSE GUARDS, *1st February*, 1816.

Sir,

I have the honour to acquaint you that His Royal Highness the Prince Regent has been pleased in the name and on the behalf of His Majesty to approve of the Fifty-seventh or West Middlesex Regiment being permitted to wear on its colours and appointments in addition to any other badge or device, which may have been heretofore granted to the Regiment the word " Albuhera " in consideration of the distinguished gallantry of that Regiment in the Battle of Albuhera on the 16th May, 1811, as particularly noticed in the public despatch of Lieutenant-General Lord Beresford to Field Marshal the Duke of Wellington, dated, Albuhera 18th May, 1811.

I have, &c.,

Signed, H. CALVERT, A.G.

The British finding the enemy had retired after the battle of the 16th May, followed them as far as Almandralijo, where the Regiment remained a fortnight.

On receipt of the information that Marshals Marmont and Soult had formed a junction, and were again advancing to relieve Badajos, the British retired to Elvas; and the 2nd Division was here joined by the main Army, under Lord Wellington in person.

The Army encamped in the Wood of Torre-de-Macera, and the Regiment remained there with little interruption for many weeks, having been only called out once in consequence of a reconnaissance made by the enemy on the 23rd June.

During the months of July and August, the Regiment remained in the Alentejo, and generally quartered at Portalegre, where for a few months it was commanded by Lieutenant-Colonel Spring, who succeeded Lieutenant-Colonel Inglis, this officer's severe wound having rendered it necessary he should be removed to England.

The Regiment received a reinforcement in Portalegre on the 24th August of three Captains, five Subalterns, and 200 rank and file.

The Officers composing this reinforcement were Captains M'Laine, Campbell and Mosman, Lieutenants Carncross, Beal, Knox, M'Donald, Watson, and Ensign Logan.

This detachment was soon followed by Lieutenant-Colonel M'Donald, who took command of the Regiment, and Lieutenant-Colonel Spring went to England to assume the command of the 2nd Battalion, then stationed in Jersey.

From the beginning of September until the 16th of October the Brigade, consisting of the 3rd, 29th, 31st, 57th, and 66th Regiments, commanded by Lieutenant-Colonel Stewart, was occupied in movements along the Valley of the Tagus, between Niza and Pena Macor, communicating with the main Army near Fuentes Guinaldo, during the combat of Elboden.

When the French Army fell back towards Salamanca,

on the 28th September, and the Army of the North resumed its cantonments, Lieutenant-Colonel Stewart's Brigade, gradually retiring, returned to Portalegre, and the 57th Regiment occupied its old quarters in that town on the 16th of October.

The Regiment increased by some small detachments of recovered sick and wounded, now amounted to 600 rank and file.

On the 22nd October the division being again put in motion entered Spain by Albuquerque. The 57th moved with Colonel Stewart's Brigade by Codicierra, Albuquerque, Aliseda, Arroyo-del-Porko and Malpartida to Alcuesca, within a few miles of Arroyo-de-Molinos, where a French Corps under General Girard was surprised and defeated with a loss of a thousand prisoners, and several hundred killed and wounded, on the morning of the 28th of October.

On the 31st the Division commenced its return towards Portugal, and the 57th Regiment marching by Aldea-del-Cano, Malpartida, and Aliseda, and resting two days at Albuquerque, re-occupied its former quarters in Portalegre on the 6th of November.

The Brigade was here placed under the command of Colonel Byng.

On the 26th December the division broke up quarters and advancing by Albuquerque and Merida, entered Spanish Estremadura.

1812 On the 1st January, 1812, the Regiment was quartered at Almendralejos, and from that time until the 7th February it was almost in constant movement with Colonel Byng's Brigade on the Guadiana and Tagus, watching the French Corps, under Count D'Erlon, the line of movement of the Brigade being between Merida and Idantra Nova. After the reduction of Ciudad Rodrigo the Regiment returned to Portalegre, where it was stationed from the 7th of February until the 4th of March.

Colonel Byng's Brigade at this time consisted of the

3rd.	Regiment	700	Total strength. 2,080 rank and file.
31st.	„	300	
57th.	„	680	
66th.	„	400	

Preparatory to the siege of Badajos, the 2nd division on the 4th of March commenced re-entering Spain, and in conjunction with the 1st, 6th, and 7th divisions of the Army manœuvred on the line of the Guadiana, and roads leading towards the Sierra-de-Morena Mountains, and the River Guadalquiver.

From the time of the taking of Badajos, on the 7th of April, until the 27th of August, the Regiment in consequence of several advances and retrogade movements of the division, was alternately quartered at Almendralejo, Villa Franca, Fuente-del-Maestro, Los Santos, Usagre, Rienvenida, Llerrena, and Merida.

At the end of August the French Corps which had occupied Estremadura, having withdrawn across the Guadalquiver, Sir Rowland Hill's Corps moved towards the Tagus to watch the roads leading to the south. In advancing the 57th moved by Llerrena, Berlango and Maquilla on the road leading to Cordova.

At Berlango on the 30th of August the Brigade sustained a slight cannonade from some field pieces of the French rear Guard which (consisting of Cavalry) after showing front for about an hour, retired and disappeared.

As the Corps now directed its movement towards the bridge of Almaraz on the Tagus, Colonel Byng's Brigade inclined to the left, and the Regiment crossing the Guadiana, by a ford near Llorenta below Dom-Deninto passed through Truxillo, crossed to the right bank of the Tagus by a Pontoon bridge near Almaraz, from thence it gradually proceeded by Oropesa, Talavera and Porrijos to Toledo, where it recrossed the Tagus moving on the left bank, entered Aranjuez on the 2nd October, in which town it was quartered until the 23rd of the same month.

About this time the advance of Marshal Soult by Ocana with 50,000 men obliged Sir R. Hill to cross to the right bank of the Tagus, and with his Corps to occupy all the fords and bridges by which the enemy might pass; Colonel Byng's Brigade watched two fords at Villamaurique, the 57th being at Columnar-de-Orega.

On the 28th of October the French had occupied Aranjuez in force, and were making every preparation for crossing the Tagus. Sir Rowland Hill concentrated his Corps, and retired across the River Jarama during the night by the bridge of Puento Laego, from this, retiring slowly, the Regiment passed Madrid on the 30th October, the Escurial on the 1st of November, and crossed the Guadaraina Mountains by the Pass of Guadaraina on the 3rd, then marching by Villa Castin, Blasco Sancho, Fuente Veros, and Penaranda, crossed the Tormes at Alba de Tormes on the 8th. From the 9th to the 14th the Regiment was encamped near a Ford five miles below Alba, and on the morning of the 14th it was withdrawn, with the other Regiments of the Brigade, and proceeded to the Arapileo, where at first it was placed in a very strong position in front of the Arapileo, and subsequently advanced into a wood in front of the position of a French Corps that had passed the Tormes during the night of the 13th. The Regiment was formed in square for two hours, and at dark withdrew, and joined the rest of the division on the road leading to Alba, encamped in contiguous columns of Regiments, during the night. At 10 o'clock on the morning of the 15th the Brigade broke into columns of route and moved towards Ciudad Rodrigo, marching daily through deep roads and exposed to severe weather, frequently forming squares to resist the threatened attacks of the French Cavalry, until the 21st when the Brigade reached the Village of Martiago in Portugal, and remained in quarters there until the 29th.

The French having re-crossed the Tormes, the Army was ordered into more extended cantonments, the 57th crossed the Sierra-de-Gata at Gata, and occupied the village of Moralijo on the 30th of November.

On the 21st of December Colonel Byng's Brigade was moved across the River Alagon at Coria, and the 3rd and 57th Regiments went into quarters at Ceclairio, four miles from the Bridge of Alcantera.

During the Campaign of 1812 the following Officers were present with the Regiment :—

Lieut.-Col. M'Donald.
Major Ackland.
Capt. Burrows.
„ Shadforth.
„ M'Laine.
„ Campbell.
„ Mosman.
Lieut. -Donaldson.
„ Knox.
„ Sankey.
„ Keogh.
Ensign Logan.
„ Aubin.
Reid.
„ Sheridan.

Lieut. Carncross
„ Mann.
„ Veitch.
Ross.
„ Macdougal.
„ Oulton.
„ G. M'Farlane.
„ Connors.
„ Hobhouse.
„ Taske
Surgeon Evans.
Assistant Brown.
„ Humphries.
Paymaster Shapter.
Quartermaster Moore.

1813 In February, 1813, Colonel Byng's Brigade having

been ordered to make a forward movement, the Regiment removed from Ceclavin to Torrejoucillo, and on the 20th of March occupied quarters at Placentia, where the Brigade was concentrated and stationed until the 19th of May.

Part of the combined Army having already moved forward, the 2nd Division was put in motion on the 19th of May. The 57th moved by Villas, Barros, Valde Fuente (where the whole division was inspected by Sir Rowland Hill on the 23rd,) Fuente Robleda, and Bozados to Salamanca on the 26th.

On the following day the Regiments of Sir Rowland Hill's Corps defiled in review order past the Commander of the Forces, and afterwards encamped on the heights near the Village of Parado, on the road leading to Tovo.

The Regiment halted there until the 2nd of June, then marching by Fuente-sanco it crossed the Douro at the Bridge of Toro on the 3rd, and proceeding by Castremonte, Villa-Alba-de-Aleor and Dinuas, passed the River Carion on the 7th, and on the following day crossed to the left bank of the Pisnerga at Pedroso Del Principe, advanced towards the Hormaza River, behind which the French Corps, under Joseph Buonaparte, had retired, and on the 20th entered upon the high road from Valadolid to Burgos at Celeda, from which place a strong reconnaisance was pushed forward on the Homaza, and a corps of the enemy was dislodged from the height of Estapas, on the left bank of that river, with the loss of two guns. The 57th having crossed that river in combination with the attacking column on the left, recrossed at sunset, when the enemy had retired upon Burgos, and bivouac'd. During the 13th, 14th, and 15th of June, marching towards the Ebro, the Regiment crossed the river on the 16th, at the Puente-de-Arena, afterwards passed by Medina, Cadenaos, Villa Alba, Espejo.

On the 19th when within two miles of Pobes, they found the French were in force in a strong position upon the River Bajas; at sunset the enemy retired, and Colonel Byng's Brigade fell back to Epeisa. On the morning of the 20th moved forward and took up a position near Pobes. On the following day, the 21st, the Regiment crossed the Bajas at day-break, and moving towards the River Zadorra, passed it at the Bridge of Pueble at 6 o'clock. When on the high road leading to Vittoria a cannonade was heard. Without any order being given, the pace of the Brigade was accelerated into a *trot*; at about half-past 7 the enemy's lines were seen, and by 8 o'clock the 57th was in position opposed to a brisk cannonade, and engaged with the enemy's numerous skirmishers, posted in a close coppice a few yards in their front. Towards the afternoon as the French were partially giving way, Colonel Byng's Brigade advanced over very broken and interrupted ground, sometimes in line, and sometimes in column, halting. This manner of marching, halting and engaging, continued until the day closed in, when the Regiment halted and bivouacked for the night, on the heights near the Village of Albazastion.

The following Officers were present in the day's action:—

Lieut.-Col.	McDonald.	Lieut.	Connor.
Major	Shelton.	,,	Knox.
,,	Ackland.	,,	Macdougall.
Capt.	Burrows.	,,	Price.
,	M'Laine.	,,	Veitch.
,,	Campbell.	,,	Oulton.
,,	Mossman.	,,	Myers.
,,	Stainforth.	,,	Keogh.
,,	Marke.	Ensign	Logan.
Lieut.	Donaldson.	,,	Aubin.
	Sankey.	,,	Sheridan.

Lieut. Mann.	Ensign Johnston.
„ Ross.	„ Chanter.
„ M'Farlane.	„ Robinson.
„ Tasker.	„ Brierly.
„ Dix (wounded).	„ Francis (wounded).
„ Hughes.	

Five men killed and 20 wounded.

1813 After the Battle of Vittoria Colonel Byng's Brigade followed the enemy to the Pyrenees, and occupied the Pass of Roncevalles in conjunction with the Spanish Division of Morillo.

In July the French having concentrated a strong force between Bayonne and Saint Jean Pied-de-Port, threatened the passage of the Pyrenees, the 57th was advanced on the 20th of July to the Village of Valcarlos, in a gorge four miles in front of Roncesvalles, on the road leading to Saint Jean Pied-de-Port, whilst the upper pass to the right was protected by the Spanish Division and the Light Companies of the 3rd, 31st, 57th and 66th Regiments, commanded by Major Ackland of the 57th. This position was attacked by an overpowering force of the enemy at daylight on the morning of the 25th. The attack was, however, effectually resisted until four o'clock in the afternoon, when the British and Spanish were withdrawn towards Espinel on the road leading to Pampaluna. The 57th was in the evening detached to protect the retreat of some of General Morillo's Troops, and during the night rejoined the Brigade. On the 26th the Regiment was in position on the heights of Zubini, along with Sir Lowry Cole's Division and part of General Picton's. The French did not attack, and the British retired during the night; and on the following day (the 27th) took up a strong position in front of Pampeluna near Huarte. The Regiment had the honour of participating in the brilliant actions of the 28th and 30th, and on the afternoon of the latter day formed the advance in pursuit of the enemy retiring by Olaque.

On the morning of the 31st of July, having moved by the Pass of Vilate, at 3 o'clock in the afternoon the head of the column had reached the position of Fruta near the River Bidassoa.

From this situation a strong force of the enemy was observed escorting a long train of mules and cars.

The Duke of Wellington immediately ordered the 57th Regiment to throw off their packs and pursue the enemy. This order and honourable mark of distinction, coming directly from His Grace was received with enthusiasm, and obeyed with alacrity. After a run of two hours the French were overtaken near Elisonda, attacked with vigour, and driven across the Bidassoa; the whole of their convoy, consisting of 150 mules and several cars, loaded with baggage, provisions and military stores, was captured. The enemy, having suffered severely in killed, wounded and prisoners, fled rapidly towards the Maya Pass, whilst the 57th Regiment with the fruits of their exertions, returned to Fruta.

On the 1st August they encamped on the Heights of Maya, where the Regiment remained three days, and thence moving along the Mountains of Aldurdos, Sir John Byng's Brigade again occupied the Pass of Roncesvalles.

The following Officers were present with the Regiment in the action of the Pyrenees:—

Lieut.-Col.	M'Donald.	Lieut.	Hughes.
Major	Shelton.	,,	Connor.
,,	Ackland.	,,	Knox.
Capt.	Burrows (wounded).	,,	Macdougall.
,,	Marke.	,,	Price (wounded).
,,	Stainforth.	,,	Veitch.
,,	M'Laine.	,,	Myers.

Capt. Campbell.
„ Mosman.
Lieut. Sankey.
„ Mann.
„ Ross.
„ M'Farlane.
„ Donaldson.

Lieut. Keogh.
Ensign Logan.
Lieut. Aubin.
Ensign Sheridan.
„ Johnson.
„ Charteris.
„ Brierly.

200 men killed and wounded.

From the 4th of August until the 6th of November, the Regiment remained at Roncesvalles, occupied in erecting Forts and Blockhouses, and was here joined by a detachment from England.

On the 7th of November General Byng's Brigade moved to the Pass of Maya, and at midnight on the 9th crossed the Pyrenees and entered France, in correspondence with the general advance of the Allied Army.

During the morning and forenoon of the 10th the Regiment was actively and particularly engaged in assisting to force the passage of the Nivelle, and driving the French from the fortified lines on the heights of Ainhoue. In this action the loss was two Officers killed and five wounded.

The following Officers were present in the Action of the 10th of November:—

Lieut.-Col. M'Donald (wounded severely).
Major Ackland (killed).
Captain Burrows (wounded severely).
„ Marke.
„ M'Laine (wounded severely).
„ Campbell.
„ Mosman.

Lieut. M'Farlane.
„ Tasker.
„ Hughes (wounded severely).
„ Connor.
„ Knox (killed).
„ Macdougal.
„ Oulton.
„ Myers.
„ Keogh.

Capt. Stainforth.	Lieut. Hartley.
„ Hely.	„ Logan.
„ Dix.	Ensign Sheridan.
Lieut. Donaldson.	Lieut. Aubin.
„ Sankey (severely wounded).	Ensign Johnson.
	„ Brierly.

Ensign Bartlett.

After the Action of the 10th of November, the 57th Regiment was alternately in huts, camps, or cantonments on the banks of the Nive, near Cambo, until the 9th December. As the Army then advanced towards Bayonne, General Byng's Brigade forded the Nive, near Cambo, on the morning of the 9th of December; and, advancing on the road to Bayonne, co-operated in the affairs and actions of the 9th, 10th, 11th and 12th, and were warmly engaged on the whole of the 13th between Vieux Mauguerre and St. Pierre, where Marshal Soult made frequent heavy and vigorous attempts to force the position so well occupied and maintained by Lieutenant-General Sir Rowland Hill.

The 57th lost three Officers killed and four wounded, having 106 Non-Commissioned Officers and rank and file killed and wounded.

The following Officers were present in the engagement:—

Captain Marke.	Lieut. Oulton.
„ Montgomerie.	„ Myers (wounded), died.
„ Stainforth.	
„ Campbell.	„ Keogh, ditto.
„ Mosman.	Ensign Hartley.
„ Hely.	„ Dix (wounded).
Lieut. Donaldson.	„ Logan.
„ Sankey (killed).	„ Sheridan.
„ M'Farlane.	„ Aubin.
„ Tasker.	„ Johnston (killed).

Lieut. Connor. Ensign Brierly.
„ Macdougall. „ Bartlett (wounded).
Ensign Pode (killed).

1814 After the Action of the 13th of December the French having crossed and extended themselves on the right bank of the Adour, the Allies were ordered into cantonments, and the 57th Regiment was quartered in Vieux Mauguerre and La Houce, on the banks of the Adour,* until the advance of the Army in March, 1814, towards Orthes, Tarbes, and Toulouse, entered Toulouse on 10th April, and passing on to Villafranche, were encamped there for a few days, when hostilities having ceased they went into cantonments at Castine; at this Village Colonel Thomas (afterwards Lieutenant-General Sir Thomas) Arbuthnot took the command of the Regiment, Colonel M'Donald, who had rejoined before his health was quite re-established from the wounds he had received on the 11th November, having received permission to return to England.

On the 11th of May the Regiment quitted its cantonments near Toulouse, and marched by Auche Condome, Castel Jaloux, and Barsac to Bordeaux, which it entered on the 24th, and on the following day encamped with the troops destined for North America, at four miles from Bordeaux, near Blanqueforte.

On the 4th June the Regiment embarked at Poliac on board three transports, and sailed from the Garonne on the 16th for America.

They anchored off Quebec on the 3rd of August, and having remained there five days for orders, sailed up the St. Lawrence, and disembarked on the 11th, thirty miles from Quebec. The Regiment then proceeded up the banks of St. Lawrence by Trois Rivieres to Montreal, where it

---

* Vide Appendix, Letter A.

halted for four or five weeks. In September the Regiment quitted Montreal and marched further up the river to Cedres and Cotean-de-Lac, where it remained cantonned during four weeks, and in October it was embarked in gun boats and conveyed to Cornwall, from whence it marched and took up quarters in Johnstown and Brockville, at the latter of which was Headquarters.

At Brockville the Regiment, under direction of Colonel Arbuthnot, constructed a very substantial Stockade and Blockhouse, enclosing commodious Barracks. Whilst at Brockville Colonel Arbuthnot returned to Europe on leave, and the command of the Regiment devolved on Major Skelton.

1815 As peace was concluded with America early in 1815 a great proportion of the troops in Canada was ordered to return to Europe. The 57th was included in the order, and commanded to march for Montreal, in June. From Montreal it was conveyed by water to Quebec, and there embarked on board three transports, viz: the Emerald, Nautilus, and Saragosa.

By the carelessness of some of the sailors, a fire broke out in the Lazaretto during the night, on board the *Saragosa*, by which accident she was burnt to the water's edge. The Officers and soldiers escaped destruction by swimming; or by being taken on board numerous boats that immediately repaired to their assistance.

The whole of the arms, accoutrements, soldiers, clothing, and necessaries, and the Officers' baggage were lost. Two soldiers and one woman perished.

The Officers and men were afterwards embarked on board the *Ocean* transport, and sailed in July.

The Regiment arrived in Portsmouth early in August, and having remained there three days without disembarking, was ordered to Ostend for the purpose of joining the Duke of Wellington's Army in France.

The following Officers were with the Regiment in America:—

Colonel T. Arbuthnot.	Captain Montgomerie.
Major Shelton.	,, Stainforth.
,, M'Gibbon.	,, M'Laine.
Bt.-Major Mark.	,, Campbell.
Captain Mosman.	Lieut. Jackson.
,, Hely.	,, Aubin.
,, Hunt.	,, Sheridan.
,, Baxter.	,, Brierly.
,, Jackson.	,, Hartley.
Lieut. Tasker.	,, Bartlett.
,, Ross.	Ensign Montgomerie.
Dix.	,, Baxter.
,, Keogh.	Surgeon Evans.
,, Connor.	Assistant Humphrys.
,, Macdougall.	,, Campbell.
,, Price.	Paymaster Shapter.
,, Oulton.	Quartermaster Moore.
,, Logan.	

In August the Regiment landed at Ostend, and was conveyed to Ghent by canal boats. It remained a week in a village close to Ghent, and then under command of Major Shelton, marched to Mons Peronne, and the Bridge of Mayence to Paris, where it joined the Army encamped in the Bois de Boulogne, at the beginning of September.

Whilst in this encampment the Regiment was reinforced by a strong detachment from the 2nd Battalion, consisting of Lieutenant-Colonel Spring, and all the Officers of the 1st Battalion, who had been serving with the 2nd, with all the effective men to the amount of 250.

On the 30th October the encampment broke up in

the Bois-de-Boulogne and the 57th was quartered at St. Cloud, and brigaded with the 81st and 90th Regiments. On the 4th of December the right wing marched to the Village of Issy, the left to Vanes, on the 8th marched from these villages to St. Denis, from thence on the 26th marched to Cressy and was quartered in that and the neighbouring villages.

On the 25th of December the 2nd Battalion was reduced, having furnished the 1st at different periods with 1,400 men, from which circumstance it had no opportunity of being employed on active service.

1816 On the 23rd January, 1816, broke up from the cantonments in or near Cressy, and marched for Valenciennes by Compiegne, Noyau, Hano, Saint Quintin, and Cambrai; arrived at Valenciennes on the 31st January, was billetted in the town a few days, and then quartered in the citadel brigaded at this time with the 3rd Battalion: of the Royals and six Companies of the 2nd Battalion 95th under Major-General Sir M. Power. In October marched and encamped near the Village of Dinan preparatory to the British, Hanoverian, Danish, and Saxon contingents of the Army of occupation being reviewed by Their Royal Highnesses the Dukes of Kent and Cambridge, which took place on the 22nd of October. After this the 57th again returned to their quarters in the citadel of Valenciennes.

1817 In May, 1817, the Regiment was removed to the Postern Barracks in consequence of its being in a sickly state, supposed to arise from the situation of the citadel.

1818 On the 24th of February the Recruiting Company was reduced, and on the 24th of March the additional Lieutenants were placed on half pay.

In September the Regiment marched from Valenciennes and encamped on the Glacis of Cambrai, and on the 11th October marched from Cambrai, and encamped near the

Village of Neuilly, close to the Fortress of Boucham. On the 15th the British, Hanoverian, Danish and Saxon Troops were reviewed by His Grace the Duke of Wellington; on the following day returned to Valenciennes, and occupied their old quarters.

At Valenciennes in June, the Garrison was inspected by His Imperial Highness the Grand Duke Michael of Russia and the Duke of Wellington, Major-General Sir James Kemp commanding.

On the 9th of October the Regiment marched from Valenciennes to Cambrai, and encamped near the Village of Douche. On the 10th the British, Hanoverian, Danish and Saxon Troops were reviewed by His Royal Highness the Duke of Kent, and on the 11th the troops returned to their respective encampments. On the 21st of October the Army again marched to the encampment near Douche, and on the 23rd the Allied Army was reviewed by the Emperor of Russia and the King of Prussia. Soon after this review the troops returned to the Camp at Cambrai, from which they marched for Calais on the 27th of October for the purpose of embarking, and embarked there on the 2nd November. The 57th Regiment arrived at Dover the same evening, where it remained until about the 15th November, when it marched to Deal, and being joined by its Depôt embarked on the 19th for Cork, arrived there on the 25th, disembarked and marched to Fermoy. On the 10th of December by detachments to Clonmel, the Head-quarters arrived on the 12th.

1819 The Regiment was at Clonmel until the 19th of August, 1819, when the Head-quarters, with five Companies, left for Kilkenny. The establishment of the Regiment was fixed this year at ten Companies of sixty-five rank and file each.

Whilst the Regiment was stationed at Kilkenny, Colonel Spring retired from the Service, and was succeeded by Lieutenant-Colonel Carey, who had been Brevet Lieutenant-Colonel, and second Major of the Regiment.

1820 From Kilkenny and Clonmel the Regiment marched on the 19th and 21st of August, 1820, in five divisions for Galway, sending out detachments to Oughterard, Headford, Craghwell and Kinvara.

In May detachments were sent to Loughrea, Mount Shannon, Mount Bellin, Athenry, Ballinasloe, Eyre Court, Meelick and Kellogue.

The establishment of the Regiment was reduced on the 24th of August to eight Companies of seventy-two rank and file.

1822 The Regiment continued to occupy the same cantonments, till it marched to Limerick in June, 1822, sending detachments to Newport and Patrick's Well. On the 22nd, 24th, and 26th of July the Regiment marched for Fermoy, and the following out-quarters: Charleville, Mitchelstown, Mallow, Killinan, Kilmallock, Kildodery, Ballyhooly, and Castletown Roche.

On the 18th of October the Head-quarters were removed from Fermoy to Buttevant, and the following detachments were distributed as follows:—Charleville, Newmarket, Bruff Castle Island, Lascarroll, Freemount, Ballyhoura, Killmallock, Killinan and Hospital.

1823 On the 21st of July, 1823, the Regiment marched for Kinsale, sending detachments to the following stations, viz: Millstreet, Macroom, Bantry, Bandon, Inchegelah, Ballyvoorna, Clonakilty, Dunmanway and Ross Carbery.

1824 On the 16th of January, 1824, the Regiment marched for Cork, and on the 18th detachments marched to the under-mentioned stations: Ganacloyn, Ringrove, Watergrass Hill, Glenville and Freemount.

On the 28th of February detachments marched to the following stations, viz: Spike Island, Haulbouline, Carlisle Fort, Cove Cloyne and Youghall.

The outposts were relieved by detachments from the 61st Regiment on the 5th of July.

An official notification from Sir H. Taylor, notifying that His Majesty had been pleased to direct that the 57th Regiment should be employed on service in New South Wales, and requesting the Corps should be held in readiness to embark for Chatham, preparatory to its removal to its ultimate destination, was received on the 20th of August.

Four Companies with Head-Quarters embarked at Cove in the "Baltic," merchant transport on the 2nd of September, sailed on the 4th, and landed on the 8th at Chatham.

The remaining Companies embarked in the "Spike," transport, on the 17th, sailed the 19th, and landed at Chatham on the 29th; Lieutenant Le Marchant with a detachment consisting of 3 Sergeants and 30 rank and file remained at Cork, for the purpose of embarking as a guard in the "Asia," proceeding with the male convicts to New South Wales.

The second division on its arrival at Chatham marched from the transports to the lines, and the Regiment manœuvred in brigade with the Royal Sappers, 2nd Queen's, 7th Fusiliers, Royal Marines, and 60th Regiment, under the command of Sir H. Torrens.

On the 30th His Royal Highness the Commander-in-Chief reviewed the troops at Chatham, consisting of the Royal Sappers and Miners, 2nd, 7th, Royal Marines, 57th, and 60th Regiments.

The line was commanded by the Adjutant-General, the 57th and 7th acted in Brigade under Sir Edward Blakeney.

His Royal Highness was graciously pleased to express his unqualified approbation of the appearance of the 57th Regiment.

The Regiments at Chatham were severally inspected, on the 1st of October, by his Royal Highness the Commander-in-Chief, who again expressed his satisfaction at the high state of discipline of the 57th Regiment.

1825 The establishment of Regiments of the line was augmented from the 24th of March, 1825, to ten Companies, and 740 rank and file.

The Regiments abroad (those in the East Indies excepted) were ordered to be formed into Service and Depot Companies, the former to consist of six Companies of 516 rank and file, the latter of four Companies of 224 rank and file.

The 57th was reported complete to its augmented establishment on the 24th of October.

On the 24th of November the Service and Depot Companies of the corps were first accounted for in separate returns.

1826 On the 7th of January 1826, the Depot Companies marched from Chatham to Weedon Barracks.

They marched in two divisions from Weedon on the 8th and 10th of July for Burnley in Lancashire.

The embarkation of the corps by detachments in convict ships for New South Wales, commenced on the 12th October 1824, and was carried on in the following order.

Return of detachments embarked for New South Wales as under.*

Names of the Ships.	Officers' Names on board each Ship.	Strength of Detachment.				Women.	Children.	Date of Embarkation.
		Sergeants.	Corporals.	Drummers.	Privates.			
Asia	Captain Heaviside Lieut. le Marchant	3	2	...	28	3	3	12th Oct., 1824.
Asia	Lieut. Bainbrigge	3	1	...	48	6	10	

* The Depôt embarked for New South Wales in the manner shown in appendix (Letter B).

Names of the Ships.	Officers' Names on board each Ship.	Strength of Detachment. Sergeants.	Corporals.	Drummers.	Privates.	Women.	Children.	Date of Embarkation.
Sir Charles Forbes.	Lieutenant Gray Ensign Gore	..	3	...	32	4	6	5th Nov., 1824.
Royal Charlotte	Major Lockyer	1	1	1	31	4	7	3rd Nov., 1824.
Hooghley	Captain Logan Ensign Taylor	2	1	2	29	4	7	12th Mar., 1825.
Norfolk	Lieutenant Brown	1	2	...	31	4	7	12th Mar., 1825.
Minstrell	Lieutenant Shadforth	2	1	...	37	4	9	18th Mar., 1825.
Medina	Captain Hartley Ensign Robertson	2	1	1	30	5	9	19th Mar., 1825.
Louch	Lieutenant Donelan Ensign Ferguson	1	2	...	29	4	8	2nd Apr., 1825.
Sir Godfrey Webster	Lieutenant Ovens	1	1	...	31	4	4	24th May, 1825.
Henry Porcher	Captain Donaldson	1	2	1	29	5	8	28th June, 1825.
Medway	Lieutenant Bate Paymaster Green	1	2	1	29	5	2	20th July, 1825.
Marquis of Hastings	Ensign Stewart (Buffs)	2	1	1	30	4	6	20th July, 1825.
Mangles	Lt.-Col. Shadforth Ensign Shadforth	1	2	...	30	4	2	8th Sept., 1825.
Sesostris	Bt.-Major Campbell Ensign Benson	3	1	3	43	9	10	4th Nov., 1825.
Woodman	Captain Wakefield (39th Foot)	2	...	...	17	4	3	8th Nov., 1825.
	Total embarked	26	23	10	504	73	101	

During the time the Regiment was stationed in New
1825 South Wales, from 1825 to the latter end of 1830, it was very much scattered, having large detachments at Norfolk Island, Melvill Island, Moreton Bay, and Van Dieman's Land. Head-quarters were constantly at Sydney, and until November, 1828, under command of Lieutenant-Colonel Shadforth. Lieutenant-Colonel Allan, who had succeeded Colonel Carey as Lieutenant-Colonel of the Regiment, now arrived at Sydney, and assumed command of the corps.

1830 On the 16th of April, 1830, Lieutenant-General Sir

William Inglis, K.C.B., was appointed Colonel, Vice Dalrymple, deceased.

On the 28th of December, 1830, the Regiment was augmented to the India establishment, and the promotion and appointment of the following Officers appeared in the Gazette.

LIST OF PROMOTION IN THE REGIMENT.

Brevet Lieutenant-Colonel Shadforth, to be Colonel; Captain Hunt to be Major, vice Shadforth; Lieutenant Brown to be Captain, vice Hunt; Ensign William Lockyer, to be Lieutenant; Ensign Edmund Lockyer, to be Lieutenant; Ensign Alexander, to be Lieutenant; Ensign Darling, to be Lieutenant.

LIST OF APPOINTMENTS TO THE REGIMENT.

Lieutenant Putman, from half-pay.
" Smith, vice Brown.
" Saunders, from Seventy-fifth Regiment.
" McCarthy, from Ceylon Regiment.
" Baynes, from Eighty-eighth Regiment.
" Bevan, from Seventy-seventh Regiment.
" Loft, from Ninety-second Regiment.

Ensign Blyth, Ensign Allen, Ensign Spence, Ensign Evans.

The Fifty-seventh Regiment received the customary augmentation of Officers preparatory to its embarkation for India, whither it eventually proceeded by detachments, all the essential particulars of which will be found exhibited in the subjoined Return; this method of collecting into one focus of condensed information the scattered elements relating to each separate Detachment has been adopted as being at once the simplest, and best calculated for the purpose of future reference.

Return of Detachments of the 57th Regiment that embarked from New South Wales for Madras (E. India.)

Date. Year.	Date. Month.	Ships' names and place of embarkation.	Rank and Names of the Officers.		Strength of Detachments. Sjts.	Cpls.	Drs.	Pts.	Women.	Children.	Arrival at Madras. Date. Year.	Month.	REMARKS.
1831	2nd March	"Resource," From Sydney.	Lieut.-Col. Captain Lieutenant " " Ensign Qr.-Master Asst.-Surg.	James Allan James Jackson John W. Donelan Henry Hill (Adjt.) John McM'Kidd Andrew J. Allan Samuel Johnson David Lister	9	8		143	20	27	1831	15th May	On the arrival of the first detachment, Lieut.-Colonel Allan obtained permission to remain at Madras, and the command in consequence devolved upon Captain Jackson, who disembarked on the 17th, and marched to Poonamallee, a Military Station about 15 miles from Fort St. George. Corporal Michael Crowley was the only man died during the passage.
1831	28th May	"Red Rover," From Sydney.	Captain Lieutenant " Ensign Asst.-Surg.	Philip Aubin Thomas Shadforth Peter Gray Thomas Aubin Robert M'math, M.D	6	4	2	90	11	23	1831	1st August	Major-Aubin also obtained permission to remain pretempore at Madras, his detachment disembarked on the 1st August, 1831, and marched to Poonamallee.
1831	15th July	"York," From Sydney.	Major Captain Lieutenant " " Paymaster	Robert Hunt James Brown George Edwards Edmund Lockyer Robert Alexander George H. Green	7	7	10	117	14	37	1831	19th Sept.	Major-Hunt disembarked with his detachment on the 21st September, 1831, and succeeded Captain Jackson in the temporary command of the Corps, which was removed on the 13th of October, 1831, from Poonamallee to Fort St. George, and Colonel Allan on the same date was appointed Commandment of the Troops in Garrison.
1831	24th Aug.	"Waterloo," From V.D.Land.	Captain " Lieutenant " " Ensign	Vance Y. Donaldson Archd. Robertson Thomas Bainbrigge John Ovens William Lockyer William Tranter	8	9		163	17	45	1831	17th Oct.	Disembarked and joined the Regiment at Fort St. George on the 17th October, 1831.
1832	11th April	"Norfolk," From V.D. Land.	Bt.-Major Ensign	Harvey Welman Charles Dunbar	2	3		54	8	24	1832	4th July	Disembarked and joined the Corps at Fort Saint George on the 4th July, 1832.
			Total Embarked -		32	31	12	567	70	156			

1832 Lieutenant-Colonel Hartley, rejoined the corps (from England), and on the 17th September, succeeded Major Hunt, in the command thereof.

Lieutenant-General the Honourable Sir Robert William O'Callaghan, K.C.B. (Commander-in-Chief at Madras), inspected the Regiment with great minuteness, and expressed himself in commendatory terms with respect to its appearance, interior economy, and discipline.

The corps was again inspected (by Colonel Vigoreux, C.B) on the 31st of December, 1832, by Lieutenant-General the Honourable Sir Robert W. O'Callaghan, and on the 8th May, 1833, by Major-General Sir Andrew McDowall.

Lieutenant-Colonel Hartley established a Regimental Savings Bank, "an institution equally calculated to fortify discipline, improve morals, and diminish crime, and which in the period of very few months from its introduction produced very important results."

1833 Major Philip Aubin assumed the command of the Regiment, Lieutenant-Colonel Hartley having obtained leave to return to England for two years, for the benefit of his health.

The Regiment was inspected by Major-General Sir Andrew McDowall, K.C.B., who was pleased to express his high approbation of its extreme cleanliness and neatness on the parade, the precision and accuracy of its movements in the field, and soldierlike conduct of the Officers and men in quarters.

The Non-Commissioned Officers and privates attending the Regimental School, passed a very creditable examination in reading, writing, and arithmetic, and received prizes.

The children were examined by the officiating Clergyman, who was highly pleased with their progress and awarded the customary prizes.

1834 Instructions were received to prepare and hold in readiness the Head-quarters, and one wing of the Regiment, to march from Fort Saint George to Bangalore, when furnished with a route and final orders.

On the 5th March orders was received for the Head-quarters and right wing, under the command of Colonel Allan to march on the 8th with directions to reach Bangalore with the least possible delay, to be ready to co-operate in *Courg*, if required, and eventually to proceed to Cannanore.

This wing reached Cannanore on the 29th March, having had but two halting days, without the loss of an individual, except Lieutenant Worsely, who died of brain fever on the 26th at Bangalore, to which place he had been sent in advance, in consequence of his illness.

The wing was inspected on 10th April by Major-General Hawker, commanding Mysore division, who was highly pleased with their healthy and soldierlike appearance, and who expressed his highest approbation of their steadiness in the field and cleanliness in quarters.

The left wing (under the command of Major Aubin), the Regimenal stores, heavy baggage, hospital establishment, and women and children, embarked from Fort St. George for Cannanore on the 12th March (and sailed on 14th), two Companies on board the *Swallow*, and the other Companies with stores, etc., on the *Isabella*, the former arrived at Cannanore on the 29th March, and the latter on the 9th April.

Colonel Allan was appointed to the temporary command of Bangalore on the 29th March, Captain Donaldson to that of the right wing, and Major Aubin resumed the command of the Regiment.

Colonel Allan on the 9th May was appointed commandant of the Provinces of Malabar and Canara, and inspected the left (now the Head-quarter) wing of the Regiment at Cannanore on the 13th June.

The right wing was again inspected at Bangalore by Major-General Hawker on 23rd June, who repeated his approval of its appearance in the field, and conduct and cleanliness in quarters.

The wing marched to join the Head-quarters at Cannanore 12th November, 1834.

Major Hunt arrived from England at Cannanore and assumed command of the Regiment on the 17th November, 1834, bringing with Ensign Souter, a detachment of 149 recruits and 7 men transferred from the Forty-sixth and Ninety-fourth Regiments.

The right wing arrived under the command of Captain Donaldson at Cannanore on the 6th December without a man on the sick list, and without any casualty during the march.

1835 The Regiment was inspected by the commandant of Malabar and Canara (Colonel Allan) on the 24th December, who expressed himself highly satisfied with its appearance, efficiency and conduct.

The Regiment was inspected by Brigadier James Allan commanding the Provinces of Malabar and Canara, who expressed himself as highly gratified with its appearance, discipline, conduct in quarters and interior economy.

Lieutenant-Colonel Jones, K.H., from Eighty-ninth Regiment, appointed Lieutenant-Colonel vice Lieutenant-Colonel Hartley, who exchanged.

His Excellency Lieutenant-General the Honourable Sir R. W. O'Callaghan, K.C.B., Commander-in-Chief of the forces in the Madras Presidency, inspected the Regiment and was pleased to address the Corps previously to its dismissal to the following effect:—

"That he should feel great pleasure in reporting most

favourably of the Corps to Lord Hill, who he knew would be highly gratified, as he had often expressed his approbation and regard for it."

He subsequently issued a General Order of which the following is a copy.

14th December, 1835.

" The Commander-in-Chief having concluded his in- "
" spection of the troops at Cannanore, desires to express "
" his approbation of their general state. Of the good "
" order and discipline of His Majesty's Fifty-seventh "
" Regiment in particular, it will afford his excellency "
".much gratification to report most favourably to the "
" General Commanding-in-Chief His Majesty's Army."

1836 Lieutenant-Colonel Jones, K.H., having arrived from England (per ship *Palmyra*) assumed command.

The Regiment was inspected by Brigadier Allan, who was pleased to compliment it on its appearance, discipline, orderly conduct in Barracks, and interior economy.

The Corps again inspected by Brigadier Allan who expressed his admiration of its movements in the field, and his perfect satisfaction with its discipline, interior economy, clean and soldierlike appearance of the men.

1837 Captain Donaldson, Lieutenants Leonard Smith, William Tranter, Henry Townsend, Gahan, Andrew, Timbra Allan and Assistant Surgeon Neville, proceeded with 5 sergeants, 2 drummers, and 100 rank and file of the flank companies to assist in quelling an insurrection near Mangalore.

The march of the detachment being chiefly along the sea beach, where the sand laid ankle deep, was very harassing to the men, they however accomplished the distance in six days.

On arrival at Mangalore most of the houses were in

ashes. The Head-quarters of the Second Regiment of Native Infantry, which had been stationed there some time under the command of Major Howard Dowker, had driven the rebels into the jungle, but had suffered considerably in killed and wounded.

A few days after its arrival, the detachment accompanied by 400 of the Fifty-first, 200 of the Second, and 100 of the Fourth Regiments of Native Infantry, with 2 Howitzers, proceeded into the jungle, but saw no rebels until the 22nd, when 200 or 300 were seen on the opposite side of the river. A party of 25 of the Fifty-seventh and 130 natives dispersed them; they, however, attacked the Camp about ten o'clock at night, but retired into the jungle after the force turned out and a few shots had been fired.

About four o'clock on the morning of the 24th, the rebels again attacked the Camp, and continued their fire for about half-an-hour. At eleven o'clock the force was put in motion along the right bank of the river, toward "Opur Ungaddy," the rebels chiefly remained on the other side, but as the stream decreased in breadth, so as to enable them to come near enough, they suddenly ran out of the jungle, fired, and retired into it again. About six o'clock the force was halted to be encamped for the night, when the rebels, to the number of six or seven hundred, took possession of a Pagoda, from which they fired rather heavily; Brevet-Major Donaldson immediately ordered his detachment to charge across the river and dislodge them; this was at once carried into effect; the Native Infantry followed, and the Pagoda was set on fire and burnt.

The force marched towards Bellary Pett, where it arrived on the 29th, and information having been received that the rebels were completely dispersed, returned to their Head-quarters on the 2nd May.

Brevet-Major Donaldson's detachment joined at Cannanore.

The Regiment was inspected by Major-General Sir Hugh Gough, K.C.B., who on his departure was pleased to direct the issue of the following order:—

REGIMENTAL ORDERS.

"*Cannanore, 7th December*, 1837.

"In obedience to instructions from Major-General Sir Hugh Gough, K.C.B., at the termination of the inspection of the Regiment yesterday, Major Hunt feels the highest satisfaction in thus promulgating to the corps the approbation of so distinguished a General."

His words were to the following effect:—"He felt proud at being at the head of a division in which are three Regiments who gained so many honorable badges in the Peninsula; that the appearance of the Fifty-seventh was highly creditable, and that he considered the corps as *second to none*; the only thing that he regretted was the extent to which the Defaulters' Book had swollen, yet he was aware that this was attributable to but a few soldiers, and he exhorted them to remember that the high name which the Regiment had so gallantly won in the Peninsula should be the pride of all to maintain, that their Sovereign and their Country expected them to do so, and that each individual for the sake of his Sovereign, his Country, and his Comrades should steadily avoid everything which could disgrace it."

He then concluded by stating how much gratification he should have in reporting favourably of the Corps to the Commander-in-Chief, Sir Peregrine Maitland.

1838 The Regiment was inspected by Major-General Allan, commanding the Province of Malabar and Canaza, who signified his approbation of its appearance, conduct, discipline, interior economy, and the regularity of its different departments.

Lieutenant F. H. Jackson, Ensign Fitzpatrick, two privates, and one hundred and five recruits arrived on board the ship *Lady Feversham*, from England.

The Regiment was inspected by Major-General Dick, K.C.B. and K.C.H., who expressed the gratification he should feel in reporting most favourably of it to the authorities.

1839 The right wing of the Regiment, consisting of Captain Caldwell's (Grenadiers), Brevet-Major William's and Captains Shadforth's, Bambrigg's, and Oven's Companies, under the command of Major Hunt, marched for Trichonopoly, where they arrived on the 29th April.

The Head-quarters and left wing marched for Trichinopoly, under the command of Lieutenant-Colonel Jones, K.H., and arrived on the 1st June, the Companies composing the wing were Captains Morphett, Saunders, Brown, and the Light.

The Regiment was inspected by Major-General Edward William Gullifer Showers, commanding the Southern division of the Madras Army, who expressed his approbation in a Division Order, of which the following is a copy :—

Deputy Assistant Adjutant General's Office.

Head-quarters Southern Division.

Trichinopoly, 28th June, 1839.

DIVISION ORDERS BY MAJOR-GENERAL SHOWERS.

1. Major-General Showers Commanding the Southern Division, having concluded the half-yearly inspection of H.M's. Fifty-seventh Regiment, derives much gratification in expressing his approbation of the appearance

of the Officers and men under arms, and highly efficient state of the Regiment.

It would be out of place were the Major-General to say more at present, but he feels a pleasing assurance that the favourable impression made on his mind, from what he has seen of this highly distinguished Regiment will be considerably strengthened, when the regular inspection and review in December affords him a better opportunity of judging of its merits.

By Order,

(Signed) J. THOMPSON,

Acting Deputy Assistant Adjutant-General,
Southern District.

The establishment augmented under authority of a letter from the Adjutant-General, Horse Guards, dated 30th March 1839, to the following:—

	Colonels.	Lieutenant-Colonels.	Majors.	Captains.	Lieutenants.	Ensigns.	Paymaster.	Adjutant.	Quartermaster.	Surgeon.	Assistant-Surgeon.	Sergeant-Major.	Quartermaster-Sergeant.	Paymaster-Sergeant.	Armourer-Sergeant.	Schoolmaster-Sergeant.	Colour-Sergeants.	Sergeants.	Corporals.	Drum-Major.	Drummers and Fifers.	Privates.	Orderly-room Clerk.
9 Service Companies ...	1	2	2	9	20	7	1	1	1	1	2	1	1	1	1	1	9	36	45	1	17	926	1
1 Depôt Company ...	...	...	...	1	2	1	...	...	...	...	...	...	...	...	...	...	1	5	5	...	1		
Total ...	1	2	2	10	22	8	1	1	1	1	2	1	1	1	1	1	10	41	50	1	18	926	1

Brevet-Major Jackson, Ensign Cassidy and one hundred privates (of whom ninety-eight were recruits), joined from England, they having arrived at Madras on 29th August, 1839.

The Regiment was inspected by General Showers, commanding the Southern Division and was highly complimented by him on its appearance, efficiency, and regularity in all respects.

Year		Company		Captain.	Lieutenants.	Ensigns.	Sergeants.	Corporals.	Drummers.	Privates.	Women.	Children.
1840	Four Companies of the left wing.	K	Consisting of	1	0	1	4	3	1	73	7	11
		H		1	2	1	3	3	1	74	8	12
		I		1	2	1	3	2	1	73	6	7
		G		1	2	1	4	4	1	72	7	16
			Total	4	6	4	14	12	4	292	28	46

marched for Bangalore under the command of Major Hunt, and arrived on the 14th February, without any loss.

The other Officers of this Detachment were Captains Wilman W., Saunders, Morphett, and Ovens; Lieutenants Lockyer, Richardson, A. T. Allen, J. Allen, Stanley and Hunt (acting Quarter and Paymaster); Ensigns McNamee (acting Adjutant), J. Ahmuty, W. Ahmuty and Raikes, and Assistant Surgeon Fraser, M.D.

Ensign Croker with 89 recruits from England and two volunteers from the Fifty-fourth Regiment joined Head-quarters.

The Regiment was inspected by Brigadier Leslie, R.H., commanding Trichinopoly, who issued the following order on the subject.

TRICHINOPOLY, 16*th June*, 1840.

GARRISON ORDERS BY BRIGADIER LESLIE, R.H.

No. 5.—Brigadier Leslie, R.H., having concluded the half-yearly inspection of H.M. Fifty-seventh Regiment has great satisfaction in expressing his high approbation of the appearance of the Officers and men under arms, and the creditable and efficient state of the Regiment, as well as of every department, alike in the orderly room, the barracks, the stores, the school and the hospital; these points in particular, and all in general, reflect the greatest credit on the zealous exertions of Lieutenant-Colonel Jones and the Officers under his command, and which the Brigadier will not fail to bring to the notice of higher authority.

By Order,

(Signed) W. CANTES.

Fort Adjutant.

1840 Left wing marched from Bangalore and arrived at Madras on the 23rd October, 1840.

Ensign McLachlan with 75 recruits from England joined Head-quarters, leaving two others at Poonamallee sick, who joined the left wing on the 28th.

The Regiment was again inspected by Major-General Showers, who expressed his unqualified approbation of all its departments, and everything connected with it.

1841 The Head-quarters, Light Company, and Drafts from the others (as herewith) marched for Madras and arrived there 13th January, 1841, without any casualty during the march.

Distribution.	Lieutenant-Colonels.	Lieutenants.	Ensigns.	Paymasters.	Adjutants.	Quartermasters.	Surgeons.	Assistant Surgeons.	Sergeants.	Corporals.	Drummers.	Privates.
Commanding Officer & Staff	1	...	...	1	1	1	1	...	5	...	1	
Light Company	...	1	1	...	...	...	...	...	4	5	2	94
Drafts and Band	...	...	2	...	...	...	...	...	3	5	2	121
	1	1	3	1	1	1	1	...	12	10	5	215

Lieutenant-Colonel Jones, Lieutenant Tranter, Ensigns

Armstrong, Croker and McLachlan, Paymaster Barlow, Adjutant Hill (c), Quartermaster Langford, and Surgeon Morgan and Assistant-Surgeon Burton, of the Honourable Company's Service, were present with Head-quarters.

Ensign Inglis, one drummer and ninety privates, four of whom were transfers from others Regiments, and the rest recruits arrived in the roads from England on board the ship *Lord Lowther*, disembarked and joined Head-quarters the same day, 15th January, 1841.

The Regiment was inspected by Major-General Fearon, C.B., the Deputy Adjutant General, Her Majesty's Forces Madras, who expressed himself perfectly satisfied with every department also the interior economy, behaviour of the men, &c.

Ensign Hunton with 422 recruits and one man transferred from the Second Foot arrived in the Roads from England on board the ship *General Kid*, disembarked and joined Head-quarters the same day, 2nd July.

This detachment increased the number of men to rather above the regulated establishment.

The Regiment was reviewed by Major-General Sir Robert Henry Dick, K.C.B. and K.C.H., Commander of the Forces, Madras, from whom it elicited the highest praise for appearance under arms, and the steady and correct manner in which the different manœuvres were performed.

Major-General R. B. Fearon, C.B., Deputy-Adjutant General of Her Majesty's Forces, Madras, made the half-yearly inspection of the Regiment, and signified his approbation of it in all respects, 27th December 1841.

1842 Lieutenant-Colonel Jones, K.H., was appointed to the command of the troops, in the Garrison of Fort Saint George, Captain Shadforth (who was in command of the right wing at Trichinopoly) succeeded to that of the Regiment, and Captain Saunders to the charge of the Head-quarters.

The right wing (consisting of the Grenadiers, the D, E, and F Companies) marched from Trichinopoly for Fort St. George, where it arrived and joined Head-quarters on the 11th February, without any loss.

The Officers comprising this wing were Captains Shadforth and Bainbrigge; Lieutenants L. Smith, Richardson, Lynch (Acting Adjutant), Stanley, Fitzpatrick and Cassidy (Acting Quartermaster and Paymaster); Ensigns Inglis and Hunt, and Assistant-Surgeon Neville.

Captain Brown joined from Staff-employ, and assumed command of the Regiment, 23rd February, 1842.

The half-yearly inspection of the Regiment, under the command of Major Brown, by Major-General Fearon, C.B., commenced on the 26th and finished on the 28th May, when the Major-General was pleased to express his entire satisfaction at the general state of the discipline, and interior economy of the Corps.

The establishment augmented under authority of a letter from the Right Honorable the Secretary at War, dated 31st March, 1842, No. 68,500, to the following:—

	Colonels.	Lieutenant-Colonels.	Majors.	Captains.	Lieutenants.	Ensigns.	Paymaster.	Adjutant.	Quartermaster.	Surgeon.	Assistant-Surgeon.	Sergeant-Major.	Quartermaster-Sergeant.	Paymaster-Sergeant.	Armourer-Sergeant.	Schoolmaster-Sergeant.	Hospital-Sergeant.	Orderly-room Clerk.	Colour-Sergeants.	Sergeants.	Corporals.	Drum-Major.	Drummers and Fifers.	Privates.
9 Service Companies ...	1	2	2	9	20	7	1	1	1	1	3	1	1	1	1	1	1	1	9	36	45	1	18	950
1 Depôt Company ...	...	..	...	1	2	1	...	...	..	...	...	...	...	...	...	...	...	...	1	5	5	...	1	
	1	2	2	10	22	8	1	1	1	1	3	1	1	1	1	1	1	1	10	41	50	1	19	950

The Regiment was inspected by Major-General E.

K. Williams, K.C.B., and reviewed on the following day, when the Major-General, in the presence of the Most Noble the Marquis of Tweedale, Govenor and Commander-in-Chief, expressed his approbation of its appearance, discipline, conduct and interior economy, and the regularity of its different departments, 5th December, 1842.

Captain Gahan, Ensign Logan, Assistant-Surgeon Jess, and 66 recruits, arrived in the Roads from England on board of the ship *True Briton*, disembarked and joined Head-quarters the same day, 6th December.

1843 Major John W. Randolph, from the Ninety-fourth Foot, appointed Major vice Brown, who exchanges.

The Regiment was again inspected by Major-General Sir E. K. Williams, K.C.B., who expressed himself perfectly satisfied with the regularity of its different departments, interior, economy, &c.

Major Randolph having joined, assumed command of the Regiment, 31st May, 1843.

Captain Edwards, Ensign Gahan, and 14 recruits, arrived in the Roads on board the ship *Ellenborough*, disembarked and joined Head-quarters the following day.

Ensign George Armstrong, 1 Sergeant, and 27 recruits, from England, arrived in the Roads on board the ship *Charles Kerr*, disembarked and joined Head-quarters the following day, 15th October.

The usual half-yearly inspection of the Regiment by Major-General Sir E. K. Williams, K.C.B., took place on the 18th December, the Review the following evening, and the Major-General was pleased to express on this, as on other occasions, his entire approbation of its appearance, discipline, interior economy, &c.

1844 The Corps was again inspected by Major-General Sir E. K. Williams, K.C.B., commanding the Centre

Division of the Madras Army, who was pleased to have his approbation expressed in a letter he ordered to be addressed to the Commanding Officer, of which the following is a copy:—

2nd May, 1844.

No. 217.

To Major RANDOLPH,

Commanding H.M. Fifty-seventh Regiment,
Fort Saint George.

SIR,

Major-General Sir E. K. Williams, having completed the half-yearly inspection of H. M. Fifty-seventh Regiment, desires I will convey to you his high sense of approbation at the very clean and uniform appearance of the Regiment, and its complete state of discipline in barracks as well as on parade. The Major-General has, throughout the inspection, with feelings of the greatest pleasure, observed in every grade, from you as Commanding Officer to the Privates in the ranks, a strenuous desire pervading the whole to maintain the well-deserved reputation of their distinguished Corps, and the Major-General begs you will convey this, his unqualified approbation, to all ranks, and to remind them that it was this noble feeling that gave them the proud badge of "Albuhera" on their colours, and which would again and ever carry them victorious through similar scenes of carnage.

I have, &c.,

(Signed) F. A. REID, *Major,*
Acting Deputy-Assistant Adjutant-General,
Centre Division, Madras.

The following detachments arrived from England during the month of September, 1844:—

Ships.	Date of Arrival.	Strength. Sergeants.	Corporals.	Drummers.	Privates.	Officers.
Wellesley............	1st Sept., 1844 ...				1	Lieut. Grant.
Ellenborough	18th Sept., 1844...				7	
Clandino............	24th Sept., 1844...				27	Lieut. Frost.

The usual half-yearly inspection of the Regiment by Major-General Sir E. K. Williams, K.C.B., K.G.T.S., took place on the 5th December, and the review on the following day, when the Major-General was pleased to express his unqualified approbation of the men's cleanly appearance, their steadiness under arms, and the correctness of their movements.

1845 Lieutenant John Ahmuty and 63 recruits arrived in the Roads from England, on board the ship *Diana*, disembarked and joined head-quarters 1st January, 1845.

Two companies of the right wing, under the command of Major Shadforth, marched to Poonamallee, where they remained until the 3rd April.

Lieut.-Colonel G. E. Jones, K.H., re-assumed command of the Regiment, 3rd April, 1845.

The head-quarters and remainder of the right wing (three companies) marched to Poonamallee, and were joined by the two companies already at that station: the whole proceeded en route to Arnee, and arrived on the 10th April.

The Officers were Lieutenant-Colonel Jones, K.H., Major Shadforth, Captains Edwards, Tranter and Bull, Lieutenants Frost, J. Ahmuty, Swetenham, Hunt, Logan, Chads and Croker, Ensigns Fraser, Annesley, Armstrong, Gahan and Brown, Paymaster Potter, Lieutenant and

Adjutant McNamee, Quartermaster Morrow, and Assistant-Surgeon Jackson.

The left wing marched from Madras for Poonamallee, and there remained until the 23rd, when it proceeded en route to Arcot, and arrived there on the 27th April.

The Officers were Major Randolph, Captain Saunders, Gahan, Hill and McCarthy, Lieutenant Smyth (Acting Adjutant), Stanley, Cassidy, Armstrong, Hunton, Grant, Boughton and Pool, Ensign Clancy, and Assistant-Surgeon Clarke.

The following Garrison Orders was issued by the Most Noble the Governor and Commander-in-Chief, the Marquis of Tweeddale, on the Corps leaving the Garrison of Fort Saint George:—

Fort Saint George,

4th April, 1845.

GARRISON ORDERS.

"On the occasion of H.M. Fifty-seventh Regiment quitting Fort Saint George, the Most Noble the Governor desires to record in Garrison Orders, His Lordship's approbation of the zealous and soldierlike manner in which the Regiment has performed its duties during the whole period that it has been under His Lordship's personal observation as a part of this Garrison.

The steady and respectful demeanour of the soldiers has repeatedly been brought to the notice of the Governor, and their general observance of the Regulations of the Garrison attests the high state of discipline of the Regiment, which His Lordship thus notices with approbation, as alike creditable to Lieutenant-Colonel Jones, Major Randolph, as well as the Officers, Non-Commissioned Officers, and soldiers of this distinguished Corps."

The corps was again inspected by Major-General Sir E. K. Williams, K.C.B., & K.C.T. & S., commanding the

Centre Division of the Madras Army, on the close of which the following Division Order was issued.

EXTRACT FROM DIVISION ORDERS.

Dated, Head-quarters, Centre Division,
MADRAS, 27*th May*, 1845.

The Major-General commanding the Centre Division has been so gratified at his late inspection of H.M. fifty-seventh Regiment (the first that has occurred since the corps entered the Division) that he feels it due to the Regiment thus publicly to record his approbation of the high state of discipline and efficiency, which continue to be maintained in this fine old Corps.

Its soldierlike appearance on parade, steadiness under arms, the compact fitting of the accoutrements, the regularity in the book keeping, and the cleanliness of the barracks and hospital, all prove how ably the responsibility to each grade and department are carried out.

The Major-General requests that Colonel Jones will accept his best thanks for the manner in which the Regiment is commanded, and that he will communicate to all ranks (especially to Major Randolph, who so well upheld the discipline of the corps, during the period of his command) the General's entire approbation of their zealous co-operation and his confident assurance, that should opportunity offer they will not fail to add fresh laurels to the already well-won and unfading wreath of the "Die Hards."

Captain Jackson, Ensign Lothian, and forty privates landed at Madras from England, per ship *Minerva*, marched to Poonamallee and joined the Queen's Depot at that station on that day.

The Regiment being under orders to proceed to England, such men of the Corps who wished to extend their services in India, were permitted by General Order, dated Fort Saint George, 7th October, 1845, to volunteer to the following corps, viz.: fourth, twenty-first, twenty-fifth, fifty-fourth and ninety-fourth foot, when the number of men hereafter specified were given to the different Regiments :—

4th Foot	...	59 men.
21st „		73 „
25th	...	133 „
84th		33 ,
94th	...	29 ,
	Total	327

These men were struck off the strength of the Fifty-seventh Regiment.

The Regiment underwent the usual half-yearly inspection (the left wing at Arcot on the 9th, and the right wing at Arnee on the 11th), by Major-General Sir Edmund R. Williams, K.C.B., and K.C.T. & S., and he was again pleased to express his approbation of its discipline, interior economy, &c.

1845 On the 19th December, 1845, the Right Wing and Head-quarters marched from Arnee for Poonamallee, preparatory to embarkation for England, arriving at Poonamallee on the 24th.

The Companies of the Left Wing from Arcot left that station on 25th of the same month, and joined the Head-quarters on the 30th, where the Regiment remained concentrated until final orders were received for its embarkation.

1846 The Regiment received orders to prepare for embarkation in the following ships:—

Mary Anne
Westmoreland
Hindostan

And sailed, the *Westmoreland* with Nos. 6, 8, and Light Company, under Captain Edwards, on 5th April.

The *Mary Anne*, with the Head-quarters, Grenadiers, Nos. 3 and 10 Companies, under Major Shadforth, on the 16th April.

The *Hindostan*, with Nos. 2, 5, and 7 Companies, under Captain Saunders, on the 18th April.

The distribution of the Officers, Non-commissioned Officers, and Soldiers, Women and Children to the different ships is shown on the following page:—

Embarkation. Date.		Names of the Ships.	Record. Rank and Names of the Officers.		Strength of Detachment.				Women.	Children.	Disembarked. Date.		Record.
Year.	Month.		Rank	Names	Sgts.	Cpls.	Drms.	Prts.			Year.	Month.	
1846	3rd April	*Westmoreland*	Captain " Lieutenant " " Ensign " " Asst.-Surg.	George Edwards R. M. Smyth D. E. Armstrong R. A. Croker T. C. Pool Frederick Gahan Jason Hassard J. H. Lothian Thos. Bissett, M.D.	9	8	4	173	10	10	1846	29th Sept.	
	14th April	*Mary Anne*	Major Captain Lieutenant " " " " Pay-Master Qr.-Master Asst.-Surg.	Thomas Shadforth J. G. Bull Edward Stanley Robert Hunt R. A Logan Sweton Grant J. H. Chads John Potter (Lt.) David Morrow (Lt.) James Jackson	15	11	5	170	12	28	"	12th Sept.	Paymaster Potter left sick at the Cape on 9th July, 1846. Died on his passage home on 18th August following.
	16th April	*Hindostan*	Captain " Lieutenant " " Ensign " Asst.-Surg.	W. J. Saunders Langford Frost Lopus Cassidy R. T. S. Boughton E. D. G. Annesly George Armstrong E. J. B. Brown F. W. Tupper	10	9	5	199	13	25	"	29th Sept.	
			Total - -		34	28	14	542	35	63			

1846 The following Order was issued by Lieutenant-General the Marquis of Tweeddale, C.B., Govenor and Commander-in-Chief at Madras on the departure of the Corps.

HEAD-QUARTERS,

Fort St. George, 11*th April,* 1846.

GENERAL ORDERS,

Her Majesty's Fifty-seventh Regiment being about to return to England after a service of fifteen years in this country, Lieutenant-General the Marquis of Tweeddale, takes this opportunity of expressing his approbation of the conduct of the Officers, Non-Commissioned Officers, and soldiers during the period they have been under his Lordship's command, and of noticing in General Orders the character the Regiment bears for steadiness, efficiency and discipline. Its smart and soldierlike appearance in the field, and its regularity and good conduct in quarters, the general good conduct of the Regiment, and the attention that has been paid to its discipline, reflects much credit on its Commanding Officer, Colonel Jones and the Officers belonging to the corps, and his Lordship trusts that wherever the Regiment may be stationed it will continue to deserve the character it has already established.

By order of the Most Noble the Commander-in-Chief.

(Signed) J. T. PRATT, *Lieutenant-Colonel.*

Deputy Adjutant-General H.M. Forces.

On the 12th September, 1846, the Companies in the *Hindostan* disembarked at Gravesend and marched to Chatham the same day.

The Head-quarters arrived on the 28th September in the *Mary Anne* and on the following day the remainder of the Regiment in the *Westmoreland*, when it was again concentrated at Chatham.

On the 28th September the Regiment was reduced to

1846 the home establishment, and the supernumerary Officers were struck off by a letter from the War Office, dated 11th November, 1846 $\frac{68557}{4}$.

The establishment was ordered to consist of the following numbers:

Companies.	Colonel.	Lieutenant-Colonel.	Majors.	Captains.	Lieutenants.	Ensigns.	Paymaster.	Adjutant.	Quartermaster.	Surgeon.	Assistant-Surgeon.	Sergeant-Major.	Quartermaster-Sergeant.	Paymaster-Sergeant.	Armourer-Sergeant.	Schoolmaster-Sergeant.	Hospital-Sergeant.	Orderly-Room-Clerk.	Colour-Sergeants.	Sergeants.	Corporals.	Drum-Major.	Drummers and Fifers.	Privates.	Total number.
10	1	1	2	10	12	8	1	1	1	1	1	1	1	1	1	1	1	1	10	30	40	1	16	760	903

Colonel Jones, K.H., who had preceded the Regiment by the overland passage, resumed command of it.

On the 5th and 6th October the Regiment marched in two Divisions for Canterbury, where they arrived on the 7th and 8th.

On the 3rd November, the Corps being not yet armed, was inspected by Major-General Brown, C.B., Deputy-Adjutant-General of the Army, who expressed himself in the highest terms of commendation of its discipline and interior economy, "that he considered the Regiment in a higher state of order and discipline than any other he had inspected on arriving from 'Indian Service.'"

1847 The Regiment remained quartered at Canterbury until 12th January, 1847, when six Companies, under Major Shadforth, marched for Dover.

The Head-quarters and remaining four Companies followed on the 13th, under Colonel Jones, K.H.; three Companies, under a Field Officer, being detached at the Castle, the Head-quarters, with remaining Companies, were stationed at the Barracks on the heights.

1847 On the 3rd May the Deputy-Adjutant-General (Major-General Brown, C.B.) again inspected the Regiment, prior to its being moved from its quarters in Dover; he expressed his entire satisfaction with its appearance and efficiency.

On the 5th and 6th of the same month the corps moved in two divisions by railroad for Weedon, marching through London: the first division, five companies, under Major Shadforth, proceeding on the 5th, and Head-quarters, with remaining five companies, under Major Randolph, on the following day.

Lieutenant-General Sir Thomas Arbuthnot, K.C.B., commanding the Northern and Midland districts, inspected and reviewed the regiment (which was completed to its home establishment,) on the 21st July; expressing to the Corps at the close of his inpection his unqualified approbation of all he had seen, both as regarded its steadiness and appearance under arms, the regularity and system of its interior economy, and his gratification at again meeting (after its long service in India) the regiment which he had commanded as Lieutenant-Colonel at the close of the Peninsular campaigns.

The Lieutenant-General directed Major Shadforth, the Commanding Officer, to make his sentiments known in Regimental Orders, and his intention of specially reporting the efficiency of the Corps to His Grace the Commander-in-Chief at head-quarters.

On the 15th August Lieutenant-Colonel Harry Shakespear Phillips, C.B., assumed command of the Regiment.

The Head-quarters, with three Companies, moved from Weedon to Hull, on the 1st October.

The remainder of the Regiment detached as follows:—
Three Companies at Leeds, one at Bradford, one at Halifax, one at Burslem, and one at Sheffield.

1848 The Detachments of the Regiment were assembled

1848 at Liverpool on the 29th, and embarked the same day for Dublin, the Head-quarters arriving on the 31st March, 1848.

During its stay in Dublin the Regiment was inspected by the Commander of the Forces, and also by His Royal Highness Prince George of Cambridge.

The Head-quarter Division marched for Enniskillen, arriving on the 17th April.

Detachments were furnished to Londonderry, Omagh, Rathmelton, Ballyshannon, Belleek, Mohill, and Ballynannon.

On the 5th August Lieutenant-Colonel Thomas Leigh Goldie assumed command of the Regiment, Vice Phillips, C.B.

The Regiment was inspected on the 21st October by Major-General Bainbrigge, C.B., commanding the Northern Division, who expressed himself perfectly satisfied with the discipline of the Corps.

The Regiment was again inspected by Major-General Bainbrigge, C.B., on the 4th May, 1849.

The Grenadiers and No. 5 Company, marched from Enniskillen; the former, accompanied by the Light Company from Armagh, proceeded to Belfast, as a Guard of Honour to Her Majesty, August 6th, 1849.

Extract from Regimental Orders.

Lieutenant-Colonel T. L. Goldie has much satisfaction in publishing in Regimental Orders the following Letter from the Assistant-Adjutant-General, conveying the thanks of the Major-General commanding the district to Captain Stanley, and to the Officer (Lieutenant Logan), Non-Commissioned Officers, and Privates of the detachment under his command at Ballyshannon, in consequence of their energetic and courageous conduct in extinguishing a serious fire at that town. Their conduct has also

1849 received the praise of the civil authorities in that locality. Colonel Goldie desires to observe to the Regiment that, in the absence of more serious business of foreign wars, no services can be more honourable, or tend more to uphold the character of the Regiment, than a prompt and ready assistance in the preservation of the lives and properties of the inhabitants amongst whom they may be quartered.

COPY.

ASSISTANT-ADJUTANT GENERAL'S OFFICE,
Belfast, 7*th August*, 1849.

Sir,

The Major-General commanding the Belfast District, having received from Captain Stanley of the Regiment under your command, a duplicate report of a serious fire in the Town of Ballyshannon, on the morning of the 5th inst., together with a copy of a letter from E. Allingham, Esq., J.P. to Captain Stanley, thanking him, his Subaltern (Lieutenant Logan) and the detachment of the Fifty-seventh Regiment under his command, for their active exertions, first in saving the town from destruction by fire, and afterwards protecting the property from pillage. I am directed by the Major-General to request you will convey to Captain Stanley and the Officer, together with the Non-Commissioned Officers and privates under his command, his best thanks for their prompt and efficient exertions on the occasion referred to.

I have, &c.,

(Signed) R. W. BROUGH, *Lieut.-Colonel,*
Assistant-Adjutant-General.

Officer Commanding Fifty-seventh Foot,
Enniskillen.

1849 EXTRACT FROM REGIMENTAL ORDERS.

20th September, 1849.

Lieutenant-Colonel Goldie has much pleasure in publishing in Regimental Orders the following letter from the Deputy-Adjutant-General, conveying the approval of Lieutenant-General Sir E. Blakeney of the conduct of three soldiers of the Fifty-seventh Regiment in affording assistance to the Police at Cavan. Colonel Goldie takes this opportunity of observing to the Regiment that the conduct of individual soldiers, whether "good or bad," is reflected upon the Corps to which they belong; and Colonel Goldie considers the conduct of Privates James Power, James Walton, and Michael Walsh so praiseworthy that he has caused the Deputy-Adjutant-General's letter of the 18th September, 1849, to be entered upon the Records of the Regiment, with the view of preserving the names of these soldiers, and holding their conduct on this occasion as an example to the Corps.

COPY.

ADJUTANT GENERAL'S OFFICE,

Dublin, *18th September*, 1849.

Sir,

By desire of the Lieutenant-General Commanding, I have the honor to refer to you the accompanying minute from Government, upon a Police Report, respecting the prompt and efficient assistance rendered, by the soldiers named in the margin, to the police at Cavan, in securing two drunken and disorderly persons, who were arrested by the police on the night of the 9th inst., and I am to request that you will be pleased to instruct the Officer commanding Fifty-seventh Regiment to express to the above-named soldiers the great satisfaction which Sir Edward Blakeney has derived, from a perusal of this

1849 report, of their praiseworthy conduct on the occasion referred to.

You will be so good as to return the enclosure to this office when no longer required.

I have, &c.,

(Signed) W. COCHRANE, D.A.G.

Officer Commanding Troops,
Belfast District.

The Regiment assisted in extinguishing a destructive fire in the town of Enniskillen, on 22nd September, 1849.

The Regiment was presented with an address by Lord Enniskillen and the inhabitants for their exertions at the late fire.

Copy.

At a meeting of the inhabitants of Enniskillen and its vicinity held in the Court House on Monday 24th inst., the Earl of Enniskillen in the Chair, the following Address was unanimously agreed upon:—

Colonel Goldie, Officers, Non-Commissioned Officers and Soldiers of the Fifty-seventh Regiment, "Accept our grateful and heartfelt thanks for your noble, generous, and untiring exertions on the morning of the 22nd inst., when this town was visited by an awful conflagration, which raged for many hours, and threatened its entire destruction.

"To your intrepid conduct its salvation may, under Providence, be mainly attributed—conduct never to be forgotten by us—and when your removal shall take place, which we hope may be a long time hence, the Heroes of "Albuhera" will carry with them the lasting gratitude of the inhabitants of Enniskillen.

(Signed) "ENNISKILLEN."

Court House, Enniskillen,
September, 24th, 1849.

1849 COLONEL GOLDIE'S REPLY TO THE ABOVE.

My Lord and Gentlemen,

I receive with feelings of the liveliest gratification the high tribute you have paid to myself and the Officers, Non-Commissioned Officers, and Soldiers of the Fifty-seventh Regiment.

To the Regiments of the British Army it is always a source of satisfaction to be of use to the inhabitants amongst whom they are quartered in any part of Her Majesty's dominions, but particularly among their own countrymen in the British Isles.

The Fifty-seventh Regiment deeply deplore the loss which the town of Enniskillen has suffered on the occasion of the late calamitous fire; but if any felicitation can be felt by them on such an occasion, it is on their having been present on the occasion, and of having been of use in extinguishing the flames.

Nothing can be more gratifying to me than the mode you have adopted in conveying the thanks of the inhabitants of the town of Enniskillen to the Fifty-seventh Regiment, and I am certain it will stimulate them to further exertion, should they be required here or in other localities to perform similar services.

I have only to add, my Lord, that through no organ could this tribute of praise have been received with greater satisfaction by the Fifty-seventh Regiment than through your Lordship, whose family name is so intimately connected with the glory and reputation of the British Army.

The Regiment was inspected by Major-General Bainbrigge, C.B., commanding Belfast District.

Copy of a District Order published by Major-General Bainbrigge, C.B.

1849 District Order.

Enniskillen,

9th October, 1849.

Major-General Bainbrigge having examined the locality of the late fire in Enniskillen, he is able to appreciate the services of Lieutenant-Colonel Goldie and the officers and men of the Fifty-seventh Regiment in extinguishing that fire. The number of houses which were burnt down on both sides the main street show at once the extent of the fire, and it must be evident, if the most prompt and decided measures had not been immediately taken, the whole town would have been destryed. Of this the inhabitants are fully sensible, as is evinced by the thanks given to the Lieutenant-Colonel, his officers and men, by them. It remains, therefore, for the Major-General to add his own thanks to those of the inhabitants, which he now does in the most cordial manner; and this incident assures him that whenever a very important piece of service is to be performed he can rely upon the gallant "West Middlesex Regiment."

By order.

(Signed) JAMES DUFF.

Captain and A.D.C.

The Head-quarters marched from Enniskillen for Dublin, arriving on the 17th of October.

The Regiment was inspected by His Royal Highness Prince George of Cambridge, K.G.G., C.M.G., commanding Dublin District, in October 1849 and again in 1850.

Extract from Regimental Orders.

7th October, 1850.

Lieutenant-Colonel Goldie is glad to bring to the notice of the Regiment the exemplary conduct of the

1850 detachment of the Regiment stationed at Aldborough House, under the command of Captain Frost, in aiding to extinguish an extensive fire which occurred in that neighbourhood on Sunday morning last.

The proprietor of a large coach factory which was consumed has expressed his gratitude to Captain Frost for the great exertions made by the troops, by whose exertions a large amount of property was saved.

This is the fourth fire that has occurred during the last two years, which the Fifty-seventh Regiment has been mainly instrumental in arresting.

Colonel Goldie is satisfied that the Regiment must be gratified at the opportunities that have been afforded them of showing their discipline and gallant bearing on those occasions, and that their services have been warmly appreciated by the inhabitants amongst whom they have been quartered.

On the 7th of the present month Lieutenant-Colonel Goldie thought it his duty to notice in Regimental Orders the excellent conduct of the detachment of the Regiment stationed at Aldborough House, under command of Captain Frost, in aiding to extinguish an extensive fire.

Colonel Goldie is now happy to observe that the conduct of the troops on this occasion has been reported to the Comander-in-Chief, and that His Grace the Duke of Wellington has expressed himself highly gratified at the conduct of the detachment, as communicated in the following letter from the Adjutant-General to the forces, dated Horse Guards, 20th January, 1851, and which letter Colonel Goldie desires may be entered on the Records of the Regiment.

HORSE GUARDS,
20th January, 1851.

SIR,

I have had the honour to receive and to submit to

1851 the Commander-in-Chief your letter of the 17th inst., with its enclosures from Messrs. Hutton, coach makers, of Dublin, reporting the great benefit derived by them on the occasion of a fire which broke out on their premises on the night of the 4th instant, threatening ruin to a portion of Summer Hill and Mountjoy Square; and I am to acquaint you that His Grace has been highly gratified in the perusal of this report, considering, as he does, the conduct of the detachment of the Fifty-seventh Regiment engaged on the occasion in the highest degree creditable to them as British soldiers.

I have, &c.,

G. BROWN, *A.G.*

Lieutenant-General the Right Hon. Sir Edward Blakeney, G.C.B., G.C.H.

The Regiment was inspected by Major-General H.R.H. the Duke of Cambridge, commanding Dublin District, on the 22nd April.

The Head-quarter Division left Dublin for Kilkenny by rail, arriving on the 27th June.

Furnished detachments to Callan, Wexford, and Newross.

The Regiment was inspected by Major-General I. M'Donald, C.B., commanding the Kilkenny District, 24th October.

1852 No. 4 Company, under the command of Captain R. A. Logan, proceeded to Festard, County Tipperary, 6th April.

The Regiment was inspected by Major-General I. M'Donald, C.B., commanding the Kilkenny District, 17th May.

The Fifty-seventh Regiment marched from Kilkenny, arriving at Cork on the 11th August, furnishing detachments at Camden Fort, Haulbowline, Youghal, Mallow, and Ballincollig.

On the Regiment leaving the Kilkenny District the

1852 following letter was received from Colonel Williams, Assistant-Adjutant-General to the District:—

ASSISTANT-ADJUTANT-GENERAL'S OFFICE,
Kilkenny, 4*th August*, 1852.

Sir,

I am instructed by Major-General McDonald to acquaint you, that he remits the remainder of the imprisonment awarded against the men named in the margin and undergoing the sentence of Courts Martial, as a mark of his high opinion of the general good conduct of the "Old Die Hards," and in order that the Regiment may enter the Cork District, with few prisoners.

You will be pleased to write on to Lieutenant-Colonel Powell and direct the immediate release of such of these men as may have marched with him.

I have, &c.,
(Signed) W. F. WILLAMS,
Assistant-Adjutant-General.

Major Shadforth, Commanding
Fifty-seventh Regiment, Kilkenny.

1853 The Regiment was inspected by Major-General R. E. Mansel, K.H., commanding the Cork District.

The Service and Depot Companies were formed and inspected by Major-General R. E. Mansel, K.H., commanding the Cork District, and on the 4th of January the Depot proceeded to Elizabeth Fort, Cork.

Brevet-Colonel T. L. Goldie, Brevet-Lieutenant-Colonel J. S. Powell, Captains E. Stanley, H. J. Warre, J. Auchmuty, J. A. Street, W. Inglis, F. G. Steward, Lieutenants J. P. Lea, H. Butler, W. F. Jones, J. F. Bland, G. B. F. Arbuckle, G. J. Forsyth, G. H. Norman, E. N. Hague, Ensigns A. M. Earle, T. N. Woodall, C. Venables, R. A. K. Hugessen, Paymaster M. Matthews, Lieutenant and Adjutant C. W. St. Clair, Quartermaster J. Balcombe and Surgeon J. Dickson, remained with the Service Companies.

1853 Major Shadforth, Captain R. A. Logan, H. Munro, C. E. Law, J. Stewart, Lieutenants L. Cassidy, J. Hassard, W. E. Brown, A. L. Copland, Ensigns H. Butler, W. W. Lee, E. C. Johnson, and Assistant-Surgeon J. C. Brady, proceeded with the Depot to Elizabeth Fort.

On the 3rd February, at Cork Barracks Colonel Goldie presented to the Regiment (the Depot attending at the presentation) new colours, which had been given to the Corps by Viscount Hardinge, the General Commanding-in-Chief.

On this occasion Colonel Goldie delivered the following address:

"Officers and soldiers of the Fifty-seventh Regiment, I am very sorry that recent instructions from the Horse-Guards, have prohibited a more public display, at the presentation of these new colours, to replace the old ones which you have now carried about with you for upwards of fourteen years. The old colours you are now parting with are to be sent to the Colonel, Lord Hardinge, the General Commanding-in-Chief—he particularly requested that they might be sent to him when I saw him in London two months ago.

"You will be glad to know that the colours borne at the Battle of Albuhera, at which action Lord Hardinge earned his early fame, and the Fifty-seventh Regiment that brave soubriquet of the '*Die Hards*,' are with the Regiment, in possession of Captain Inglis, whose father nobly commanded the Regiment in that action."

"In handing to you to-day these new colours emblazoned with the victories which our predecessors have won, it is hardly necessary for me to remind you how sacredly you should guard them, and how you should strive when the opportunity offers, to add fresh victories to your banners; this can be only done in time of war, but in the course of our service, what opportunities are

1853 offered to the Regiments of the British Army, dispersed as they are through all portions of the globe. Consider the position of our army: in the Mediterranean three stations, Gibraltar, Malta, and the Ionian Islands, to the latter pleasant station we are about to proceed."

"In Africa what a considerable force we have, and how actively employed (Cape War)."

"In Asia what extensive territories we garrison, and how busy are our troops (Burmese War) in acquiring fresh victories, and more extended dominion."

"In America how vast are the possessions of our country which our Regiments are called upon to occupy; and Australia, how immense the continent, and how numerous the detachments of our troops. When you reach Corfu the Fifty-seventh Regiment will have been at a great portion of the British Colonies and possessions, since the close of the Peninsular War; for after the action of Toulouse the Regiment proceeded to North America, and at the close of the American War returned to Europe, and formed part of the army of occupation in France; after some years there and at home the Regiment in 1824 proceeded to New South Wales, from thence to the East Indies, and then home, where we have completed our term of home service."

"Called upon by our country to perform such various duties, how essential it is that we should be civil and courteous to the inhabitants of the countries we are stationed in, and firm and courageous in crushing rebellion, in upholding the laws, and thus bearing true allegiance to our Sovereign."

Soldiers, I have not discanted to you upon the victories which our predecessors have won, because neither you nor I had any share in them, finished nearly 40 years ago; to us they are matters of history, but I should be wanting in my duty towards the memory of those men who fell in

1853 the Peninsular War, to those veterans who still survive, as well as wanting in feeling to their descendants, many of whom I see around us, if I omitted to read an extract from the Regimental Record, which will show you the character the Fifty-seventh Regiment bore in those days of action and strife.

Extract from Lieutenant General Beresford's Order after the action of Albuhera.

"It is impossible by any description to do justice to "the distinguished gallantry of the troops, but every "individual most nobly did his duty, as will be proved "by the great loss we suffered through repulsing the "enemy, and it was observed that our dead—particularly "the Fifty-seventh Regiment—were lying as they fought "in ranks, and every wound was in front."

"In speaking of individuals who distinguished themselves, the Lieutenant-General says, and nothing could exceed the conduct and gallantry of Colonel Inglis at the head of his Regiment."

"The Regiment has since been permitted, by his Royal Highness the Prince Regent, to bear on its colours and appointments the word "Albuhera," which was notified to General Sir Hew Dalrymple (the Colonel) in a letter from the Adjutant General, of which the following is a copy:—

HORSE-GUARDS,

2nd February, 1816.

SIR,

I have the honour to acquaint you that His Royal Highness the Prince Regent has been pleased, in the name and on the behalf of His Majesty, to approve of the Fifty-seventh or West Middlesex Regiment being permitted to bear on its colours and appointments, in addition to any other badge or device which may have been heretofore granted to the Regiment, the word

1853 "Albuhera," in consideration of the distinguished gallantry of that Regiment in the Battle of "Albuhera," on 16th May, 1811, as particularly notified in the Public Despatch of Lieutenant-General Lord Beresford to Field-Marshal the Duke of Wellington, dated Albuhera, 18th May, 1811.

I have, &c.,

(Signed) A. CALVERT, A.G.

To General Sir Hew Dalrymple, Bart.,
Colonel Fifty-seventh Regiment.

"Soldiers of the Fifty-seventh Regiment, I have but a few more words to say to you. During the last four years I have commanded I have little fault to find with you. Some few irregularities have occurred, it is true, and, I fear, always will, among large bodies of men; but I trust that evil-doers and the thoughtless will endeavour to amend, and that those new colours, when, in course of time, worn out, and others command you, may be given in, if not adorned with more victories, as free from taint as these old ones, now about to be sent to the General Commanding-in-Chief."

The Service Companies of the Fifty-seventh Regiment proceeded to Corfu, Mediterranean, in three divisions, in the following order:—

First Division: Nos. 3 and 8 Companies, under the command of Captain Stanley, with Captains Auchmuty and Jones, Lieutenant Hague, Ensign Venables, Assistant-Surgeon Scott, 11 Sergeants, 7 Corporals, 3 Drummers, and 172 Privates, embarked at Cork on the 18th February, 1853, on board the freight ship, *Anna Maria*, and proceeding to Corfu, disembarked at Vido on the 7th of the following month.

Second Division: Head-quarters, Grenadiers and No. 4 Companies, under the command of Colonel Goldie, with

1853 Captain Street, Lieutenants Butler, Bland, and Forsyth, Ensign Woodall, Paymaster Matthews, Adjutant St. Clair, Quartermaster Balcombe, Surgeon Dickson, 10 Sergeants, 9 Corporals, 5 Drummers, and 177 Privates, embarked at Cork on 26th February, 1853, on board the freight ship *Andromache*, and proceeded to Corfu, where they disembarked on the 22nd March, 1853.

Third Division: No. 2 and Light Company, under the command of Lieutenant-Colonel Powell, with Captain Inglis, Lieutenants Ardbuckle, Norman, Earle, and Ensign Hugessen, 10 Sergeants, 8 Corporals, 3 Drummers, 177 privates, embarked at Cork on the 1st March, 1853, on board the freight ship, *Lady Clarke*, and proceeding to Corfu, disembarked at Vido on the 23rd of the same month.

Extract from Regimental Orders.

Colonel Goldie has read, with much satisfaction, a detailed Report from Captain Stanley, respecting the running on shore of the freight ship, *Anna Maria*, on which occasion the conduct of the detachment on board was exemplary. Their conduct having already met with the praise of the General Officer commanding in these Islands. Colonel Goldie thinks it unnecessary to say more, but he will send copies of Captain Stanley's Report, and General Conyer's Orders to the Colonel of the Regiment, Viscount Hardinge, and to the Depot, being certain that the soldiers of the Depot will be gratified to hear that the conduct of their comrades on a trying occasion was such as to add to the credit of the Regiment, and to the service.

The Depot Companies marched from Cork to Tralee, Co. Kerry, in three divisions, Head Quarters of the Depot, arriving on the 19th March, 1853.

HORSE-GUARDS, 10*th May*, 1853.

1853 Sir,

I have the honour to acknowledge the receipt of your letter of the 30th March last, reporting the safe arrival of the several divisions of the Fifty-seventh Regiment at Corfu, and transmitting for the information of Viscount Hardinge, the details of the only casualty which occurred, in the freight ship, *Anna Maria*, having run on shore at the southern point of the Island; and to convey to you the expression of the satisfaction of the General Commanding-in-Chief at the conduct of the Troops on the occasion alluded to.

I have, &c.,

Colonel Goldie, (Signed) RICHARD AIREY
57th Regiment. *Adjt.-Genl.*

The Regiment continued at Corfu during the remainder of 1853.

Major-General Conyers, C.B., commanding in the Ionian Islands, made the usual inspections of the Service Companies at Corfu.

1854 In July an order was received to hold the Regiment in readiness for immediate embarkation for service in the East; but so great was the pressure for transport that no ship could be provided until September, when, after receiving Volunteers from the First Royals, Thirty-first, Forty-eighth, and Seventy-first Regiments, the Regiment embarked on the 12th September, 1854, on board the hired steam ship *Mauritius*, and sailed from Corfu the same evening, strength as below.

Field Officers.	Captains.	Subalterns.	Staff.	Sergeants.	Drummers.	Rank and File.
2	5	8	6	45	10	685

1854 The following Officers embarked with the Regiment at Corfu for the Crimea:—

Colonel	Goldie (Br. General)	Lieutenant	Norman.
Major	Powell (Bt. Lt. Col.)	„	Hague.
Captain	Stanley		Earle.
„	Auchmuty		Hugessen.
„	Street	„	Venables.
„	Inglis	„	Buller.
„	Bland	Paymaster	Mathews.
Lieut.	Butler	Quarter-mstr.	Balcombe.
„	St. Clair (Adjt.)	Surgeon	Dickson.
„	Forsyth	Asst. Surgeon	Scott.

The steam ship *Mauritius* anchored for 36 hours in Vatika Bay, in consequence of a gale of wind, and arrived at Constantinople on 18th September, where the ship was again detained to coal. These detentions on the voyage caused the Regiment to be too late for the battle of the Alma on the 20th September.

Assistant-Surgeon Brady joined the Regiment at Scutari.

The *Mauritius* anchored among the fleet off the Alma River on the 22nd September, and on the following day the army marched to the Katcha River. The *Mauritius* proceeded to the mouth of the river, and the Regiment disembarked during the afternoon, and joined the Fourth Division of the army under Lieutenant-General the Honourable George Cathcart, K.C.B.

Brigadier-General Goldie assumed command of the First Brigade of the Fourth Division, appointing Captain Street, Brigade-Major, and Lieutenant Earle, Aide-de-camp. The command of the Regiment devolved on Brevet Lieutenant-Colonel Powell.

The army continued to advance, the Fourth Division forming the rear and baggage guard, and on the 27th continuing the march, passing "Balaklava" bivouacked

1854 on the hills above Sebastopol, about 1½ miles from the town.

The town opened fire for the first time on the 30th September.

The Regiment received Tents on the 4th October, and the Division took ground to the right. The 3rd Division taking up the old ground vacated by the 4th Division.

The regular siege of Sebastopol commenced on the 7th October, when ground was broken up for the first time; the Regiment formed part of the covering party, and continued from that time to take its share in the operations of the siege.

On the 25th the Russians in force attacked "Balaklava" and took some field works from the Turks; at 8.30 a.m. the 4th Division were under arms, and marched down to the plains of "Balaklava," where the 1st Brigade, deployed in rear of the Artillery, acted as a support to them during the day, and at dark returned to camp. "Clasp."

On the 5th November shortly before day-light the enemy attacked the extreme right of the allied position in great force. During the night, favored by a heavy fog and drizzling rain, the enemy transported batteries of heavy guns on to the high ground on the left front of the 2nd Division, posted on the heights of Inkerman, and covered by a cloud of skirmishers, supported by dense columns of Infantry, advanced up the ravine on the centre, and by the valley of the Tchernaya, on the right and rear of the Allied camp.

The Fifty-seventh (forming part of the 4th Division) was quickly under arms, and was sent forward towards the point of attack, deploying with the other Regiments of the Division, across the ravine leading from the Tchernaya, where it held in check the heavy columns of

1854 the enemy, who were advancing under a tremendous fire from their skirmishers, and their numerous batteries posted on the surrounding heights.

The struggle continued for several hours, with varied success, the fire from the enemy's heavy guns was very destructive, but the English (supported later in the day by two Battalions of the French) maintained their ground, the enemy became disheartened, dense masses were observed recrossing the bridge over the Tchernaya, at length the retreat became general and the victory was complete. It is stated that 40,000 men of the enemy were engaged, and that 15,000 were placed *hors de combat*, including 3,000 taken prisoners; but the losses of the Allies were severe, and of the 4th Division alone, Major-General Sir G. Cathcart, G.C.B., and Brigadier-General Goldie (57th) were killed, and Brigadier-General Torrens was severely wounded.

The loss of the Regiment is given below:—

	S.	D.	R. & F.	
Strength in the Field.	29	14	294	Actually present.
Casualties { Killed ...	3	1	11	
Casualties { Wounded ...	5	1	69	
Total ...	8	2	80	

The following Officers were engaged on 5th November, 1854:—

Captain E. Stanley, Senior Officer (killed).
" J. Auchmuty, sick, absent.
" W. Inglis, brought the Regiment out of the field.
" J. F. Bland, dangerously wounded, died of wounds.
Lieut. H. Butler.
" G. J. Forsyth.
" Hague, dangerously wounded, died of wounds.
Venables.

1854 Lieut. C. W. St. Clair (Adjutant), horse shot under him. Asst.-Surgeon Scott.

Lieutenant-Colonel Powell, Lieutenant Norman and the remainder of the Regiment were on duty in the trenches, Lieutenant Hugessen was on Inlying Regimental Picquet.

Captain Street, Brigade-Major, received a Brevet-Majority.

Captain Inglis received a Brevet-Majority.

Brevet Lieutenant-Colonel Powell, an unattached Lieutenant-Colonelcy, for distinguished service in the field.

Lieutenant-Colonel Shadforth arrived from England and assumed command of the Regiment on the 8th November.

A draft arrived on the 15th November, in the *Jura* steam ship, strength as follows :—

Captains.	Subalterns.	Staff.	Sergeants.	Drummers.	Rank and File.
2	4	1	4	4	243

Captain Hassard, Captain Lea, Lieutenant Copland, Ensign Mitchell, Ensign Shortt, Ensign Slade, Assistant-Surgeon Phelps.

1855 Captain Brown, Lieutenants Ingham and Ashwin, and 8 rank and file, arrived from Cork in H.M. Ship *St. Jean d'Acre*, and joined head-quarters on the 4th February.

Major H. J. Warre appointed Lieutenant-Colonel on the 9th March, 1855, in augmentation.

Lieutenant Mitchell wounded in the trenches and died in camp on the 28th March.

1855 Lieutenant-Colonel Warre joined Head-quarters from sick leave on the 27th March, 1855.

Lieutenant Coope, Ensign and Adjutant Waugh and 2 rank and file, joined Head-quarters from the Reserve Companies at Malta on the 18th May.

Lieutenant Bird, one Sergeant, and 50 rank and file joined from the Reserve Companies at Malta on the 2nd June.

Fifteen Sergeants and 300 rank and file under the command of Captain St. Clair, together with Captains Forsyth and Norman, Lieutenants Venables and Coope, Shorlt, Bird, Slade and Grace, on the 7th June, acted as a Reserve at the attack on the Quarries.

Major Inglis was in command of 600 officers and men of other corps acting as supports on the Woronzoff road; the remainder of the Regiment stood to their arms in camp during the night.

Lieutenant Macartney and 1 rank and file joined Head-quarters from the Reserve Companies at Malta on the 11th June.

The whole of the officers present at Head-quarters, 25 sergeants, and 400 rank and file, under the command of Lieutenant-Colonel Shadforth, reinforced the right attack, in rear of the Quarries, on the 13th June and returned to camp at daylight on the 14th June. No casualties.

Lieutenant Wilmot and 1 rank and file joined Head-quarters from the Reserve Companies at Malta on the 17th June.

Extract from Division Orders.

June 17*th*, 1855.

1. Major-General Sir John Campbell will take command of the attacking column, 1,750 men to be furnished from the First Brigade, as follows: Seventeenth, Twen-

1855 tieth, Twenty-first, and Fifty-seventh Regiments; Rifle Brigade, 100 rank and file.

EXTRACT FROM BRIGADE ORDERS.

A combined attack by the Allied Forces upon the enemy's works having been decided upon, 400 of the Fifty-seventh Regiment, with the officers named below, were selected to lead the assault on the right flank of the great Redan.

At 1 o'clock a.m., on the 18th June (covered by 100 rank and file of the Rifle Brigade) the "Forlorn Hope" of the Fifty-seventh Regiment, consisting of 19 officers and 400 men, under the command of Lieutenant-Colonel Shadforth (with the officers named below) marched off the Divisional Brigade Ground, followed by the other Regiments of the Brigade, under the immediate command of Major-General Sir John Campbell, Bart. commanding the 2nd Brigade, supported by the 1st Brigade, under Brigadier-General Garrett, the whole forming the 4th Division, under the command of Lieutenant-General Sir Henry Bentinck, K.C.B.

It was nearly daylight before the Fifty-seventh filed into its position in the fifth parallel in front of the "Quarries" and within about 300 yards of the Great Redan, against the right flank of which the attack by the 4th Division was to be made.

The other Divisions took up similar stations, but it was evident that the Russians had, during the night, repaired the breaches in their parapets and were expecting the attack.

The French commenced the assault and fought most bravely; 2,500 men *hors de combat*, shows the determination with which they assaulted the Malakoff, but the Russians were too strong for them, and the order for the English advance was given at the

1855 moment when it was evident that the French attack had failed.

The impatient spirit of our Brigade leader, Sir John Campbell, would brook no delay; "Who will be the first on the Parapet?" was the gallant soldiers' first thought, and was the only order given to advance. It was instantly obeyed by Lieutenant-Colonel Shadforth and the left wing of the gallant Four Hundred, but before it reached the right, Sir John Campbell had been killed, and Colonel Shadforth was brought back mortally wounded, having advanced towards the Redan but a few yards across the intervening ground, which was enfiladed by a small battery on the flank, the guns of which had never been silenced. Lieutenant-Colonel Warre immediately went to the front, but no order could be heard amid the roar of cannon and the rush of shrapnel, which rained upon the devoted band. Colonel Lord West (with the Twenty-first Regiment) had assumed command of the brigade, but the smoke hung like a curtain upon the Redan; and of the attacking party of 400, 104 Non-Commissioned Officers and men were lying scattered and exposed to the mitraille that swept across the ground. An endeavour was made by Colonel Warre to turn the flank of the small Russian outwork, and this was so ably supported by Major Inglis, Captains Butler and Browne, and about 100 soldiers of the Fifty-seventh, and other corps, that it might have been successful; but reinforcements could not be obtained. It was in vain that Major Inglis and Sergeant Bosworth crossed and recrossed the fatal ground. The assault had failed, and the order was given to return to the original position from which the attack had been made. To retire was even more dangerous than to advance, but the retreat was at length effected, by retiring in skirmishing order, carrying back not only

1855 the wounded of the Fifty-seventh, but Colonel Tylden of the Royal Engineers and Captain Snodgrass, Sir John Campbell's Aide-de-Camp, who with many others were shot down on the first attempt to storm the apex of the Redan.

The assault had failed, and the attack on the left flank being equally unsuccessful, the 57th Regiment remained at its post in the most advanced trench under a tremendous fire from the Russian lines until mid-day, when it was relieved and returned to camp. Of the 19 Officers and 400 Non-Commissioned Officers and men who had formed the assaulting party, 6 Officers and 110 Non-Commissioned Officers and men were killed or wounded. Many remained in the front between the English and Russian batteries without being able to retire. Captain Forsyth and several men took refuge in a shell hole, from whence piling the dead bodies of their comrades in their front, and making use of their ammunition, they continued to fire against the enemy until quite late in the afternoon, when a dust storm enabled them, unobserved, to effect their retreat. Instances of individual bravery were conspicuous. Many wounded men lying in front of the parallel, under the fire of the enemy, were brought into the trenches by their comrades, who sought no recognition of their heroism. The conduct of the Medical officers was most praiseworthy, and that of Assistant-Surgeon Phelps was rewarded by a commission as Ensign in the Regiment, an honour selected by himself. Colour-Sergeant Gardiner eventually obtained the Victoria Cross for gallant conduct, when, with Captain Forsyth, he was exposed to almost certain death.

The cool and gallant conduct of Major Inglis and Sergeant Bosworth deserves special mention; they crossed and recrossed the fatal ground in front of the Redan in the vain hope of obtaining reinforcements which

1855 the failure of the first attack rendered impossible to afford.

THE FOLLOWING OFFICERS WERE PRESENT ON THE 18TH JUNE:—

Lieut.-Col. T. Shadforth (killed).
„ H. J. Warre.
Major Wm. Inglis.
Captain J. Hassard.
„ F. P. Lea (severely wounded).
„ H. Butler.
„ C. W. St. Clair (severely wounded).
„ G. J. Forsyth.
„ H. Norman, severely wounded, died of wounds.
„ W. E. Browne.
Lieut. C. Venables.
„ J. E. Ingham.
„ J. E. Ashwin (killed).
„ W. J. Coope.
„ W. A. J. Shortt.
H. Bird.
„ J. N. S. Macartney.
„ A. F. A. Slade (severely wounded).
„ T. Grace.
Ensign and Adjutant G. R. Waugh.
Asst.-Surgeon T. E. Brady.
„ J. S. Phelps.

Assistant-Surgeon Phelps was appointed Ensign at his own request for his gallant conduct on this occasion.

Lieutenant-Colonel H. J. Warre succeeded to the command on the death of Lieutenant-Colonel Thos. Shadforth killed in action.

The death of Field-Marshal Lord Raglan was deeply felt by the Allied Armies. He died at 9 o'clock p.m. on the 28th June, of cholera, produced, doubtless, by anxiety

1855 of mind and distress at the result of the unsuccessful attack on the Redan on the 18th inst.

The General Order published by the French Commander-in-Chief fully expresses the grief of the Army, and the loss sutained by the death of a true English nobleman. A translation of it appears a fitting memorial for these Regimental Records.

" Death has suddenly taken away, while in the full " exercise of his command, Field-Marshal Lord Raglan, " and has plunged the British Army into mourning. " We all share the grief of our brave Allies. Those who " knew Lord Raglan, who knew the history of his life— " so noble and so pure—so replete with service rendered " to his country—those who witnessed his fearless " demeanor at Alma and at Inkerman—who recall the " calm and stoic greatness of his character throughout " this rude and memorable campaign—each and all, " with every generous heart, will indeed deplore his loss. " The sentiments here expressed by the General Com- " manding-in-Chief are those of the whole Army. " Marshal Pelissier himself has been cruelly struck by " this unlooked-for blow: the public grief only increases " his sorrow at being separated from a companion in " arms whose genial spirit he loved, whose virtues he " admired, and from whom he has always received the " most loyal and hearty co-operation."

General La Marmora also published a similar Order to the Sardinian Army, in which he eulogised the important services Lord Raglan had rendered to his country, deplored his death, and venerated his memory.

Lord Raglan's body was sent to England on the 3rd July, when the Regiment furnished a funeral party consisting of 1 field officer, 1 captain, 1 subaltern, and 50 rank and file.

The procession was accompanied by the Generals

1855 commanding the French, Sardinian, and Turkish Armies. The whole of the available Staff and every officer off duty attended this melancholy duty. 3,000 English and about 10,000 French troops lined the way to Kazatch Bay, where the boats of every ship formed in procession in double lines, while the body was removed from the gun-carriage to the barge which conveyed it to the *Caradoc*. Minute guns continued to be fired, until the vessel that carried the remains of the beloved Commander had disappeared in the distance.

As a military spectacle, nothing grander could be desired; but the grief of all was more eloquently expressed in the deep depression that fell upon the English Camp, and remained for days after the mortal remains of their General had quitted the scene of his triumphs and defeats.

On the death of Lord Raglan, Lieutenant-General Simpson assumed the command of the army as Senior Officer pending further orders from the Home Government.

On the 1st July, Captain C. W. St. Clair was appointed Assistant-Adjutant-General of the Staff at Scutari, where he had been sent on being wounded, on the 18th June.

On the 3rd July, Colonel The Honourable A. A. Spencer, C.B., of the Forty-fourth Regiment, was appointed to command the 1st Brigade of the 4th Division, vacant by the death of Major-General Sir John Campbell, Baronet, killed in action on the 18th June.

The Russians, as might naturally be anticipated, were greatly elated at the result of the attack made upon their defences on the 18th June. They were very active, not only in repairing their works, but also in organizing sorties, whereby the repose of the Allied Armies was constantly disturbed.

1855 The 'trench' duties were very severe on the reduced numbers in the several Regiments, also the men being constantly under arms at all hours of the day and night to resist anticipated attacks; the incessant firing of cannon and musketry kept up constant excitement, and the discipline of the army suffered from the numerous sutlers, through the facilities they afforded to the soldiers to obtain strong drink.

A fortnight's comparative quiet enabled the Fifty-seventh to get the Camp into tolerable order. Drains now carried off the superabundance of water, which formerly rendered it a swamp after the almost tropical rain and thunderstorms, frequent in this country during the hot season. The railway from Balaklava to the Camp was making rapid progress. Supplies being plentiful there was little chance of the army suffering as it did last winter from short rations, or the impossibility of getting supplies owing to the impassability of the roads.

Brigadier-General The Hon. A. A. Spencer had frequent Brigade drills and inspections. Although not always obtaining his unqualified approval the Fifty-seventh maintained its old reputation, its Camp being a pattern of neatness and order. Divine service was regularly conducted on every Sunday—weather permitting—many officers and soldiers availing themselves of the Communion Service, celebrated once a month in one of the huts in Camp.

Early in August the promotions and appointments, consequent on the deaths at the Redan, were received from England.

Lieutenant-Colonel H. J. Warre was appointed an Ordinary Member or Companion of the Most Honourable Order of the Bath, the appointment being dated 5th July, 1855.

1855 Major and Brevet Lieutenant-Colonel J. A. Street to be Lieutenant-Colonel, vice Shadforth killed in action.

On the 16th August, the Russians attacked the Sardinian army and endeavoured to force the passage of the bridge over the Tchernaya River, to get possession of the heights commanding the plain of Balaklava; the Sardinians fought splendidly, and being reinforced by the French, and supported by our Artillery and the Highland Brigade, soon obliged the Russians to retire, with considerable loss.

The Russian attack was well planned and was said to have been conducted by Prince Gortschakoff in person, but they had not calculated upon the depth or breadth of the Tchernaya River. Covered by a cloud of skirmishers and the field batteries lining the high ground beyond the river, the enemy pushed forward a line of portable bridges, which they expected would facilitate their passage across the rivulet; but the bridges were too short, and although the assailants actually crossed the Trachtir bridge at Tchorgum, and approached the heights, they were not supported in sufficient numbers to effect their purpose, and were forced to relinquish the attempt, and reoccupy their former ground on the high land overlooking the ruins of Inkerman. On the 17th August, another bombardment showed that the end was approaching, the Russian losses were so heavy, it was said, that they with difficulty could keep their men in their works, and seldom relieved them.

Owing to the constant fire they could no longer repair their parapets which presented in places a most dilapidated appearance; the bridge across the harbor was nearly completed.

On the 29th August, Surgeon W. H. Macandrew, M.D., joined on appointment.

Lieutenant C. G. Clarke, with 50 rank and file, arrived

1855 on the 3rd September and were followed on the 5th by Captain J. Stewart, Lieutenants F. S. Schomberg, Sir R. Douglas, Baronet, D'Arcey Curwen, with 100 rank and file, and Lieutenant H. H. Chanter joined on the following day, all from the Reserve Depot at Malta.

The Fifty-seventh Camp being situated on the slope in rear of what is known as "Cathcart's Hill"—from the fact that Sir G. Cathcart and many other Officers were buried there—is within about one and a half miles of the batteries of Sebastopol. The Russians had recently mounted some heavy guns which they fired at very uncertain hours, with a high elevation, causing considerable uneasiness, particularly at night, when the shot and shell pitched actually in the Camp, or in its immediate vicinity. Several casualities occurred from their long shots which the men christened "Whistling Jimmies," from the peculiar sound they produced in their flight.

On the 6th September another bombardment commenced. The cannonade was incessant both from the English and French attacks, and the traffic across the Russian bridge never ceased. The enemy was evidently clearing out all that was portable from the South side, ready to abandon his defences when no longer tenable.

Early on the morning of the 8th September an Order was issued for the 1st Brigade to be ready at noon to support another attack on the Redan, in conjunction with the French attack on the Malakoff and Flagstaff Battery. The assaulting party, under Brigadier-General C. Windham was composed of 1,000 men of the Light and 2nd Divisions.

It having been ascertained that the Russians quitted their works for their mid-day meal at noon, the French took advantage of their remissness to attack the Malakoff and the Flagstaff Battery, establishing themselves

1855 successfully in the former, but being driven back after a desperate fight from the latter, the English troops under their gallant leader, at the same time, making their attack upon the apex of the Great Redan. The Fifty-seventh Regiment after remaining for two hours in position overhanging the Woronzoff Road, was ordered forward to occupy the second parallel, and relieve the unfortunate troops who had again unsuccessfully borne the brunt of the assault. The failure of this attack and the heroism of the troops employed are now matters of history, but the heroic conduct of the Russians troops in defence of their works has hardly been sufficiently extolled. From the position occupied by the Fifty-seventh the reckless gallantry of the Russians was apparent, they stood upon the crest of the parapet and exposed themselves to the fire of their enemies without apparently a thought of the consequences; their guns were exposed by the destruction of the parapets, but the Artillery men continued to serve them, and in one instance after all the gunners had been knocked over, several men in succession endeavoured to serve the gun, only to meet with a soldier's death from the galling fire to which their gun was exposed.

At 5 o'clock the Fifty-seventh Regiment (with the 63rd, whose commanding officer was placed *hors de combat*) under the command of Colonel Warre, C.B., went to take up its quarters for the night, near the mortar batteries at the head of the Ravine, between the Malakoff and the Redan; darkness had hardly set in when it became evident that the Russians were abandoning their works, and by the aid of that bridge which their prudence and foresight had constructed, were evacuating that portion of Sebastopol situated on the south side of the harbour, now no longer defensible.

Fires sprung up on every side; fearful explosions

1855 filled the air with shells and stones. Batteries and ships had disappeared before the morning's light enabled one to see that the town was deserted.

The Regiment was relieved at 10 o'clock a.m., on the 9th September, and returned to Camp. Lieutenant Bayntun joined on the same day from Malta.

On the 12th September Lieutenant H. R. Russell, and on the 22nd Lieutenant H. Powell joined the Service Companies.

The Regiment was inspected by the Lieutenant-General commanding the 4th Division on Saturday the 15th September, and on the 18th September Sir Henry Bentinck, K.C.B., inspected the whole division on the ground in front of the camp overlooking Sebastopol.

The following Regiments composed the division divided into two brigades, viz.:

The 1st Brigade, under the command of Major-General The Honourable A. A. Spencer, C.B., consists of Seventeenth, Twentieth, Twenty-first (R.N.B.) Fusiliers, Fifty-seventh and Sixty-third Regiments. The 2nd Brigade, under the command of Brigadier-General R. Garratt, C.B., consisting of Forty-sixth, Forty-eighth, Sixty-eighth (Light Infantry), and 2nd Battalion Rifle Brigade.

On the 19th September the Crimean War Medals, with Clasps for Balaklava and Inkermann, were issued on a Heavy Marching Order Parade, to every officer and soldier who had been present during the campaign.

On the 24th Lieutenant E. G. Hasted joined from Ireland.

The Regiment under the command of Lieutenant-Colonel H. J. Warre, C.B., strength as below marched from the heights from before Sebastopol to Hazatch Bay to join an expeditionary force, the head-quarters and right wing, embarked on board H.M. Steam Ship *Sidon*,

1855 and the left wing under the command of Lieutenant-Colonel J. A. Street, C.B., embarked on board H.M. Steam Ship *Leopard*, on the 4th October.

Lt.-Colonels.	Major.	Captains.	Subalterns.	Staff.	Sergeants.	Drummers.	Rank and File.
2	1	7	14	4	37	13	663

Sailed with the Allied Fleets under Admirals Bruat and Lyons for Odessa, on the 7th October.

Lieutenant D'Arcy Curwen died in camp, Crimea, of disease, on the 8th October.

The Allied Fleets anchored on the 8th October, about 5 miles off Odessa, awaiting orders.

Remained at anchor off Odessa, on the 9th, 10th, and 11th October.

The head-quarters and right wing were transhipped off Odessa from H.M. Steam Ship *Sidon*, to the Steam Troop Ship *Vulcan*, on the 12th October, but remained at anchor off Odessa, until the 14th, when the *Vulcan* weighed anchor and steamed with the fleet to the mouth of the Dnieper River off Otshak. The fleet anchored about 5 o'clock p m. The Troops landed at noon on the 15th October, about three miles from Fort Kinburn, and bivouacked for the night on the sands connecting the spit of land on which the Fort is situated with the mainland.

On the 17th, the Regiment paraded at 4.30 a.m. in light marching order, and made a reconnoissance about 4 miles along the coast, met with no opposition from the enemy, and returned to camp about 10 a.m. The Garrison of Fort Kinburn surrendered after five hours' bombardment to the Allied Fleets of England and France.

1855 Shifted camp ground and moved nearer to Fort Kinburn on the 18th October.

Quartermaster Balcombe joined the Regiment from leave of absence.

On the 20th, the Regiment under the command of Lieutenant Colonel H. J. Warre, C.B., with the Infantry Brigade, under Brigadier-General the Honourable A. A. Spencer, C.B., marched from Kinburn to Patrouska (5 miles), halted and bivouacked in quarter distance column. On the following day the Regiment attended a divisional field day under Brigadier-General the Honourable A. Spencer, and bivouacked for the night.

On the 22nd the Regiment advanced about seven miles, drove some Cossacks out of the Village of Schadoffka and returned to its old ground and bivouacked for the night.

The Brigade marched back to Kinburn, on the 23rd, and occupied the camp ground vacated on the 20th instant.

On the 29th, the Head-quarters and right wing under the command of Lieutenant-Colonel H. J. Warre, C.B., embarked on board H.M. Steam Ship *Valorous*, and the left wing under the command of Lieutenant-Colonel Street, C.B., on board H.M. Ship *Firebrand*, weighed anchor and steamed with the allied Fleets of England and France for Hazatch Bay.

Anchored in Hazatch Bay, on the 30th October, at about 10 o'clock p.m., and remained at anchor until Sunday morning the 11th November, when the Regiment disembarked and marched to its original camp in the 4th Division of the Army before Sebastopol.

On 2nd November, Major William Inglis was promoted Brevet-Lieutenant-Colonel, and Captain Jason Hassard, Brevet-Major for service in the field.

Lieutenant-General Sir W. Codrington, K.C.B.,

1855 succeeded Lieutenant-General Simpson, C.B., as Commander-in-Chief, on 13th November.

On the 18th November, Major Robert Abraham Logan, and 2 privates, joined Head-quarters from the Reserve at Malta, and on the 20th, Assistant-Surgeon M. J. Griffin joined from Medical Staff.

During the year the Non-Commissioned Officers and soldiers of the 57th Regiment sent to their families and friends in England £2,446 15s. in addition to money forwarded by private hands.

The men were employed during November in getting from Balaklava planks and roofing to erect huts for their comfort during the ensuing winter.

The Russians on the North side of Sebastopol occasionally fired upon working parties employed on the South side; otherwise there was very little active duty to perform.

Lieutenants H. D. M. Shute and Edward Mills joined from the Reserve at Malta on the 28th December,
1856 and on the 5th January, 1856, Assistant-Surgeon W. Fergusson joined from Medical Staff.

The destruction of the Sebastopol Docks was completed on the 7th February.

Dispenser of Medicines, W. D. North joined Head-quarters from England, on the 8th February.

On the 1st March, an Armistice by land was proclaimed with the Russian forces, until the 30th March; during which period there was to be no firing by the Allied Army upon the enemy.

Lieutenants H. R. Russell, S. H. Powell, and E. G. Hasted received the Crimean Medal without Clasps, for operations against the enemy at Kinburn, having joined after the fall of Sebastopol.

On the 19th March, Captain G. V. B. Arbuckle, T. W. J. Lloyd, Lieutenant Edward Brutton, 2 Ser-

1856 geants, 4 Corporals, 1 Drummer and 43 Privates, joined Head-quarters from the Reserve Companies at Malta.

A salute of 101 guns was fired in honour of the birth of the Prince Imperial of France on the 23rd March.

The Commander of the Forces published to the Army the translation of a General Order, issued by Field Marshal Pelissier, to the French Army.

Head-Quarters, French Army,
23rd March, 1856.

The firing you have just heard has informed you that the Empress has given to France an Imperial Prince. Our brave and loyal Allies, the English and Sardinians have also desired to fire a salute in honour of this happy birth. "*Soldiers*," you will be sensible on this day of the same joy that the country has felt; for like her, you will see in this desired event, another satisfaction for our Emperor, a new pledge of the great destinies of France, and a striking mark of the blessings of Heaven.

The Field Marshal Commanding-in-Chief,
(Signed) A. PELISSIER.

On the 30th March, the treaty of peace with Russia was signed at Paris.

On the 2nd April, a salute of one hundred and one guns was fired in honour of the treaty of peace being signed with Russia.

The field allowance of 6d. per diem. to the Non-Commissioned Officers and men was discontinued on the 2nd April, 1856.

After the declaration of peace, the English army was no longer restricted from crossing the Tchernaya River.

Lieutenant A. F. A. Slade rejoined Head-quarters from sick leave, having been severely wounded on the 18th June.

1856 EXTRACT FROM DIVISION ORDERS, 5TH MAY, 1856.

The breaking up of the 4th Division being about to commence, by the embarkation of the Sixty-third Regiment to-morrow, to be followed by the Seventeenth Regiment, both of them destined for North America, Major-General Garrett took leave of them, and congratulated them on their good fortune in being called on to serve in that quarter, and assured them of his best wishes for their welfare and success.

EXTRACT FROM BRIGADE ORDERS.

"The breaking up of the 1st Brigade 4th Division having commenced by the departure to-morrow of the Sixty-third Regiment, Brigadier-General The Honourable A. Spencer, C.B., takes this opportunity to return his thanks to Lieutenant-Colonel Cole, C.B., and Major Gordon, Seventeenth Regiment, Lieutenant-Colonel Eveliegh, Twentieth Regiment, Lieutenant-Colonel Stewart, Twenty-first Regiment, Lieutenant-Colonel H. J. Warre, C.B., Fifty-seventh Regiment, and Colonel Hill, Sixty-third Regiment, for the assistance he has received from them as Commanding Officers during the period he has had the honor of commanding the Brigade."

"Brigadier-General Honourable A. Spencer at the same time takes leave of the Officers, Non-Commissioned Officers and privates of the gallant regiments composing the brigade, wishing them every happiness in whatever part of the world their destinies may lead them."

On the 8th May Lieutenant-Colonel Street, C.B., took command of the Regiment on the departure of Lieutenant-Colonel Warre, C.B., on leave of absence.

Six decorations of the French Military War Medal were sent by the Emperor of France to the Regiment, and conferred, at a general parade on the 24th May,

1856 on the following men for meritorious conduct in the field:

No. 1061 ......Colour-Sergeant John McCardle
No. 1569 ...... „ John Coughlan
No. 3080 ...... „ J. F. Andrews
No. 1166 ......Corporal Thomas Connell
No. 1940 ......Lnce.-Corporal William Kinnarney
No. 2501 ...... „ John Murray

GENERAL AFTER ORDER.

Head-quarters, Sebastopol,

15*th May*, 1856.

Peace being now definitely arranged, the Commander of the Forces had the satisfaction of publishing an extract of a despatch from the Secretary of State for War, in which reference is made to the services of this army.

" I avail myself of so fitting an opportunity as the " moment when Her Majesty's Troops, under your com- " mand, are about to quit the scene of their endurance " and triumph, to place on record the feelings entertained " towards them by Her Majesty, the Government, and " the People.

" Since the period when the Army first quitted the " shores of England there is no vicissitude of war which " it has not been called upon to encounter. Shortly " after its arrival in Turkey, and while doubtful as to " the manner in which it was to be brought in contact " with the enemy, it had to sustain the terrible attacks " of cholera which prematurely closed the career of many " a gallant and eager spirit. On this occasion the Army " proved that moral as well as physical courage pervaded " its ranks.

" Led to the field, it has triumphed in engagements " in which heavy odds were on the enemy's side, it has

1856 "carried on, under difficulties almost incredible, a siege "of unprecedented duration; during which the trying "duties of the trenches, privations from straightened "supplies, the fearful diminution of its number by "disease, neither shook its courage, nor impaired its "discipline.

"Notwithstanding that many a gallant comrade "fell in their ranks, and they were called to mourn the "beloved commander who led them from England, and "who closed in the field his noble life as a soldier, Her "Majesty's Troops never flinched from their duties, or "disappointed the sanguine expectation of their country. "The zealous manner in which the Army prepared to "take the field, had the war been prolonged, its eager-"ness for active operations, and its fitness to meet any "emergency are known to all. These continued events "and circumstances have thus afforded to the Queen, "the Government and the Country, the opportunity of "witnessing the conduct of the Army under every aspect, "and the feeling is universal, that it has worthily main-"tained its own high character, and the honour of British "Arms, and you may be perfectly assured that on its "return home, it will be welcomed with the fullest "approbation of its Sovereign and with every demonstra-"tion of admiration by the country at large.

"I add with pleasure, that the services of the various "departments attached to the Army, are of a character "to entitle them to the fullest credit. The zeal and "energy of the Medical, Commissariat and Clerical "Departments, have contributed to bring the Army into "its present most effective condition.

"(Signed) PANMURE.

"By Order,

"(Signed) C. A. WINDHAM,

"*Chief of the Staff.*"

1856 On the 27th May, 1856, the Fifty-seventh received an order to embark for Malta, and on the 28th the Regiment, under the command of Lieutenant-Colonel Street, C.B., strength as below, vacated the ground on the heights before Sebastopol, where it had been encamped for one year and six months, marched from thence to Balaklava, and embarked on board the steam transport *Etna.* The *Etna* steamed out of the harbour at six p.m., and reached the Island of Malta on the night of the 1st June. The regiment disembarked the following day at 3 p.m., and was quartered in Fort Verdala Barracks.

Field Officers.	Captains.	Subalterns.	Staff.	Sergeants.	Corporals.	Drummers.	Rank and File.
2	7	15	5	49	44	13	645

The following Officers sailed with the service companies from the Crimea:—

Lieut.-Col. J. A. Street, C.B.
Major R. A. Logan.
Capt. James Stewart.
„ G. V. B. Arbuckle.
„ Henry Butler.
„ G. J. Forsyth.
„ W. E. Brown.
„ T. W. J. Lloyd.
„ J. C. Ingham.
Lieut. W. E. J. Shortt.
„ T. N. G. Macartney.
„ J. R. Wilmot.
„ F. S. Schomberg.
„ Sir R. Douglas (Bart.)
„ A. F. A. Slade.
Lieut. H. D. M. Shute
„ C. G. Clarke.
„ H. R. Russell.
„ G. R. Waugh (Adjutant.)
„ B. C. Bayntun.
„ S. H. Powell.
„ E. Mills.
„ E. G. Hasted.
„ E. Brutton.
Ensign J. S. Phelps.
Surgeon W.H. MacAndrew, M.D.
Asst.-Surgn. M. J. Griffin.
„ W. Furguson.
Dispenser of Medicines W. D. North.

1856 The Reserve Companies stationed in Malta under the command of Brevet Lieutenant-Colonel William Inglis, (strength as below) joined Regimental Head-quarters, also the following Officers:—

Brevet-Major Jason Hassard.	Ensign S. F. Sewell.
Captain T. N. Woodall.	" H. F. Emly.
" Jesser Coope.	" W. de W. Waller.
Lieut. W. A. K. Thompson.	" J. Parkinson.
" J. H. Tragett.	H. Wayne.
" C. F. Houghton.	

On the 6th June, Captains Henry Butler, C. W. St. Clair, and A. M. Earle were promoted to Brevet-Majorities for service in the field.

The Insignia of the 5th Class of the Imperial Order of the Legion of Honour was conferred by His Majesty the Emperor of the French upon the under-mentioned Officers and soldiers of the Regiment for distinguished services before the enemy during the late war, viz:—

Brevet-Major Henry Butler.	1626 Sergeant-Major G. Cumming.
Captain G. J. Forsyth.	2101 Color-Sergeant W. Griffith.
Brevet-Major A. M. Earle.	1782 Private J. Burgess.

Field Marshal Henry Viscount Hardinge, G.C.B., Colonel of the Fifty-seventh Regiment died on the 26th September. See Appendix.

On the 29th September, Lieutenant-Colonel H. J. Warre, C.B., resumed command of the Regiment, from leave of absence on Medical Certificate.

Major-General Sir J. F. Love, K.C.B., K.H. (Governor of Jersey), appointed Colonel of Fifty-seventh Regiment in succession to the late Lord Hardinge, G.C.B.

On the 29th October, the Regiment was inspected by Major-General H. F. Williams, K.H., commanding the Brigade at Malta.

1856 Ensign W. Hedger, 1 Sergeant, 3 Corporals and 47 Privates joined Head-quarters from Ireland.

1857 The Flank Companies were clothed in the new pattern single-breasted tunic on the 1st April, 1857.

The Regiment moved by wings to the encampment St. George's Bay for musketry instruction, the Head-quarters and right wing on the 15th and the left wing on the 20th April.

Major-General F. Horn, C.B., made the usual half-yearly inspection of the Regiment on the 11th May, 1857.

By memorandum dated Assistant-Adjutant-General office Malta, 16th May, 1857, the effectives of the Service Companies were ordered to be reduced to the following:—

Sergeants.	Corporals.	Drummers.	Privates.
46	32	21	628

On the 28th May, the French War Medal was presented by Lieutenant-General Sir J. L. Pennefather to No. 2499 Private Thomas Anderson for distinguished conduct in the field.

The French War Medal was also conferred upon No. 1802 Colour-Sergeant John Jones, at the Regimental Depot.

On the 30th June, Ensign P. F. Clarke joined Head-quarters from Ireland.

The right wing having completed its course of musketry instructions returned to the barracks at Floriana, on the 1st July, 1857.

The grant of the Victoria Cross with an annuity of £10 to 1971 Private Charles McCorrie for distinguished

1857 conduct in the trenches before Sebastopol, on the 23rd June, 1855, in throwing a live shell over the parapet, thereby saving the lives of his comrades; published in General Orders, dated Malta, 16th July, 1857.

This brave soldier died at Malta on the 9th April, 1857, before the Cross was received.

The Head-quarters returned to the barracks, Floriana, on 18th June, and the left wing on the 29th June.

The Regiment generally supplied with the new pattern accoutrements, shoulder belts, waist belts and double pouches in August, 1857.

Sardinian Medals were conferred upon the under-mentioned officers and soldiers who had served with the Regiment in the Crimea:

Lieutenant-Colonel J. A. Street, C.B. (Commanding Depot Battalion, Colchester); Brevet-Major C. W. St. Clair; Brevet-Major G. J. Forsyth; Lieutenant A. F. A. Slade; (983) Dr. Michael Norton; (2583) Private Jeremiah Healy.

Brevet-Major St. Clair, Lieutenant Slade and Private Healy were presented with the medal by Lieutenant-General Sir J. L. Pennefather, K.C.B., commanding troops at Malta on a Brigade Parade, on the 19th August, 1857.

On the 29th September Orders were received for two Companies to proceed overland, *via* the Isthmus of Suez, to Aden to be there stationed.

Major Logan, Captain Brown, Lieutenants Wilmot, Sir R. Douglas, Baronet, Tragett, and Hedger, Ensigns Phelps and P. F. Clarke Assistant-Surgeon Griffin, 10 Sergeants, (including the Regimental Quarter-master Serjeant), 4 Drummers, 10 Corporals, and 176 Privates accordingly embarked on board the Peninsular and Oriental Company's Steamship *Ripon*, on the 30th, and sailed the same night.

1857 The Regiment ordered again to recruit to its full establishment of 1,000 rank and file.

No. 1782 Private James Burgess, who received the Legion of Honour for gallant conduct in the field, died on the 19th September, at Malta.

Major-General C. Warren, C.B., made the usual half-yearly inspection of the Regiment on the 6th October.

1858 Lieutenant-Colonel Warre, C B., had much pleasure in publishing to the Regiment the following observations of H.R.H. the General Commanding-in-Chief on the autumn half-yearly inspection, viz.: "The excellent " report on the Fifty-seventh Regiment has been perused " by H.R.H. with great satisfaction."

On the 1st March, the following Officers proceeded overland *via* the Isthmus of Suez, to join the detachment of the Regiment at Aden: Lieutenant H. R. Russell, Ensign J. Parkinson, Ensign H. F. Emly.

On the 17th March, Major R. D. Logan, commanding detachment at Aden, received an order to detail 1 captain, 2 subalterns, and 100 rank and file, to march at 2 a.m. on the 18th March, and, as next senior, was left in command of the garrison with 50 Europeans and a portion of the 29th Regiment Bombay Native Infantry, to take charge of the camp and town during the absence of the expeditionary force, and also to be ready to act in the event of any outbreak amongst the inhabitants, chiefly composed of Arabs.

The admirable manner in which Captain Brown commanded his party, the judgment and coolness displayed by this officer, and the conduct and gallantry of officers and men, elicited the marked approbation of the Brigadier as shown on the following Brigade Order.

ADEN, 19*th March*, 1858.

Extract from Brigade Orders by Brigadier W. M. Coghlan commanding Aden Field Force.

1858 The Brigadier Commanding tenders his best thanks to the officers and men of all ranks (including those of the Indian Navy), engaged in yesterday's operations; for the gallantry and cheerfulness they displayed, and it will afford the Brigadier great pleasure to bring their particular services to the notice of His Excellency the Commander in Chief and Government of India.

Horse-Guards,

Copy, *29th April*, 1858.

Sir,

I am directed by the General Commanding in Chief, to acknowledge the receipt of your letter of the 15th instant, enclosing the Report received by you, relative to the proceedings of a detachment of the Fifty-seventh Regiment stationed at Aden, when acting against the Arabs, in the vicinity on the 18th ultimo, and to inform you that it is very satisfactory to His Royal Highness to receive so favourable a report of the conduct of the troops on the occasion in question.

Lieutenant-General, I have, &c.,

Sir J. L. Pennefather, K.C.B. (Signed) C. YORKE.

The Regiment was completed with new pattern accoutrements and knapsacks on the 31st March, 1858, and at the same time was clothed in the new pattern single breasted tunic.

The Service Companies augmented to ten companies, but no addition of Non-Commissioned Officers or men by Horse-Guards Circular, 29th January, 1858.

The Queen has been pleased to give and grant unto the undermentioned officers, Her Majesty's Royal License and permission that they may accept and wear the Insignia of the several classes of the Imperial Order of the Medjidie attached to their respective names, which

1858 His Imperial Majesty, the Sultan, has been pleased to confer upon them as a mark of His Majesty's approbation of their distinguished services before the enemy during the late war, and that they may enjoy all the rights and privileges thereunto belonging, viz:—

Lieut.-Col. H. J. Warre, C.B.	Capt. W. E. Brown.		Fifth Class.
„ J. A. Street, C.B.	„ C. Venables.		
(On the Staff, 4th Class.)			
Fifth Class.	Bt. Lieut.-Col. W. Inglis.	„ J. C. Ingham.	
	Capt. & Bt.-Mjr. F. P. Lea.	Lieut. W. A. J. Shortt.	
	„ Jason Hassard.	„ A. F. A. Slade.	
	„ A. M. Earle.	Ensign J. S. Phelps.	

Lieutenant-Colonel Henry J. Warre, C.B., having completed three years' actual service in command of Fifty-seventh Regiment to be Colonel in the Army, under the Royal Warrant of the 6th October, 1854, dated 9th March, 1858.

A draft consisting of Ensigns Cox and McClintock, 1 Sergeant and 40 rank and file, joined the Service Companies from Ireland on 25th April.

It having been determined to send the Regiment to India, the following order was issued on the 10th May:

Assistant-Adjutant-General's Office,
10*th May*, 1858.

The Fifty-seventh Regiment will embark on board Her Majesty's Ship *Princess Royal*, Captain The Hon. Thomas Baillie, C.B., at 3 o'clock p.m. to-morrow, from the Calcara Marina.

The Regiment, under the command of Colonel Warre, C.B., embarked on the 11th May, at 3 p.m. from the Calcara Wharf, Malta (strength as under,) on board H.M. Steam Line of Battle Ship *Princess Royal*, and steamed out of the harbour en route for Alexandria and Bombay:—

1858

Field Officers.	Captains.	Subalterns.	Staff.	Sergeants.	Corporals.	Drummers.	Privates.	Total.
1	3	9	5	35	27	16	558	654

THE FOLLOWING OFFICERS EMBARKED.

Lieut.-Col. H. J. Warre, C.B., (Brevet-Colonel.)	Lieut. C. G. Hasted.
Captain H. Butler (Brevet-Major.)	„ W. A. K. Thompson.
„ A. L. Copland.	Ensign W. de W. Waller.
„ H. Bird.	„ A. M'Clintock.
Lieut. W. A. J. Shortt.	Paymaster M. Matthews.
„ F. S. Schomberg.	Lieut. and Adjt. G. R. Waugh.
„ H. D. M. Shute.	Quartermaster J. Balcombe.
„ B. C. Bayntun.	Surgeon W. Macandrew.
„ S. H. Powell.	Asst.-Surgn. W. Ferguson.

The *Princess Royal* arrived off Alexandria on the 16th May.

First Division, Head-quarters (13 Officers, 434 Non-Commissioned Officers and men) disembarked at Alexandria about 2 p.m., on the 18th May, and proceeded to the railway station.

The train started at 6 p.m., crossed the Nile in boats, and reached Kafa Zayhat about 12 o'clock midnight, where the Officers and men dined. After an hour's stay, again proceeded, and arrived at Cairo about 4 a.m. On reaching No. 13 Station, the last in the desert, at about 9 a.m., the men breakfasted, and after an hour's detention were provided with donkeys, on which to continue the journey to Suez.

The Nile was not bridged, and the railway was not completed beyond this station. Boats conveyed the Regiment (Officers and men with their baggage, &c.,

1858 across the rapid river, and donkeys were provided to carry the 400 men the 22 miles still to be traversed over the hot sandy desert. Having been told off into sections—single ranks—at intervals of 100 yards, the march commenced, and owing to the admirable conduct and steadiness of the men, under circumstances so novel, the otherwise fatiguing march was performed in about seven hours, without inconvenience from the clouds of dust, which were blown through the intervals of Companies clear of the Column.

On arriving at Suez at about 4 o'clock p.m., the Head-quarter Companies embarked at once on board the Honorable East India Company's Steamer *Prince Arthur*, which had been sent expressly to convey the Regiment to Bombay.

The 2nd Division, Nos. 3 and 4 Companies, (5 officers, 200 Non-Commissioned Officers and men,) followed on the 19th and reached Suez the next day, where they embarked on board the Penisular and Oriental Company's Steamer *Bengal*, it having been found that the *Prince Arthur*, would not afford proper accommodation for more than the Head-quarter Division. These two Companies were landed at Aden, and joined that detachment on the 26th May.

The *Prince Arthur* with the Head-quarters, left Suez on the 20th and reached Aden on the 27th. No. 5 Company disembarked the same evening and joined the Aden detachment.

The Head-quarter wing left Aden on the 28th May, and reached Bombay on the evening of the 6th June.

There was only one casualty during the voyage.

The head-quarter wing disembarked on the 8th June, at 6 a.m., marched into the Town barracks, Bombay, and the Regiment was taken on the strength of the Indian establishment.

1858 On the 11th June, the Victoria Cross was conferred on No. 1356 Colour-Sergeant George Gardiner, (Authority War Office letter, of the 11th June, 1858) with an annuity of £10 from the 22nd March, 1855.

Lieutenants A. F. A. Slade, E. Mills, and E. Brutton, joined by the Overland Route off leave on the 23rd June.

On the 11th July, a detachment consisting of Captains Schomberg, Sir R. Douglas, Baronet, and Lieutenant Tragett, with 4 Sergeants, 1 Drummer, and 194 rank and file, arrived from Aden and marched to Colaba, to reinforce the Head-quarter Companies, which were removed on the 23rd June from the Town barracks to Colaba.

Captain Stewart joined Head-quarters from England on the 12th, and Lieutenant-Colonel Inglis, Brevet-Major Earle, Ensign C. M. Clarke, and Assistant-Surgeon Davis, with 25 Privates, joined from England on the 13th October.

The Regiment received orders to proceed by detachments from Bombay, by railway and bullock train to Malligaum, for "Field Service." Head-quarters arrived at Malligaum on 3rd December, and encamped on the Maidan in front of the Cantonment; the other Companies joined in succession.

On the 24th November, Ensign Brown and 28 privates joined from England.

On the 11th December, the Head-quarters and two Companies proceeded by bullock train to Dhoolia, and from thence to Seerpore, on the Taptee River; the remaining Companies followed in succession, and continuing their march to Chopra, the Regiment was encamped for about six weeks, forming a small Brigade, with the Poona Horse and Bheel Rifles; the whole under the immediate command of Colonel Warre, C.B.

1858 The Brigade, or Field Force, was encamped at several stations, between Berhampoor and Tulloda, a distance of about 150 miles, to prevent the incursions into Khandeish of rebel natives, who under Tantia Topee, occupied the jungle on the Satpoora Hills, and in the valley of the Taptee River.

On the 28th December, Captain and Brevet-Major St. Clair joined from England, having been employed as Aide-de-Camp to the Earl Mulgrave, Governor of Nova Scotia.

1859 Ensign P. F. Clarke and 4 Privates joined at Malligaum from England on the 12th January, 1859.

Received 5 Volunteers from Her Majesty's 78th Highlanders on the return of that Regiment to England on the 1st February.

The following distribution of Companies was ordered on the Head-quarters being relieved at Chopra by the 26th Native Infantry:

No. 1 or Grenadiers to ....Asseerghur
No. 2.................. „ ....Ahmednuggur
No. 3.................. „ ....Aden
No. 4.................. „ ....Aden
No. 5.................. „ ....Tulligaum
No. 6.................. „ ....Ahmednuggur
No. 7.................. „ ....Aden
No. 8.................. „ ....Ahmednuggur
No. 9.................. „ ....Adjunta
Light.................. „ ....Ahmednuggur

The Head-quarters and No. 6 Company left Chopra en route for Maligaum, via Dhoolia, on the 9th February, 1859, arrived at Maligaum on the 16th, and continued their march to Ahmednuggur on the 18th, arrived at Ahmednuggur on the 28th February, and were encamped on the cantonment under the fort; remained encamped until the 16th May, when temporary Barracks

1859 were completed for them. The men suffered severely from fever during the months of April and May, owing to being under canvas during the hot weather.

Received 25 Volunteers from H.M. 86th Regiment, on the return of that Regiment to England in March, 1859.

Ensign R. H. Cox joined from England in the ship *Cospatrick*, and arrived at the Head-quarters of the Regiment at Ahmednuggur, on 15th June.

The red serge frocks authorised for Regiments serving in India, were received at Ahmednuggur, on 30th May, 1859, and taken into wear on 2nd July, as a substitute for shell jackets.

On the 25th September Quartermaster Balcombe was promoted and removed from the Regiment, after a service of over twenty years, on which occasion the following Regimental Order was issued:—

"In publishing the Gazette of the 25th September, which promotes Captain Balcombe, and deprives the Regiment of his valuable services as Quarter-master, Colonel Warre gladly avails himself of the occasion to remind Non-Commissioned Officers and men that they may also, by a similar attention to their duties, attain the highly honorable position Captain Balcombe now occupies. Brought up in the Regiment and having gained his rank, entirely by his own merits, Captain Balcombe may justly be proud of his position, and it is with feelings of very great regret that Colonel Warre, on behalf of his brother officers, and in the name of the Regiment takes leave of him, and in wishing him every future success, assures him of their sincere friendship and esteem."

On the 2nd October Colonel Warre, C.B., having been appointed to the command of the Brigade at Mhow, resigned, while he was so employed, the command of the Regiment to Lieutenant-Colonel Inglis, on which

1859 occasion the following order was issued by Colonel Warre, C.B., on leaving the Regiment.

"In taking leave of the Regiment which he has had the pleasure to command, under such varied and often peculiarly trying circumstances, Colonel Warre desires to place upon record his grateful appreciation of the undeviating good conduct of the Officers, Non-Commissioned Officers and men. Their courage and devotion were conspicuously shown and acknowledged in the Crimea, at Kinburn, on the voyage from Malta, on the march across the Egyptian Desert, and their good conduct and discipline have been at all times remarkable. From Malta, where the Regiment remained for two years, Lieutenant-General Sir John Pennefather writes constantly of the deep interest he takes in that splendid Regiment, the 'Die Hards,' while H.R.H. the General Commanding-in-Chief is pleased to admit that 'the remarkable absence of crime in the 57th Regiment has attracted the particular notice of His Royal Highness,' who deems the Report of this Corps 'highly creditable in every respect.' Under such circumstances, Colonel Warre cannot but feel grieved to quit, even for a time, a Regiment that has so distinguished itself, and has gained for him and for itself so much credit and honour."

Lieutenant-Colonel W. Inglis assumed command of the Regiment from the 2nd October, 1859.

Six hundred and sixty-seven Turkish Crimean medals were received from the Secretary of State for War, for distribution among the officers and men engaged in the Crimean Campaign of 1854-5.

The undermentioned officers were present with the Regiment and the Companies distributed as follows, Head-quarters being at Ahmednuggur.

1859 DISTRIBUTION OF OFFICERS AND COMPANIES.

No.	RANK AND NAMES.		REMARKS.
1	Lieut-Col.	H. J. Warre, C.B. (Col.)	Brigadier at Mhow.
2	„	W. Inglis.	Ahmednuggur.
1	Major	R. A. Logan.	Aden.
2	„	H. Butler.	Ahmednuggur.
1	Captain	J. Stewart.	Ahmednuggur.
2	„	C. W. St. Clair.	At Sattara.
3	„	W. E. Brown.	Ahmednuggur.
4	„	E. M. Earle, (M.)	On leave (Europe).
5	„	T. R. Woodall.	At Aden.
6	„	H. Bird.	Staff College.
7	„	J. R. Wilmot.	At Aden.
8	„	F. S. Schomberg.	Ahmednuggur.
9	„	Sir R. Douglas, (Bt.)	On leave (Europe).
10	„	A. F. A. Slade.	On leave (Europe)
1	Lieutenant.	W. A. J. Shortt (I. M.)	Ahmednuggur.
2	„	H. D. M. Shute.	Admednuggur.
3	„	H. R. Russell.	On duty with time expired men to England.
4	„	B. C. Banytun.	At Aden.
5	„	S. H. Powell.	At Aden.
6	Lieutenant.	E. Mills.	On leave (Europe).
7	„	E. G. Hasted.	At Sattara.
8	„	E. Brutton.	Ahmednuggur.
9	„	W. A. K. Thompson.	Ahmednuggur.
10	„	J. H. Tragett.	Ahmednuggur.
11	„	John Parkinson.	At Aden.
12	„	R. A. H. Cox.	At Sattara.
1	Ensign.	H. F. Emly.	At Aden.
2	„	W.-de-W. Waller.	On leave (Europe).
3	„	A. McClintock.	Ahmednuggur.
4	„	P. F. Clarke.	Ahmednuggur.
5	„	C. M. Clarke.	Adjt.-Bgde. Depot.
6	„	R. E. Brown.	At Sattara.
1	Paymaster.	Mark Matthews.	Ahmednuggur.
1	Adjutant.	G. R. Waugh.	Ahmednuggur.
1	Surgeon.	W. Macandrew (M.D.)	On leave (Europe).
1	Asst.-Surg.	M. J. Griffin.	At Aden.
2	„	W. Ferguson.	Ahmednuggur.
3	„	J. Davis.	At Sattara.

DISTRIBUTION OF COMPANIES.

No. 1 Company....................Ahmednuggur.
No. 2 „ ....Sattara.
No. 3 „ ....Aden.
No. 4 „ ....Aden.

1859 No. 5 Company.....................Ahmednuggur.
No. 6 " ....Ahmednuggur.
No. 7 " ....Aden.
No. 8 " ....Ahmednuggur.
No. 9 " ....Ahmednuggur.
No. 10 " ....Sattara.

During the month of January, 1860, the several Companies of the Regiment, which had been detached at various stations in Khandeisch and on the Taptee River, rejoined Head-quarters; and the Regiment, with the exception of three Companies at Aden, was concentrated at Poona.

The Barracks being fully occupied, the Regiment was encamped upon the Maidan, or parade ground in front of the Barracks.

On the 31st January, Brevet-Major Hassard, Ensign Robert Murray and Quartermaster Martindale, accompanied by 1 Sergeant, 2 Drummers and 89 rank and file, joined Head-quarters from England, and on the same day the regiment gave 25 volunteers to the Thirty-first Regiment on its proceeding on Active Service to China.

On the departure of the 31st Regiment on the 14th February, the Fifty-seventh took possession of the Ghorpoorie Barracks.

When the Regiment left Malta, the soldiers' families remained in that Garrison, and were subsequently sent to England. On the 21st February, 1860, after nearly two years' absence, forty-two women and fifty-three children, under charge of Armourer-Sergeant A. Holland, rejoined the Regiment, having been sent from England on board the ship *Water Witch*, via Cape of Good Hope, &c.

1860 On the 15th March, 1860, the detachment under command of Major R. A. Logan, from Aden, rejoined Head-quarters at Poona.

As a depot for coaling the Indian mail steamers, or

1860 occasionally giving shelter in its open roadstead to British men-of-war, Aden may be necessary as a protection to our commerce in the Red Sea, but as a military station it would be difficult to find a more desolate place or a climate more unsuitable to European soldiers. The Barracks are situated within the steep scarps of an extinct volcano: these scarps are nearly 1,800 ft. in height, rising abruptly from the sea, but afford neither vegetation nor water to relieve the scorching heat or the intense glare of a tropical sun. Rain seldom falls; and although the remains of old cisterns, cut out of the solid rock, show that Aden was once a place of considerable resort, it was, until recently, entirely dependent upon water brought by small acqueducts from a distance, and periodically the hostile tribes of wandering Arabs used to attempt to cut off the supply.

European troops were kept on this barren spot to protect the shipping and to prevent the water from being cut off. Modern inventions have, however, rendered Aden independent of external aid: condensing machines now render an adequate supply of water, but the troops remain in charge, and are necessary for the protection of Government property.

The Companies under Major Logan rejoined their Regiment in very good order, and the conduct of the men was made, prior to their departure, the subject of a special panegyric by the Brigadier under whom they had been serving.

Colonel Warre rejoined at Poona on the reduction of the Brigade at Mhow, and, on the 25th March, 1860, resumed command of the Regiment.

The Regiment was inspected by Brigadier-General Hale, commanding Poona Brigade, and by Lieutenant-General Sir Henry Somerset, K.C.B., commanding the Bombay Army.

1860 On the 1st June Colonel H. J. Warre, C.B., proceeded to Calcutta as Military Secretary to His Excellency Sir Hugh Rose, K.C.B., who was appointed General Commanding-in-Chief in India; and Major Logan assumed the temporary command of the Regiment.

The usual inspections were held by the Brigadier, and by His Excellency Sir W. Mansfield, K.C.B., commanding the Bombay Army. His Excellency expressed his great satisfaction at the soldier-like appearance of the men, the cleanliness of the Barracks Hospital, &c., and remarked "that everything connected with the Regiment "was in perfect order and just as it should be."

On the 3rd November orders were received to hold the Regiment in readiness for service in New Zealand.

Ensign Clayton and 80 rank and file, on 16th November, joined from England in the ship *Clyde*.

On the 17th November, the regiment was inspected and reviewed by the Commander-in-Chief of the Bombay Army at Poona, prior to its embarkation for New Zealand.

On the conclusion of the parade, His Excellency addressed the Regiment in the following highly complimentary terms:—"Fifty-seventh, I now, having "finished my inspection, have formed this square to "address you, prior to taking leave of you; you are now "about to proceed to a country where you will meet a "wily and a cunning foe, and I know from experience as "an old soldier, the style of warfare you will be engaged "in; I urge the Officers Commanding Companies to look "well after their men when under fire, the young soldiers "in particular to be cautious in not throwing away their "fire, and to make every shot tell. During the time "you have been under my command, I have seen you "both on parade and in quarters, and I have no hesitation "in saying you are just what a British Regiment should "be, your conduct has been exemplary. I have now

1860 "tried you with what I consider a difficult movement, "that is an *Advance of Line*, the distance you marched "so steadily, proves that you are a well drilled regiment, "as well as a well conducted one.

"I have already reported you most favourably to "H.R.H. the General Commanding-in-Chief, and it will "afford me much satisfaction again reporting your very "efficient state, and which reflects the highest credit on "your Commanding Officer, Major Logan, and the "Officers in general.

"Fifty-seventh, I wish you success in your present "undertaking, and shall feel the greatest interest in the "future career of so fine a Regiment. I now bid you "*Farewell.*"

On the 22nd November, in compliance with instructions received from the Quartermaster-General's Department, the following officers and right wing, strength as per margin, under the command of Major Butler, embarked at Bombay on board the Freight ship *Star Queen*, for service in New Zealand, sailed the following day, and disembarked at Taranaki, the seat of war, on the 23rd of January, 1861. The casualities during the voyage were: Privates John Kelly, Charles Daly, Thomas Savage, Thomas Crawley, Daniel Malley.

Major H. Butler.
Capt. W. C. Brown.
Lieut. B. C. Bayntun.
" E. G. Hasted.
" W. K. Thompson.
" R. A. H. Cox.
" W. de W. Waller.
Ensign P. F. Clarke.
" R. Murray.
" F. H. Clayton.
Asst.-Surgn. J. Davis.

Field Officer.	Captain	Lieutenants.	Ensigns.	Staff.	Sergeants.	Corporals.	Drummers.	Privates.
1	1	5	3	1	16	18	9	292

1860 On the 26th November the Head-quarters, Band, and Left Wing (strength as per margin), under the command of Major R. A. Logan, with the annexed officers (leaving a Depot at Poona, consisting of 104 Non-Commissioned Officers and Men, together with the soldiers' families, under the command of Brevet-Major Hassard) embarked on the 26th November at Bombay, on board the Freight ship *Castilian*, and sailed the following day, for service in New Zealand, arrived in Auckland Harbour on the 21st January (casualties during the voyage by death were: Captain H. D. M. Shute, Privates P. Bonard, Joseph James, Thomas Waller, and Michael Fitzpatrick,) disembarked at Auckland, N.Z., on the 26th January, 1861, and encamped on the Albert Barrack Square.

Major R. A. Logan.
Capt. C. W. St. Clair.
„ J. N. Woodall.
„ D. M. Shute.
Lieut. W. A. J. Shorlt.
„ Jno. Parkinson.
„ C. M. Clarke.
Ensign H. F. Emly.
Lt.-Adjt. G. R. Waugh.
Qtr.-msr. Martindale
Surgn. W. Macandrew.

Field Officer.	Captains.	Lieutenants.	Ensign.	Staff.	Sergeants.	Corporals.	Drummers.	Privates.
1	3	3	1	3	24	10	15	366

1861 Brevet-Major St. Clair, with Lieutenant C. M. Clarke, and 150 Non-Commissioned Offices and men marched from Auckland to Onehunga the same day, and embarked on board H.M. Ship *Cordelia* for passage to the seat of War, in Taranaki, and landed at the Waitara on the 28th January, 1861.

Lieutenant-Colonel Inglis, gazetted on 29th January 1861 to 1st Battalion, 9th Regiment, at Corfu. The

1861 following Regimental Order was published by Colonel Warre, C.B., on the appointment of Lieutenant-Colonel Inglis to the above corps being notified.

New Plymouth, 13th *May*, 1861.

REGIMENTAL ORDER.

"Lieutenant-Colonel Inglis desires to express, on his "removal from the Regiment, his kind farewell to all "ranks, and his fervent hope, that by strict attention to "discipline and obedience to orders, they will ever main-"tain the high character the Regiment has gained for "itself on all occasions."

"In publishing these parting words, Colonel Warre desires also to record his sense of the great loss the Regiment has sustained by the removal of Lieutenant-Colonel Inglis. His name belongs to the Regiment, under this name the first laurels of the Regiment were so nobly won at Albuhera, and the lesson there learned has never been forgotten."

"Colonel Warre trusts that Lieutenant-Colonel Inglis' parting words will ever be remembered, and that although deprived of his able assistance, his influence in the Regiment will remain."

"Colonel Warre feels assured that Lieutenant-Colonel Inglis carries with him the sincere good wishes of every officer and man of the Regiment, for his future welfare and success."

On the 17th February a draft, consisting of Captain C. J. Clarke and 45 rank and file from England, arrived at Bombay in the Transport Ship *Instamboul*, disembarked and proceeded the same day to join the Depôt at Poona, under the command of Brevet-Major Hassard.

On the 20th February the Head-quarters and Band, as per margin, with the following officers under the command of MajorLogan, embarked at Onehunga (for the seat of war in Taranaki), on board H.M. Ship *Niger*, and disembarked at the River Waitara the following day, where they were encamped, and took part in the field operations against the Rebel Maories, until the cessation of hostilities on the 20th March, 1861.

Major R. A. Logan.
Captain T. N. Woodall.
Lieut. W. A. I. Shortt.
„ John Parkinson.
Ensign H. F. Emly.
Lt. & Ajt. G. R. Waugh.
Qtr.-msr. Martindale.
Sgn. W. Macandrew, M.D.

Field Officer.	Corporal.	Lieutenants.	Ensign.	Staff.	Sergeants.	Corporals.	Drummers.	Privates.
1	1	2	1	3	16	13	7	215

KILLED AND WOUNDED.

Distribution.	S.	C.	D.	P.
Died of Wounds ...	...	...	...	1
Wounded	...	1	...	5

On the 4th March the Depôt and families of the Regiment, under the command of Brevet-Major Hassard, left Poona by railway, and arrived at Bombay the following day, embarked on board the Transport Ship *Victory;* but in consequence of there not being sufficient accommodation, 1 Officer, 1 Sergeant, 20 privates, 30 women, 65 children disembarked on the 9th March, were encamped on the esplanade, Bombay, for 9 days, when they again embarked on board H.M. steam ship *Prince Arthur*. On the 18th March the *Prince Arthur* left for New Zealand, called at Point de Galle and Launceston, arrived at Auckland on 31st May, and left for New Plymouth in the Province of Taranaki, where the Depot arrived and disembarked on the 4th June, 1861; casualties during the voyage, 2 privates, 2 women, and 1 child.

Colonel H. J. Warre, C.B., rejoined the Fifty-seventh Regiment on the 5th March, 1861, at Fort Kairau, on the Waitara River, Taranaki; having resigned his appointment as Acting Military Secretary to the Commander-in-

1861 Chief in India, on the embarkation of his regiment for active service in New Zealand.

Being at the time on a tour of inspection with the Commander-in-Chief at Lucknow, in Oude, Colonel Warre returned to Calcutta, embarked on board a Peninsula and Oriental Company's Steamer, via Madras, for Pointe de Galle, Ceylon. Here he re-embarked on board another Peninsula and Oriental Company's Steamer for Australia, touching at King George's Sound, Western Australia, at Melbourne, and arriving at Sydney, New South Wales, on the 10th February, 1861. Availing himself of the Colonial Mail Steamer to New Zealand, Colonel Warre arrived at Auckland on the 25th February. Finding himself Senior Officer in Auckland he reported his arrival to His Excellency Colonel Thos. Gore Browne, C.B., the Governor, by whom he was granted a passage in the Colonial Steam Man of War "*Victoria*" to the seat of war.

On arrival at Camp Kairau, on the Waitara River, and having reported his arrival to the General, Sir Thomas Pratt, K.C.B., Colonel Warre was ordered to return to Auckland on the 9th March to take command of the troops in that Province, with the rank of "Colonel on the Staff."

The Governor having proceeded to the seat of war a few days after Colonel Warre's return to Auckland, this officer was sworn in Deputy-Governor, under the seal of the province, and continued to hold that office until the return of the Governor, on the 23rd April, when Colonel Warre proceeded to New Plymouth to resume command of his Regiment.

In the meanwhile peace had been proclaimed, and the troops (with the exception of the Fifty-seventh) were withdrawn from the Province of Taranaki. Colonel Warre, as Senior Officer, was appointed Agent for the

1861 New Zealand Government, a post similar to that he had occupied in Auckland as Deputy-Governor: the Province of Taranaki being continued under "Martial Law."

The Fifty-seventh Regiment, aided by the Militia and Volunteers, continued to hold the several blockhouses and outposts on the Waitara River on the north, and at Omata on the south of New Plymouth, during the two following years, without actual collision with the rebel natives.

Major-General Cameron, C.B., arrived at the Waitara on the 9th March 1861, and relieved Major-General Sir Thomas Pratt, K.C.B., in the command of the troops in New Zealand.

Head-quarters and left wing were inspected at Camp Kairau, on the 7th, and the right wing on the 12th April, by Major-General D. A. Cameron, C.B., Commanding the Troops in New Zealand, who expressed himself highly satisfied with the state of the Regiment.

The Head-quarters under the command of Major R. A. Logan, with the following number of Officers and men marched from Camp Kairau, and joined the right wing at New Plymouth:—

Major	R. P. Logan.	Ensign	P. F. Clarke.
Capt.	C. W. St. Clair.	"	F. H. Clayton.
"	J. R. Woodall.	Adjutant	G. R. Waugh (Lt).
Lieut.	W. A. J. Shortt.	Quartermaster	J. Martindale.
"	E. Brutton.	Surgeon	W. Macandrew.
"	C. M. Clarke.	Asst.-Surg.	W. A. Illingworth.

F. Officer.	Captains.	Lieutenants.	Ensigns.	Staff.	Sergeants.	Corporals.	Drummers.	Privates.	Total exclusive of Officers.
1	2	3	2	4	17	12	7	236	272

1861 In June, the following detachments left New Plymouth for Wanganui, per steamer *Wonga-Wonga*:—

Officers' Names.	Strength of detachment.				Women.	Children.	Date of Embarkation and Arrival.	
	S	C	D	Pts.			Embd.	Arrived.
							1861.	
Major R. A. Logan. Captain Sir R. Douglas, Bt. Lieutenant E. G. Hasted. Ensign H. F. Emly. Ensign H. C. Manners.	3	4	1	64	2	1	20th June	21st June
Captain J. Clarke. Lieutenant R. Murray	3	3	1	64	3	2	23rd June	24th June
Captain J. Stewart.	3	3	2	62	1	—	1st July	2nd July

On the 12th August, a Draft consisting of Ensigns H. A. C. Barton, H. M. Powell, and P. E. Powys, with 110 rank and file, joined at New Plymouth, N.Z. from England in the ship *Henry Fernie*.

On the 24th September, Surgeon William H. Macandrew, M.D., died of disease.

New-pattern shako sent out on trial, agreeable to instructions contained in Horse Guards letter dated 5 January, 1861, was taken into wear on the 29th September, 1861.

On the 12th October, Ensign J. T. Down joined from England, in the Transport Ship *Northumberland*.

The following detachments left New Plymouth for Wanganui, per steamer *Wonga-Wonga*, to join the detachment stationed there under the command of Major Logan.

Officers' Names.	Strength of detachment.				Women.	Children.	Date of Embarkation and Arrival.	
	S	C	D	Pts.			Embarked.	Arrival.
							1862	
Lieutenant F. H. Clayton.	3	—	—	85	2	5	17th Dec.	18th Dec.
							1862	
Captain J. Hassard (M.) Ensign H. M. Powell.	3	4	3	68	3	6	7th Jan.	8th Jan.

1862 On the 1st January, 1862, Lieutenant Charles Mans-

1862 field Clarke was appointed Adjutant, vice Lieutenant G. R. Waugh, who resigned that appointment.

Ensign Andrew B. Duncan joined from England, 10th February.

Lieutenant H. M. Muttit joined on the 16th April, on exchange from 65th Regiment.

On the 5th June, leather leggings were received for the use of the Regiment and taken into wear, none having been previously received since Order of 17th October, 1859, introducing them into the service.

The establishment of the Regiment was reduced by authority from the War Office, to the following strength:

Distribution.	Field Officers.	Captains.	Lieutenants.	Ensigns.	Staff.	Sergeants exclusive of Schoolmaster & Armourer.	Corporals.	Drummers.	Privates.
10 Service Companies...	3	10	11	9	5	46	40	21	730
2 Depôt Companies ...	...	2	3	1	...	10	10	4	120
Total ...	8	12	14	10	5	56	50	25	850

Ensign A. K. Douglas joined from England, on the 10th July.

Lieutenant E. Mills appointed Musketry Instructor, vice Captain W. A. J. Shortt promoted, 5th September, 1862.

Surgeon Mackinnon joined from England on 12th November.

Ensign C. Picot joined on appointment, 18th Dec.

Lieutenant-General D. A. Cameron, C.B., commanding the forces in New Zealand, arrived at New Plymouth and made the annual inspection of the Regiment (six

1862 Companies at Head-quarters) under the command of Colonel H. J. Warre, C.B., on the 22nd December, 1862.

The following is the distribution of the Service Companies in New Zealand:—

No.	Rank	Names	Remarks.	No.	Rank	Names	Remarks.
1	Colonel	H. J. Warre, C.B.	New Plymouth		Lieut.	T. H. Tragett	New Plymouth
1	Major	R. A. Logan	Wanganui		,,	R. A. H. Cox	,,
2	,,	H. Butler	New Plymouth	10	,,	W. De W. Waller	,,
1	Captain	J. Stewart	Wanganui		,,	H. F. Emly	Wanganui
	,,	J. Hassard (M.)	,,		,,	F. H. Clayton	,,
	,,	C. W. St. Clair	New Plymouth	13	,,	H. M. Muttit	,,
	,,	W. E. Brown	,,	1	Ensign	H. C. Manners	,,
5	,,	T. N. Woodall	,,		,,	H. D. C. Barton	,,
	,,	Sir R. Douglas, Bt.	Wanganui		,,	H. M. Powell	,,
	,,	C. J. Clarke	,,		,,	P. E. Powys	,,
	,,	E. Gorton	Waitara	5	,,	A. K. Douglass	New Plymouth
	,,	W. A. J. Shortt	New Plymouth		,,	J. T. Down	Wanganui
10	,,	H. K. Russell	,,		,,	G. J. Cumming	New Plymouth
1	Lieut.	G. R. Waugh	Auckland		,,	A. B. Duncan	Mahoetahi
	,,	B. C. Bayntun	,,	9	,,	C. Picot	New Plymouth
	,,	E. Mills (I. of M.)	New Plymouth	1	Py.-Mr.	M. Matthews	,,
	,,	E. G. Hasted	Wanganui	1	Adjt.	C. M. Clarke	,,
5	,,	R. Brutton	New Plymouth	1	Qmr.	T. Martindale	,,
	,,	W. A. K. Thompson	,,	1	Srgn.	W. A. Mackinnon	,,
	,,	J. Parkinson	On 2 yrs. leave in Europe.	1	As.-Srg.	J. Davis	Wanganui
				2	,,	W. A. Hope (M. B.)	New Plymouth

1862

Companies.

	Companies.	Stations.	Field-Officers.	Captains.	Subalterns.	Staff.	Sergeants.	Corporals.	Drummers.	Privates.	Remarks.
1	No. 1, 4, 6, 7 & 10	New Plymouth	2	5	9	5	25	22	11	419	Head-quarters under command of Colonel Warre, C.B., in Province of Taranaki.
3	No. 2, 3, 8, 9	Wanganui	1	4	9	1	15	14	7	326	Detachment under command of Major Logan in Province of Wellington.
		Waitara		1			1	2	7	31	
2	No. 5	Mahoetahi (Nw. Plmth.)			1		1	1		23	Detachment under command of Captain Gorton in Province of Taranaki.
		Bell Block					1	1	1	20	

From the cessation of hostilities in March, 1861, during 1862 to the present time, the Province of Taranaki had been abandoned to the rebel natives. More than 200 farm buildings had been destroyed during the recent war, but the country was too insecure to admit of their being rebuilt.

The settlers, with their families, were crowded into the small town of New Plymouth, without means of support. The men were employed during the interval in building block-houses at suitable strategical points, and making roads to the most accessible parts of the settlement. The whole population was more or less supported by Government aid.

New Plymouth, situated on the sea coast, is naturally protected by a high mound, on which the Barracks are situated. In this citadel a sufficient number of troops were kept under Colonel Warre's command to prevent the incursions of rebel natives.

Sir George Grey, K.C.B., succeeded Colonel Thomas Gore Browne, C.B., as Governor of New Zealand in September, 1861, but it was not until March, 1863, that His Excellency was able to turn his attention to the Province of Taranaki, which had been placed under martial law.

1863 On the 12th March His Excellency the Governor having decided to occupy a strong position on the southern boundary of the English Settlement before he re-occupied the land at Tatairamaka, the whole of the men at Head-quarters, strength as under, paraded at 7 o'clock a.m., under command of Colonel Warre, C.B., and marched to Poutoko, where a camp was formed preparatory to erecting a Redoubt, which was commenced next morning and occupied on the 24th March. Bad weather retarded the completion of the work for several days; this Redoubt was called St. Patrick's Redoubt.

List of Officers and return of Non-Commissioned Officers and rank and file employed:—

Col. H. J. Warre, C.B.
Capt. J. N. Woodall.
„ E. Gorton.
Lieut. E. Brutton.
„ W. A. Thompson.
„ R. A. H. Cox.
Lieut. W. de W. Waller.
„ J. H. Tragett.
Ensign C. Picot.
Adjt. C. M. Clarke.
Asst.-Srgn. W. A. Hope, M.D.
Quartermaster J. Martindale.

Field Officer.	Captains.	Subalterns.	Staff.	Sergeants.	Corporals.	Drummers.	Privates.
1	2	6	3	13	11	8	250

The Governor (Sir G. Grey, K.C.B.,) accompanied by Lieutenant-General Sir Duncan Cameron, commanding the forces, and the Colonial Secretary arrived at New Plymouth on the 29th March, 1863.

Finding that it would be impossible to carry out his views without additional troops, Sir G. Grey directed the Lieutenant-General Commanding, to reinforce the Garrison. Accordingly a Battery of Royal Artillery, under the command of Captain Mercer; wing of the

1863 Sixty-fifth Regiment, and the Seventieth Regiment under Lieutenant-Colonel Mulock, arrived from Auckland.

There being no Port at New Plymouth (the anchorage for all vessels being an open roadstead,) and the surf on the beach being at all seasons heavy, great difficulty is at all times experienced in landing heavy goods or baggage, and animals of all kinds.

Nevertheless one hundred horses belonging to the Royal Artillery were landed in one day (12 hours) without a single casualty, under the direction of Lieutenant and Adjutant C. M. Clarke, Acting-Deputy-Assistant-Quartermaster General.

As the country afforded no provisions or stores, every article required for the subsistence of the troops was also landed on the open beach. Few people, unacquainted with the coast, upon which, at all seasons, a heavy surf breaks, can imagine the difficulties experienced in landing guns, waggons, and supplies of all kinds. The boat service was admirably performed by settlers trained to the work.

His Excellency having decided upon re-occupying the Tatairamaka block of land which had been abandoned during the war of 1860-61; a strong force, under the immediate command of Lieutenant-General Cameron, C.B., marched at 10 o'clock a.m. on the 4th April, 1863, and after some difficulty in crossing the several rivers and gullies, but without being opposed by the Rebel Maories, encamped at 4 o'clock p.m. on an open field, near the centre of the block, about thirteen miles south of New Plymouth.

	Field Officer.	Captains.	Subalterns.	Staff.	Sergeants.	Corporals.	Drummers.	Privates.
Fifty-seventh Regiment.	1	2	6	2	11	10	6	240

1863 A site having been selected for the erection of a Redoubt, near the southern boundary of the Block, St. George's Redoubt was commenced on the 6th April, and occupied without opposition on the 13th April, the work having been greatly retarded by bad weather.

The following Officers and Non-Commissioned Officers and men occupied St. Georges Redoubt, under the command of Major Logan, who arrived on the 13th April, having been relieved by Major Butler, in command of the Detachment at Wanganui.

Capt.	J. N. Woodall.	Lieut.	F. H. Tragett.
Lieut.	E. Brutton.	,,	R. H. Cox.
,,	W. A. Thompson.	Asst.-Srgn.	W. A. Hope.

S.	C.	D.	Privates.
6	8	2	130

The natives threatened to intercept the communication with Tatairamaka, but no overt act having been committed, the ordinary escorts and convoys proceeded as usual.

On the 4th May, 1863, Colour-Sergeant Samuel Ellers, Sergeant Samuel Hill, Private Edward Kelly, Private John Flynn, Private Bartholomew McCarthy and Private Patrick Ryan were sent from Tatairamaka on escort duty, having in charge Private William Banks, a prisoner to be brought to trial before Court Martial at New Plymouth.

Lieutenant Tragett (Fifty-seventh) and Staff Assistant-Surgeon Hope (late Fifty-seventh, recently transferred to Staff), accompanied this escort, but without any idea of danger, the Rebel Maories, up to this time, having been in the habit of bringing vegetables, and supplying the Troops at the Redoubt.

On reaching the "Wairau," a small stream half way

1863 between Tatairamaka and Poutoko, the escort was suddenly fired upon by an Ambuscade of 30 or 40 Rebel Natives, and the whole party were killed or wounded. Private Florence Kelly, although wounded, escaped into the fern, subsequently joining a party under Lieutenant Brutton, which was sent from Tatairamaka on the report of the murders being conveyed to that Post by a mounted Orderly. On the news of the murders reaching Poutoko Captain Shortt, then in command, immediately proceeded to Wairau with about 30 men, and succeeded in recovering the mutilated remains of all but Private Ryan, whose body was subsequently recovered, having been concealed in a hole by the natives near the scene of the massacre.

So entirely unexpected was this attack, that Lieutenant-General Cameron, C.B., and Colonel Warre, C.B., were en-route for Tatairamaka at the time; and the latter proceeded with an escort to Captain Shortt's assistance.

The melancholy death of the above-mentioned Officers and men was deeply and universally lamented.

His Excellency the Governor determined at once to confiscate the land on which the murders were committed, and with this object, the Lieutenant-General directed a Redoubt to be constructed at Oakura (half-way between the Redoubt at Poutoko and Tatairamaka,) a commanding position near the scene of the massacre, which was occupied, on the 12th, by Detachments Fifty-seventh and Seventieth Regiments, under the command of Major R. A. Logan, Fifty-seventh Regiment.

His Excellency the Governor, the Lieutenant-General Commanding and their respective Staff Officers, the whole of the Military and Civil Force in New Plymouth attended the funeral of the Officers and men who were murdered on the 4th instant.

1863 Lieutenant Tragett, Assistant-Surgeon Hope, Colour-Sergeant Ellers, Sergeant Hill, and Private Banks were interred with military honours in the churchyard of the Parish Church at New Plymouth.

Private E. Kelly, Flynn and McCarthy were interred with military honours in the Roman Catholic Burial Ground.

On the 7th of May the Lieutenant-General's Head-quarter Staff arrived from Auckland, and Colonel Warre took command of the Outposts; the Head-quarters Fifty-seventh Regiment being removed to Poutoko.

The murders of the 4th of May being, according to Maori custom, tantamount to a declaration of war, every precaution was henceforth taken to guard against surprise.

The rebel natives commenced operations by digging rifle pits and strongly entrenching themselves on the left bank of the Katikara River, the boundary of the Tatairamaka Block, about ½ mile south of St. George's Redoubt. Other Redoubts were formed to harass the natives and cut off their communications.

The Detachment of the Fifty-seventh was withdrawn on the 13th May from the Waitara, which had been occupied by Detachments Fifty-seventh and Sixty-fifth since the termination of hostilities in March 1861.

Lieutenant Brutton, in command of a Volunteer party from Tatairamaka Redoubt, on the 18th May waylaid and bayonetted one Maori, wounding several others.

Lieutenant Waller, in command of a Volunteer reconnoitring party from Oakura Redoubt, went within 3 or 400 yards of the rebel position at Kaitake on the 21st May and exchanged shots with the natives, gaining much valuable information regarding their numbers and position.

1863 Lieutenant C. M. Clarke, with his Volunteer party from Poutoko, also explored the country, and examined the native tracks towards Kaitake.

Major Logan promoted Lieutenant-Colonel by Brevet, Gazette dated 22nd February, 1863.

Lieutenant Waller, in passing from Oakura to Poutoko on horseback, fell into a Maori ambuscade, on the 29th May. Lieutenant Waller's horse was shot, but with his revolver he beat off his assailants, and effected his escape to Poutoko. One hundred men were immediately turned out, under command of Colonel Warre, C.B., to scour the bush, and succeeded in capturing one Maori (a half-caste named Hori), who was subsequently tried before the Supreme Court and condemned to death, but the sentence was commuted to penal servitude for life, and eventually this native was set free, although clearly and legally convicted of attempting to murder Lieutenant Waller.

A reconnoitring party, under the command of Colonel Warre, C.B., proceeded to Wairau on the 1st June, and succeeded in recovering the body of Private Ryan who was found, as described by the prisoner Hori, in a Maori pit about 300 yards from the scene of the massacre. The remains of Private Ryan were interred, with military honours, at Oakura.

Information having been received that large numbers of natives from the South had joined the rebels in arms against the Queen's Government, it was determined to attack their position on the Kaitikara River, where the main body of southern natives, about 600 strong, were said to be entrenched, and accordingly instructions were given to Lieutenant-Colonel Logan to march from Oakura at midnight of the 3rd June for Tatairamaka, in charge of convoy, guns, &c.

The Lieutenant-General, with a strong force from

1863 New Plymouth, reached Poutoko at midnight, and joined by the Companies at Head-quarters under Colonel Warre, C.B., continued the march to Tatairamaka, where the whole force assembled at 4 o'clock a.m., on 4th June.

At 6 o'clock a.m., the attacking column under the command of Colonel Warre, C.B., Commanding Fifty-seventh, and composed as under, viz.:

Major	R. A Logan, (Bt.-Lieut.-Colonel.)	Ensign	C. Picot.
Captain	T. N. Woodall.	„	E. Broderip.
„	W. A. Shortt.	„	A. B. Duncan.
„	R. H. Russell.	„	A. K. Douglass.
Lieut.	E. Brutton.	Adjt.	C. M. Clarke.
„	W. A. Thompson.	Surgeon	W. A. Mackinnon.
„	R. H. Cox.	Qtr.-msr.	T. Martindale.
„	W. de Waller.		

	Field Officers.	Captains.	Subalterns.	Staff.	Sergeants.	Drummers.	Rank and File.
Strength of Officers Non-Commissioned Officers, and men.	2	3	8	3	18	9	383

under cover of a battery of Armstrong guns, commanded by Captain Mercer, Royal Artillery, crossed the Katikara River, and advanced rapidly to the attack ; the Companies under Lieutenant Brutton and Waller wheeled towards the right to take the enemy's position on the river in reverse, and open the road for the remainder of the force, the other Company under Ensign Duncan and the supports under Lieutenant-Colonel Logan, were ordered to occupy the ravine by which the troops had advanced across the river until the road was open, when joined by the other Companies the whole were to proceed to the attack of the enemy's Redoubt.

1863 So rapid was the advance, and so completely surprised were the rebels, that the whole of the attacking column proceeded simultaneously and carried the whole of the enemy's position at the point of the bayonet, with the loss of 1 man killed (Private Edward Martin), and 9 wounded, viz.:—

Pte. Jno. Osborn, mortally, since dead.
„ H. Shipman, „
„ P. Flaherty, severely.
„ J. Evans, „
„ J. Deegan, slightly.
Pte. Bartholomew Stagpool severely.
„ M. Fox, slightly.
„ D. Hurley, „
„ J. Morton, severely.

The bodies of 22 Maories (among them that of their principal chief Hori Patini) were taken from the Redoubt stormed by the supports under Lieutenant-Colonel Logan. Several other Maories were killed and wounded. The success which attended this attack is best recorded by the General Order published by the Lieutenant-General Commanding on the 4th June, and so disheartened were the rebel Maories that they abandoned the neighbourhood.

GENERAL ORDER No. 519. HEAD QUARTERS.

New Plymouth, *4th June*, 1863.

The Lieutenant-General Commanding has great satisfaction in complimenting the Troops under his Command on the result of the action this morning at the Kaitakara River, when a well-merited chastisement was inflicted on the rebel natives for their cruel and murderous attack, in time of peace, on 2 Officers and 7 Non-Commissioned Officers and men, Fifty-Seventh Regiment, on 4th May last.

The Lieutenant-General thanks all the Troops engaged for their conduct on this occasion, and particularly Colonel Warre and the Fifty-seventh Regiment, for their rapid advance across the river, and the gallantry with which

1863 they carried the enemy's principal intrenchment on the opposite bank, and drove him in complete confusion before them. The operation was materially assisted by the precision with which the fire of three Armstrong guns under Captain Mercer, R.A., and of the heavy guns of H.M.S. *Eclipse,* under the command of Captain Mayne, R.N., was directed against the enemy's position.

By Command,

(Signed) W. H. HUTCHINS, Lieut.-Col.,

Assistant Military Secretary.

The following dispatch, dated 28th August, 1863, was received by the Lieutenant-General Commanding the Forces, and published for general information on 17th December, 1863:—

Sir,

Having laid before the Field-Marshal Commanding-in-Chief your letter of the 9th June last, enclosing the copy of a dispatch, which you have addressed to the Secretary of State for War, giving an account of the action on the 4th June, by a force under your command on the left bank of the Katikara River, I am directed to acquaint you that His Royal Highness has derived much pleasure in the perusal of your communication, and considers that the whole operation was admirably performed by the Troops, the conduct of the Fifty-seventh Regiment, under Colonel Warre, being particularly deserving of commendation.

(Signed,) W. H. FORSTER.

Captains Shortt and Russell, Lieutenants Brutton and Waller, Ensign Duncan, were particularly distinguished on this occasion, as also were Privates Bartholomew Stagpool, and J. Dannahey.

Captain Shortt and Private Dannahey were recom-

1863 mended by the Lieutenant-General Commanding for the "Victoria Cross," for their distinguished gallantry in being the first to jump over the parapet into the enemy's Redoubt.

On the 20th June, Lieutenant-General Cameron, C.B., embarked for Auckland on board H.M. ship *Eclipse*, leaving Colonel Warre in command of the Province of Taranaki, when Major (Brevet-Lieutenant-Colonel) Logan took command of the Regiment.

Owing to the removal of Troops to Auckland, it became necessary to withdraw the Detachment, Fifty-seventh Regiment, from Tatairamaka, and abandon the land (for the second time) to the Rebel Maories. This was effected by Lieutenant-Colonel Logan, Fifty-seventh, without opposition.

The whole of the Seventieth Regiment, with the exception of one Company, having been withdrawn from New Plymouth, it became necessary to abandon the Oakura Redoubt, which was effected on the 11th August without casualty, after a desultory skirmish with the rebel natives, who were driven out of the Redoubt they had taken possession of, after the Troops had been withdrawn.

The Detachment from Oakura joined Head-quarters and returned to New Plymouth, on the 12th August.

A Detachment of the Fifty-seventh continued to occupy St. Patrick's Redoubt at Poutoko.

A Reconnoitring Party, on the 25th August, under the command of Captain Russell, while endeavouring to recover some sheep taken by the rebels, fell in with a strong party of natives at the upper ford of the Tapuae River, near Poutoko, and, after a sharp skirmish, withdrew, with one officer (Ensign Picot) and two men wounded.

The natives having become very troublesome since

1863 the troops had been withdrawn, Volunteers from Australia were enlisted in order to replace the troops and form Volunteer Companies of Militia.

A settler having been shot within about three miles of New Plymouth, 100 men of the Fifty-seventh and Seventieth Regiments, under the command of Captain Shortt, were sent out on 13th September to cut off the rebel natives, who escaped by the bush to their stronghold at Kaitake.

To punish the rebel natives for their cowardly attempt to murder three unarmed settlers, on Sunday, 13th September, Captain Russell was permitted to place a party of men in ambuscade at the Wairau, leaving a smaller party in the abandoned Redoubt at Oakura.

On the 15th September a body of natives fell into this ambuscade, and were attacked with great gallantry and driven back, with the loss of 9 killed and several wounded. Among the killed was "Aparo," a head chief of the Wanganui River Tribes, from whom a handsome "tiaha" or native spear was taken, which was presented to the Lieutenant-General Commanding.

There were no casualties in this successful encounter, which the Lieutenant-General characterised as having "been planned and carried out with great ability; and "it deserved to be successful, for it was the result of "previous careful observation."

On the 24th September a settler having been shot within a short distance of the Stockade at Bell Block, 100 of the Fifty-seventh Regiment, under Major Butler, with 50 Volunteer Militia, under Captain Webster, left New Plymouth at three o'clock a.m., on the 25th to punish the offenders. The Troops fell in with several parties of natives, who were dispersed and driven back into the bush, with the loss of 5 wounded, without casualty on our side.

1863 On the 30th September Quartermaster-Sergeant R. Collins was presented, on muster parade, with a medal and annuity of £20 for long service and exemplary conduct. In congratulating the Quartermaster-Sergeant on being the recipient of this honourable mark of Her Majesty's favour, Colonel Warre took occasion "to thank the Officers, Non-commissioned Officers, and Men of the Fifty-seventh Regiment for their excellent conduct, not only in the field against the rebel Maories (whom they have invariably met successfully, inflicting severe loss, with comparatively little or no loss to themselves), but also in Quarters, thereby gaining for the Regiment high distinction, and showing that men can adapt themselves to every service without losing discipline or being forgetful of their high character as British Soldiers."

The rebel natives having been mustering their forces for some time to revenge the loss they had sustained on so many occasions, assembled in large numbers on the 1st October at the Tapuai River, near Poutoko, with a view to attack the Redoubt or to draw out the Troops, consisting of 1 Company, Seventieth Regiment, under Captain Wright, and Detachment, Fifty-seventh Regiment, under Lieutenant Mills.

At 3 o'clock a.m. on the 2nd October, Lieutenant Mills (when covering a working party, obtaining firewood for the Redoubt,) fell in with a considerable number of rebel natives who had bivouacked for the night in the vicinity of the Redoubt.

Lieutenant Mills at once charged the outposts of the rebels (killing one and wounding others,) but finding the main body strongly posted on an elevation, covered with 'bush,' he withdrew his party without loss, and sent a report of the occurrence at once to Head-quarters at New Plymouth. In consequence of this report, Major Butler was sent (with reinforcements) to take command

1863 at St. Patrick's Redoubt. The rebels having assembled on the north of New Plymouth, as well as at Poutoko on the south, they threatened the communications with the outposts, on all sides.

Holding all the available Troops in readiness to meet the attack, which now threatened the town of New Plymouth, Colonel Warre awaited further intelligence by telegraph, which fortunately had been established between the outposts and the town.

Finding that the demonstration on the north, at Bell Blockhouse, was intended to take off attention from the attack at Poutoko, Colonel Warre was able to reinforce the latter post, on news being transmitted that the Troops, under Major Butler, were seriously engaged.

The Garrison had been so greatly reduced, that but few regular Troops were available; nevertheless, it was necessary not only to preserve the Redoubt at Poutoko, a valuable outpost to check the advance of the rebels, and keep them away from the town of New Plymouth, but also to send relief to the Troops by whom the Redoubt was garrisoned.

Accordingly two weak Companies (about 100 men) of the Fifty-seventh, under Brevet-Major Shortt, were sent by a bush road in rear of the native position; while a similar number of Volunteer Militia, under Captains Atkinson and Webster, accompanied Colonel Warre by another track which led towards the Redoubt.

Major Butler, with a small party of the Seventieth Regiment, having gone out to reconnoitre, had been seriously engaged with a very superior number of Maories who advanced with considerable determination, driving back Major Butler's party (with some casualties) towards the Redoubt; the Companies under Major Shortt arrived at the moment when, embarrassed with his wounded men, Major Butler was endeavouring to force his way back to

1863 Poutoko. Although very inferior in numbers, Major Shortt did not hesitate to cut his way through the rebels, whom he took by surprise in the rear, and inflicted considerable loss. Major Butler quickly recovered his ground, and being joined by the Volunteer Militia under Colonel Warre, was able to drive the natives off the Plateau into the deep ravines, from which, being densely covered with bush, it was not possible to dislodge them. During this attack so gallantly repulsed upon the north, another party of 200 or 300 natives crept up the gullies on the south side, with a view to surprise the Redoubt; these were met by Lieutenant Mills, in charge of the small garrison, whose effective fire, with that of the howitzer permanently defending the Redoubt, soon obliged the rebels to retire. This severe engagement, in which the Maories far outnumbered the Troops, was not brought to a successful termination without loss. Ensign Powys was severely wounded, Sergeants S. Harvey and P. Bourke being dangerously, and Corporal Rae, Privates W. Reeves, F. Flinn (died of wounds), H. Cain, M. Foley very severely, and Drummer Dudley Stagpool slightly wounded.

Major Shortt was highly commended for the gallant manner in which he led his party right through the rebel Maories upon whom he inflicted heavy loss.

The conduct of the Volunteer Cavalry, acting as Guides and Escort, under Captain Mace, was also deserving of special notice. When ammunition failed, these men rode to the Redoubt, and returned, through a very heavy fire, carrying the ammunition (tied up in clothes), in their hands, and several instances occurred of the removal of wounded men on the horses of the Mounted Orderlies.

Ensign Down and Drummer D. Stagpool were recommended for, and eventually received the Victoria

1863 Cross, for their gallant conduct in rescuing a wounded comrade from the clutches of the rebel natives, and many other soldiers behaved with marked courage and coolness, when nearly surrounded by a howling multitude of naked savages, whose loss on such occasions it is always difficult to determine; the killed and wounded being dragged off the field, and carried off (by the women), to a place of safety. That the Rebels suffered severely was evident, not only by the size of the pit in which they—during the night—buried their dead, but by the procession of carts, evidently bearing off the wounded, which were seen later in the evening winding their way to Kaitake, a very strong position in the neighbouring mountains. The stranger natives retired from the District, and the resident rebels made no attempt to renew the war for several months.

1864 A draft, under Captain T. W. J. Lloyd, of 1 Sergeant and 60 rank and file, joined the Head-quarters at New Plymouth from England on the 24th January.

The war in New Zealand assumed larger proportions. Military settlements were formed on the Waikato River, and Taranaki was reinforced by 600 men, volunteers to take the place of the Militia. The Militia was disbanded with the exception of three Companies called *Bush Rangers.*

The war in Taranaki recommenced on the 28th February by the murder of a settler, Mr. Patterson, who was waylaid whilst visiting his farm, about 3 miles from New Plymouth.

The military settlers were sent to occupy the abandoned Blockhouses at Mahohetaki on the north, and Oakura on the south.

Major Butler, Fifty-seventh Regiment, took command of the southern outposts.

In reconnoitring the rebel position at Kaitake, Major

1864 Butler advanced too near to the Stockade, from which he had to withdraw under a heavy fire from the rifle pits during which 1 private was killed, and 1 Officer (Lieutenant Larcom, Royal Artillery) and 4 privates were wounded.

On the 22nd March the Lieutenant General's permission was obtained to reconnoitre the country and destroy the rebel positions.

Reinforced by Half-Battery of Royal Artillery (Armstrong guns) under Capt. Martin and a Detachment Seventieth Regiment, Colonel Warre determined and effected the destruction of the Rebel Pahs at Tataraimaka and "Ahu Ahu," on the 23rd and 24th March.

Having collected a mixed force of Regulars and (Military Settlers) Militia, amounting to about 650 Non-Commissioned Officers and men, Colonel Warre told them off into several parties, in order to attack simultaneously the strong and very important position at Kaitake. The attack was entirely successful. Major Butler, Fifty-seventh Regiment, led two companies (that of the Fifty-seventh, under Captain Schomberg) up the steep ground on the right to turn the enemy's rifle pits on the left flanks of the Maorie Stockade.

The Militia, under Captain Atkinson, guided by Lieutenant C. M. Clarke (Fifty-seventh), who had previously explored the path, marched by a very intricate and circuitous track, in order to take the position in the rear.

Captain Corbett's Volunteers were in ambuscade before daylight on the proper right (our left) of the enemy's Pah; while Captain Lloyd's Company of Fifty-seventh and Captain Wight's Company of the Seventieth Regiment forced the right flank; and Captain Russell's Company, under cover of the Armstrong guns and a rocket battery, attacked the stockade directly in front.

1864 Captain Martin's guns were admirably served, and were supported by Captain Carthew's Company of the Militia Volunteers.

Everything being prepared, a lucky shot from the Armstrong guns set fire to the Wharries within the Stockade.

Captain Corbett immediately took advantage of this occurrence, and, under cover of the smoke, stormed the Stockade, which was simultaneously attacked by all the other parties.

The Company, under Captain Russell, forced its passage through the double line of palisades in front, and as the enemy's rifle pits and defences were taken in reverse, as soon as Captains Corbett and Lloyd had established themselves on the higher ground, the rebels abandoned their position, leaving a long line of Stockade —two Stockades or Pahs—and a very large supply of food, their mats, ammunition and cultivations in the hands of the captors. The thick bush and high mountain range, upon which Kaitake was built, enabled the rebels to escape without serious loss, but their communications with the north were intercepted, and on the site of the rebel Pahs a Redoubt was soon completed.

The rebels abandoned the district. The loss of the Troops was trifling, so sudden and simultaneous was the attack.

On the 20th February, 1864, H.R.H. The Duke of Cambridge recommended that the undermentioned distributions and rewards shall be bestowed upon the Officers and men in consideration of the gallant and important services which they have performed under the distinguished leader (Sir Duncan Cameron,) whose name His Royal Highness is happy to recommend for the distinction of K.C.B. The Military Secretary further states:—

"I have to add that Colonel Mould, C.B., R.E., "and Colonel Warre, C.B., Fifty-seventh Foot, being

1864 "already full Colonels and C.Bs., H.R.H. does not con- "sider that any further advancement can be granted for "their recent services, but the testimony that has been "rendered to their excellent conduct will be duly recorded "in their favour."

On the 27th June, the Secretary of State for War wrote to Lieutenant-General Sir D. Cameron, K.C.B.:—

"The operations conducted by Colonel Warre, C.B., were marked by ability and skill, and the result of the attack on Kaitake was highly satisfactory."

(Signed) DE GREY & RIPON.

The capture of Kaitake was a severe blow to the rebel natives; it was one of the strongest of their fastnesses, admirably placed on the borders of impenetrable jungle, and commanded about 2 miles of open level land between the mountain range upon which it was situated and the sea. Nothing could pass safely between the Tatairamaka block of land and New Plymouth so long as the rebels occupied Kaitake; the whole line of road was now clear, but the rebels continued in the vicinity and constant Patroles were necessary to prevent native ambuscades.

RETURN OF TROOPS AT CAPTURE OF KAITAKE.

STRENGTH.								OFFICERS ENGAGED.
Corps.	F. Officers.	Captains.	Subalterns.	Staff.	Sergeants.	Drummers.	Rank & File.	Commanding Officers' Rank and Names.
Staff	1			2				Col. Warre, C.B., Commdg.
Medical Staff				2				Surg. Mackinnon, 57th Staff
Royal Artillery... ...		1			2		35	Capt. Martin, R.A.
Royal Engineers ...			1				2	Lieut. Fergusson, R.E.
57th Regiment	1	3	5		8	3	175	Major Butler, 57th Regt.
70th Regiment		1	1		1	1	26	Capt. Corbett, Militia.
Total ...	2	5	7	4	11	4	238	Capt. Carthew, Militia.
Militia		8	9	1	25	3	389	Capt. Webster, Militia.
								Capt. Atkinson, Militia.
Total ...	2	13	16	5	36	7	627	

1864 The Regular and Militia Forces engaged were highly complimented by Lieutenant-General Sir D. Cameron, K.C.B., for the high spirit and gallantry they displayed.

On the 6th April, Captain Lloyd, Fifty-seventh Regiment (and party as under), had an engagement with the rebels at "Ahu Ahu," while reconnoitring the country. The troops were surprised, while halted, by rebel natives, who after a gallant struggle killed Captain T. W. J. Lloyd, Private J. Dooley, Private G. Sadler, and several of the Military Settlers.

Strength.	Capts.	Subs.	Sergts.	Drs.	R. & F.	Engaged.
Corps.						Officers' Names.
Fifty-seventh Regiment ..	1	1	1	1	53	Captain T. W. J. Lloyd.
Militia	1	1	2	...	41	Lieutenant R. A. H. Cox.
Total ...	2	2	3	1	94	

Captain Lloyd killed or wounded 3 natives with his revolver, after he had been himself shot down, and his thigh broken. The natives decapitated his body (on which they inflicted 18 wounds), and carried his head in triumph down the coast. The bodies of the other men were also terribly mutilated and several were decapitated.

One of the heads taken by the rebels, supposed to have been the head of Captain Lloyd, was subsequently recovered by Mr. Broughton, interpreter to Colonel Logan, Fifty-seventh Regiment, commanding the Wanganui District. The progress of this head through the country gave rise to a religious fanaticism, which gradually spread amongst the rebels, and was known as the "Haw Haw," or "Pai Maori" religion. This fanaticism caused the defection of several tribes hitherto supposed to be friendly to the British rule, and thus prolonged the war.

1864 On the 18th April, a Force under Major Butler proceeded on special service for the purpose of ascertaining (Fifty-seventh 3 Captains, 3 Subalterns, 6 Sergeants, 3 Drummers, 150 rank and file), whether the hostile natives had entrenched themselves in any position south of the Tàtaraimaka Block, and of destroying their crops and cultivations with a view of placing a large tract of uncultivated country between New Plymouth and their habitable "Pahs," and thus securing the immediate neighbourhood of the town from sudden predatory attacks.

The deserted Pah of Paketaioa and some cultivations were burnt and destroyed, and some of the enemy's horses in the vicinity captured. Major Butler moved his force by a cross-road towards the mountains and soon found a native Pah "Kopua" in a clearing surrounded by bush. On the force entering the bush, the natives opened fire and Private Dowling was severely wounded. The fire was replied to, and silenced by an Armstrong gun and the fire of the troops; but not having any knowledge of the locality or the number and position of the enemy, Major Butler did not consider it advisable to push further into the bush. A quantity of cultivation was destroyed and some Wharres (native houses) were burnt, also an unoccupied Pah in the neighbourhood; several horses were captured. Having returned to Tataraimaka, Major Butler moved to "A'hu A'hu," and found a newly-erected Pah higher up on the Patua Ranges (bush covered mountains) which had been previously unexplored. More cultivations were destroyed as well as several Wharres.

The following letter, dated Head-quarters, Tauranga, May 9th, 1864, was received in due course:—

AUCKLAND, *May 9th*, 1864.

Sir,

I have had the honour of receiving and submitting to

1864 the Lieutenant-General Commanding your letter of the 23rd ultimo, with enclosures reporting in detail the circumstances of the recent successful reconnoissance of the country south of Tataraimaka made by the Force under command of Major Butler, Fifty-seventh Regiment, and I am to request you will have the goodness to express to that Officer, and all who took part in the expedition, the Lieutenant-General's entire satisfaction with the manner in which the operations were carried out.

I have, &c.,

(Signed) G. J. GAMBLE, Lieut.-Col.,
Deputy-Quartermaster-General.

To Colonel Warre, C.B.,
Commanding the Troops at Taranaki.

On 24th April medals were presented to the undermentioned men:—

Private Thomas Carr and Private John Smith, by the Royal Humane Society, for their courage and humanity in having rescued Charles Newland and Mrs. Adamson on the 14th and 17th March respectively from the Wanganui River.

A letter dated Horse Guards, 24th February, 1864, was received appointing Captain W. A. Shortt and H. R. Russell Majors in the Army for service in the field.

Although dispersed by the capture of Kaitake and subsequent operations, the rebel natives were not conquered; they reappeared in force on the north side of New Plymouth, and assembled in considerable numbers at Maitatawa and Te Are.

After one or two attempts to waylay and murder settlers, they determined to attack the Morere Redoubt at Sentry Hill, then occupied by a Detachment of Fifty-seventh Regiment, under Captain and Brevet-Major Shortt, supported, at about one and a-half miles' distance,

1864 by another redoubt and blockhouse at Mahohetahi, where Major Butler was placed in command.

After a false alarm, on the 29th April, which enabled Major Shortt to train his small garrison (about 40 men) to reserve their fire and keep under cover of the parapet, some three or four hundred natives, led by their newly-created prophet, Te Ua, and stimulated to victory by their incantations and war dances, advanced at daylight on the 30th April to the attack of the Redoubt.

The small garrison, being fully prepared, the sentries took no notice of the approach of the natives, who evidently expected that the Troops would go out of the Redoubt to meet them.

When the natives were within about fifty yards of the ditch, and were preparing for the assault, the Troops lined the parapet, and received the natives with so destructive a fire, that, although some of them fell upon the crest of the glacis, the main body fell back more quickly than they advanced, carrying off their wounded, but leaving thirty-five dead upon the glacis of the little work.

The rebels were too numerous to admit of Major Shortt following up his success; and before Major Butler's arrival with reinforcements, the living had departed and the dead were left to be buried by the soldiers.

Big Joe and two others, fearfully wounded, were captured and pointed out several chiefs among the slain. It was afterwards discovered that 109—of the 400 natives who advanced to the attack—were killed or wounded; the natives showed real courage in the dexterity with which they carried off their wounded.

On the previous day, but many miles distant, on the east coast, a similar fight had occurred; but the troops were the attacking party, and the fearful loss in Officers

1864 and men of the 43rd Light Infantry showed that the Maories who reserved their fire are no mean enemies, nor are their warlike tactics to be despised. The Lieutenant-General complimented Majors Shortt and Lieutenant Waller and men for their gallant conduct, and expressed his warm approval of the good service performed by them, "when, owing to the high state of discipline and "control of the Officers, a heavy loss was inflicted upon "the enemy, at the cost of one man only wounded."

The exigencies of the service now required that the Fifty-seventh Regiment should be concentrated at Wanganui.

As the whole of the Fifty-seventh Regiment was eventually removed from Taranaki, leaving Colonel Warre, C.B., in command of that Province, it may not be out of place to record the gallant services performed during the period the Fifty-seventh had been stationed at New Plymouth by Captain Mace and about 25 mounted Volunteer Civilians who not only removed the wounded from the field, especially at Poutoko on the 2nd October, but were ready on all occasions to act as escorts to Officers, or as messengers, to brave the ambuscades of the enemy, during the whole period of the war.

It is but bare justice to these gallant men to say that they were always ready to aid and accompany the Troops (as also were the Volunteer Companies of Bush Rangers) on every service of danger.

Sufficient commendation can hardly be given also to the manner in which the transport service was performed under Lieutenant C. M. Clarke, Fifty-seventh Regiment, District-Assistant-Quartermaster-General.

Acting under "martial law," it was frequently necessary to *press* carts, drivers and bullocks to perform all duties. In no instance were the drivers wanting in pluck to face the enemy, and it is owing to their excellent

1864 conduct that, under escort of the Troops, the numerous outposts were kept properly supplied. The outposts extended 25 or 30 miles to the south, and 15 or 20 to the north of New Plymouth.

Ensign Robert Joseph Holmes joined the Service Companies from England on the 21st May.

No. 6 and 10 Companies, commanded by Brevet-Major Shortt (strength as under,) embarked on the 26th May at New Plymouth for Wanganui, to join Detachment at that station, with following Officers:—

Officers		Srgs.	Drs.	R. & F.
Lieutenant	E. Mills.			
„	W. de W. Waller.	7	2	148
Ensign	P. E. Powys.			

No. 5 and 7 Companies (with band,) under command of Major Butler (strength as under), embarked on 31st May, at New Plymouth, for Wanganui, with following Officers:—

Captain T. N. Woodall. Captain F. S. Schomberg.
Ensign A. K. Douglas. Ensign J. T. Down.
„ C. Picot. „ R. J. Holmes.

Sergeants.	Drummers.	Rank & File.
9	4	158

Captain E. G. Hasted, and Lieutenant C. G. Clarke, joined the Service Companies from England on the 29th June.

Surgeon William Mackinnon, appointed Companion of the Most Honorable Order of the Bath, October, 1864.

Captain James Stewart, gazetted a Brevet-Major, and Major Henry Butler Brevet-Lieutenant-Colonel for his services in the field.

The distinguished Conduct-Medal was presented on a general parade to Drummer Dudley Stagpool, for his gallant conduct on 25th September, 1863, at Taranaki.

On the 13th December, Brevet-Major Stewart's Detachment joined Head-quarters from Taranaki.

1864	Capts.	Subs.	Srgts.	Drms.	R. & F.
	2	3	7	4	140

Before the end of 1864 the whole Regiment, under command of Brevet-Lieutenant-Colonel Logan, was concentrated at Wanganui, preparatory to commencing the opening of the West Coast road to Taranaki by Lieutenant-General Sir Duncan Cameron, K.C.B., in personal command of the expedition.

1865 Early in January a Detachment of the Fifty-seventh, under Major Butler, Fifty-seventh Regiment, was sent out to occupy Alexander's Farm situated on the Morohanaw River, about nine miles from Wanganui; and soon afterwards Colonel (now Brigadier) Waddy, C.B., of the Fiftieth Regiment, with a mixed force of about 1,200 Non-Commissioned Officers and men taken from the 2nd Battalion Eighteenth (Royal Irish) Regiment, the Fiftieth and Fifty-Seventh Regiments, formed an encampment on a high plateau on the left bank, and close to the mouth of the same river, which flows through a deep ravine into the sea.

Temporary bridges were thrown across the Kai Iwi River, and the line of advance was cleared and bridged about 7 miles beyond Alexander's Farm.

On the 20th January, Lieutenant-General Sir D. Cameron arrived at Wanganui. Having left Auckland on the 14th, the Lieutenant-General landed at New Plymouth to arrange with Colonel Warre, C.B., for the occupation of the country south of the Tataraimaka block of land, and for the simultaneous movements of the two Brigades destined to open out the Coast road which had hitherto belonged to, and had been strictly guarded by, the rebel natives.

The Lieutenant-General established his Headquarters at Alexander's Farm on the 22nd January. In order to protect the town of Wanganui during the

1865 absence of the Expeditionary Force, the Head-quarters of the Fifty-seventh Regiment, under command of Brevet-Lieutenant-Colonel Logan, were left in charge. Two additional posts were formed, and occupied by two Companies Fifty-seventh Regiment, under Brevet-Major Stewart and Captain Woodall; and one Company was left at Alexander's Farm on the advance of the Expeditionary Force on the 24th January.

The Lieutenant-General considered it necessary to move by night, and successfully accomplished the passage of the Waitotara River at daylight on the 25th January.

Colonel Weare, Fiftieth Regiment, held the position at Nukumaru with a mixed force of about 1,100 Non-Commissioned Officers and men from the Regiments already named, and 250 of the Seventieth Regiment.

On the 14th February the Lieutenant-General directed a combined movement by night march. Brigadier Waddy, Fiftieth Regiment, was to advance from Waitotara to the Patea River, a distance of about 15 miles, while Colonel Weare, Fiftieth Regiment, with his Force from Nukumaru, was to occupy the Redoubts vacated by Brigadier Waddy at Waitotara. The combined movement was effected without opposition.

The Patea River marks the boundary of the Ngatiruanui Country, and being of considerable breadth with strong current, it became necessary to erect Redoubts upon both banks, and leave a Force for the protection of the supplies, and to guard the entrance of the river.

It was not, therefore, until the 13th March that the Lieutenant-General found himself in a position to advance to Kakaramea, and in the meanwhile the natives had assembled in considerable force to oppose his onward march.

The route lay over open fern land, bounded by a

1865 ridge of sand hills running parallel to the track, and within musket shot of the line of march. The Maories occupied these sand hills, and fired upon the Cavalry Advance Guard, who were relieved by several Companies of the Fifty-seventh in extended order. These skirmishers having changed front to the right, rushed over the ridge and drove the natives from their ambuscade into the swamp beyond, in escaping from which the natives were exposed to a heavy fire, and suffered some loss. Twenty Maories were killed, and five taken prisoners, two of whom died of their wounds. Many other natives were wounded, but they displayed considerable courage in carrying off their wounded, and held their position with great tenacity against a much superior force.

Private James Nixon, Fifty-seventh Regiment, was the only man killed. Three privates of the Fifty-seventh were wounded, also one of the Military Train, and one of the Sixty-eighth Light Infantry. The force continued its advance, and encamped at Kakaramea on the same day.

STRENGTH ENGAGED ON THE 13TH MARCH, 1865.

Corps.	Field Officers.	Captains.	Subalterns.	Staff.	Sergeants.	Drummers.	Rank and File.
Military Train	...	1	3	1	2	1	56
Royal Artillery	1	1	1	2	3	...	35
Royal Engineers	1	1	1	...	2	...	20
Fiftieth Regiment	1	5	6	3	22	10	386
Fifty-seventh Regiment ...	1	5	9	1	23	14	486
Sixty-eighth Regiment ...	1	3	5	1	10	7	208
Volunteer Cavalry	...	...	...	...	3	...	27
	5	16	25	8	65	32	1213

The following Officers of the Fifty-seventh Regiment were engaged, viz:—

1865	Major	H. Butler.	Lieut.	H. D. C. Barton.
	Bt.-Major	J. Hassard.	„	P. E. Powys.
	Captain	C. J. Clarke.	„	J. T. Down.
	„	Sir R. Douglas, Bt.	Ensign	C. Picot.
	„	E. G. Hasted.	„	J. K. Tredennick.
	„	C. M. Clarke.	„	A. J. Holmes.
	Lieut.	W. de W. Waller.	Asst.-Srgn.	J. Davis.
	„	F. H. Clayton.		

The Fifty-seventh was specially noted for the conduct of Officers and men on this occasion, and Captains Sir R. Douglas, Bart., and Sergeant D. O'Connor were particularly named.

A Detachment of the Fifty-seventh moved on the 18th March to Maniwapow, under Major Butler, to occupy the position, and were employed in cutting a road down the precipitous left bank of the Inghapi River and in constructing a Redoubt with a view to the permanent occupation of the position as a Depôt and as a post of communication.

Strength of Detachment.

Field Officer.	Captains.	Subalterns.	Staff.	Sergeants.	Drummers.	Rank and File.
1	5	7	1	18	12	337

Major Henry Butler was gazetted Brevet-Lieutenant-Colonel in the Army on the 21st March, 1865.

On the 22nd March, Convoys from the Patea brought up supplies. The Force at Manawapow was reinforced by 100 men of the Fiftieth and 100 of the Fifty-seventh. They were engaged in building a Redoubt (for 100 men) on left bank; and another (for 150) on right bank, in continuing the formation of the road to Inghapi, and in making a heavy cutting up the right bank of the Tongahoe River, 600 yards further north.

1865 The Redoubts at Maniwapow being completed on 28th March were garrisoned by 100 of the Fifty-seventh Regiment, under Brevet-Major J. Hassard, and that on right bank by 100 of Fiftieth Regiment under Major Locke.

A Force moved from Tongahoe to the Waiongongora River, on the 31st of March, with four days' supplies. The Troops were detained an hour and a-half making the ford at the Waika and at the next stream passable. The Maories showed themselves at about 1,000 yards in front, but were soon dispersed. 100 infantry were pushed across the Waiongongora River, and the heights were occupied as a picquet ground.

Two Redoubts were constructed on right and left banks of the river, and occupied by the Fifty-seventh Regiment, under Brevet-Lieutenant-Colonel Butler.

The Detachment of Fifty-seventh Regiment was employed chiefly in conveying provisions from Manawapow to Waiongongora, entailing very arduous duties on Officers and men.

Ensign Charles John Matthews joined Service Companies on appointment on the 9th April.

On the 5th July, 1865, Major and Brevet-Lieutenant-Colonel Logan was appointed Companion of the Most Honourable Order of the Bath.

Lieutenant-General Sir Duncan Cameron, K.C.B., relinquished command of the Troops in New Zealand, and published the following General Order:—

No. 1188.

Head-quarters, Auckland,

1st August, 1865.

1. " On relinquishing the command in New Zealand, the Lieutenant-General desires to express to the Troops he has so long commanded his entire satisfaction with their conduct, and with the high state of discipline and efficiency maintained throughout the war."

1865 2. "The Lieutenant-General thanks Officers, Non-commissioned Officers and men of all arms who have served under him, for the cheerful alacrity with which they have performed the harassing and arduous duties required of them, and for the gallantry which they have displayed on all occasions when engaged with the enemy."

3. "His thanks are particularly due to Officers commanding Corps and the Heads of Departments for the cordial support and assistance they have afforded him, as well as for the assiduity with which they have conducted their various duties."

"The Lieutenant-General has often had occasion to submit to His Royal Highness the Field-Marshal Commanding-in-Chief the names of individuals who have distinguished themselves, and it will afford him great satisfaction further to bring to the notice of His Royal Highness his appreciation of the general good conduct of the whole force."

"He now takes leave of the Troops, and assures them he will always continue to feel the greatest interest in the welfare of those to whose energy, discipline, and gallantry he is so much indebted."

The Head-quarters of the Fifty-seventh Regiment, under Lieutenant-Colonel Logan, C.B., left Wanganui on 19th August, for Pipiriki, a rebel post, seventy miles up the Wanganui River, and were located in three Redoubts.

Field-Officer.	Captains.	Subalterns.	Staff.	Sergeants.	Drummers.	Rank and File.
1	3	6	1	14	8	294

The Regiment was conveyed to its destination in canoes.

1865 The following Officers accompanied the Regiment:—

Brevet-Major J. Stewart
Captain F. S. Schomberg
Brevet-Major W. A. J. Shortt
Lieut. E. Mills (I. of M.)
„ W. A. Thompson (Acting Adjutant)
Lieutenant F. H. Clayton (Acting Quartermaster)
„ A. C. Manners
„ H. D. C. Barton
Ensign E. Brodrip
Assistant-Surgeon J. Davis.

Captain and Brevet-Major Jason Hassard appointed Brevet-Lieutenant-Colonel in the Army, date of Gazette 28th August, 1865.

Major-General Trevor Chute, commanding the Forces in the Australian Colonies and in New Zealand, having arrived in Auckland, assumed command of the Troops.

1866 The Service Companies were distinguished alphabetically instead of numerically as hitherto.

The following was published in Regimental Orders:—

"The Commanding Officer has much pleasure in notifying for the information of the Regiment that a medal for distinguished conduct in the field, has been conferred on No. 2,774 Sergeant Daniel O'Connor for gallant conduct in the skirmish near Kakaramea, New Zealand, on 13th March, 1865. The medal was presented by Lieutenant-Colonel Logan, C.B., on parade, 3rd January, 1866, at Camp Tanhitunie."

A Field Force under Major-General Chute marched at 4 a.m., on the 10th January, crossed the Winnakura and Patea Rivers, proceeded to Kakaramea and encamped.

One Non-Commissioned Officer and 15 Gunners, with two 6-pounder Armstrong field gun, joined the force from the Patea.

Armed parties were employed, reconnoitring the bush near Kakaramea and destroyed two native cultivations.

The field force marched and encamped on the plains about a mile and a-half from the supposed position of Katemarai, and was augmented by detachments under

1866 Lieutenant-Colonel Butler, Fifty-seventh, from Waiongongora, consisting of:

Officers.	N. C. O.	R. & F.	
5	6	120	From Waiongongora under Brevet Lieutenant-Colonel Butler
4	6	120	From Manawapow under Brevet Lieutenant-Colonel Hassard

En route from Waiongongora and Manawapow, Lieutenant-Colonel Butler, on the 6th January, drove the rebels from their position of Ketemitea, and Lieutenant-Colonel Hassard destroyed some villages.

At 2.30 a.m., on the 13th January, the Force (as under) moved towards Otapawa, a fortified Pah, five miles to the north-east of the Camp.

Royal Artillery ...... 3 6-pounder Armstrong guns, with proportion of N.C. Officers and gunners under Lieut. Carre.

2/14th Regiment....Lt.-Col. Trevor and 200 rank and file.

57th Regiment ......Lt.-Col. Butler and 130 rank and file.

Militia and Native Troops.................2 Officers and 236 of all ranks.

The Troops advanced under cover of the guns against the position, which consisted of an entrenched work strongly palisaded, having a front of about 100 yards.

The approach was over level ground, flanked on the right by a tongue of bush at 70 yards. The Major-General having taken advantage of an undulation in the ground at a distance of about 150 yards from the work, formed the Force in the following order, viz.: the Detachment of the Fifty-seventh Regiment on the left in skirmishing order, with Militia in support.

The 2nd Battalion 14th Regiment was extended on the right with a support.

The signal for the assault being given, the Troops

1866 dashed at the works. The rebels kept perfectly quiet until the Troops were within 40 yards when they opened a most severe and unusually well directed fire from the whole front of the entrenchment as well as from the bush on its right.

Under this heavy cross-fire a portion of the Fifty-seventh, under Brevet-Lieutenant-Colonel Hassard, wheeled to the left, and drove the rebels from the bush; then turned and advanced against the right angle of the "Pah."

At the same moment the remainder of the Fifty-seventh, gallantly led by Lieutenant-Colonel Butler, reached the left angle of the work. The Maories fought desperately for a time, but in vain; a portion of the palisading being cut down by Private Doakes, Fifty-seventh Regiment, the troops entered the works, and carried all before them. The enemy broke, and fled down a precipitous, densely wooded gully, immediately in the rear of the Pah, through which it was impossible for the Troops to follow.

The capture of Otapawa was of importance, inasmuch as it was a position of historical repute for its natural strength. It had never fallen in any of the native wars, and in a manner justified the opinion of the rebels, that they held an impregnable position.

The loss of the enemy was estimated at 50 killed and wounded, the body of their leader was found in the ditch.

The Regiment lost 1 Officer (Brevet-Lieutenant-Colonel Hassard), 2 Sergeants and 5 privates killed, and many wounded.

The Major-General in his despatch observes, that, "in Lieutenant-Colonel Hassard, the service has lost one of its bravest Officers; he led his men with the greatest gallantry, and fell inside the Pah, nobly performing his duty."

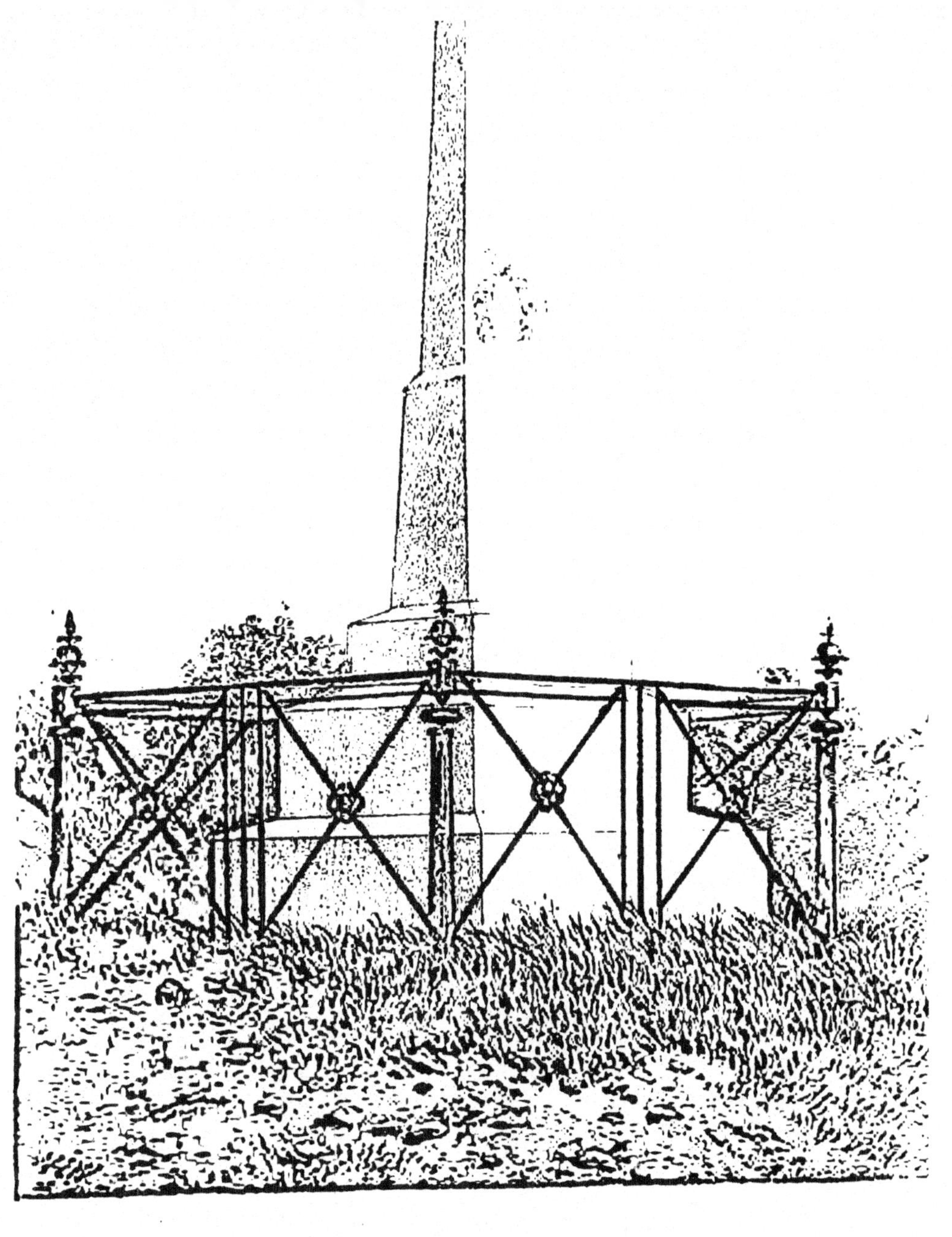

1866 KILLED.

Sergeant F. Day. Private Robert Doakes.
„ J. Sullivan. „ John Moran.
Private Hugh McGregor. „ George King.
Private John Manning.

WOUNDED.

Brevet-Lieutenant-Colonel Jason Hassard (mortally), since dead

Corporal T. R. Bowyer (severely)
Private J. Hartley „
„ F. Roycroft
„ McCorcoran „
Dr. George Donoghue „
Private William Kinnarney (slightly)
„ M. Connolly (severely)
„ T. Gannon (slightly)

Private Doakes, for his conspicuous bravery, would have been recommended for the Victoria Cross had he survived. The Regiment deeply regretted the loss of so brave a soldier.

By the capture of their stronghold at Otapawa and the dispersion of the rebel natives the war on the west coast was virtually concluded, and the troops returned to their several garrisons, the Fifty-seventh reoccupying Wanganui.

The following Numerical Return will show the number of Officers, Non-commissioned Officers, and men of the Regiment who have been killed, wounded, or died of wounds in the several engagements with the rebel Maories from 1st May, 1863, to the 31st March, 1866:—

	KILLED.		WOUNDED.		DIED OF WOUNDS.		TOTAL.
	Officers.	N.-C.-O. and Men.	Officers.	N.-C.-O. and Men.	Officer.	N.-C.-O. and Men.	Officers and Men.
1st May, 1863, to 30th March, 1866.	2	17	3	51	1	7	73

1866 1. Assistant-Surgeon Hope, although actually transferred to the Staff when he fell into the Maori ambuscade and was killed, on the 4th May, 1863, had been attached for some years to the Fifty-seventh Regiment. He is not included in the above Return, but his loss was deeply regretted, as was also that of Lieutenant Tragett, Fifty-seventh Regiment, and the six Non-commissioned Officers and men, forming a small escort, who were all cruelly murdered by the rebel Maories before war was declared.

2. Captain Lloyd was killed in a Maori ambuscade on the 6th April, 1864, while patrolling the country around Kaitake, recently captured from the rebels. Captain Lloyd served for many years as Adjutant, and was much thought of as an excellent Officer. His loss was severely felt. He left a young widow and child.

3. Captain and Brevet-Lieutenant-Colonel Jason Hassard was killed while gallantly leading his Company in the attack on a native Pah on the 13th January, 1866, having served for twenty years in the Fifty-seventh Regiment. He was greatly beloved and much regretted. He left a widow to mourn his loss.

Ensign Edward Percy Benn joined the Service Companies from England on appointment on the 24th January, 1866, and on the same day Drummer Dudley Stagpool was presented with the decoration of the "Victoria Cross," which Her Majesty had been graciously pleased to grant him, by Brigadier General R. Waddy, C.B., at a general parade of the Troops at Wanganui. (See Appendix.)

Lieutenant John Thornton Down was presented with the decoration of the "Victoria Cross," which Her Majesty had been graciously pleased to grant to him, by Brigadier- General R. Waddy, C.B., at a general parade of the Troops at Wanganui on the 7th February. (See Appendix.)

1866 General Charles Fox was appointed to be Colonel of the Fifty-seventh Regiment *vice* General Sir F. Love, K.C.B., transferred to 43rd Light Infantry.—Gazette, September 15th, 1865.

Head-quarters under Lieutenant-Colonel Logan, C.B., were taken on the strength of the Wanganui garrison, preparatory to the concentration of the Regiment.

During March the Regiment was concentrated at Wanganui, preparatory to embarkation for Auckland to occupy the Waikato District.

The Sergeants have also been completed with new short rifles, sword bayonets, and scabbards.

On the 18th April, Head-quarters under Colonel Logan, C.B., embarked at Wanganui on board the hired steam ship *Ahurire*, for Onehunga, with the following Officers: —Lieutenant and Acting-Adjutant W. A. Thompson, Lieutenant P. E. Powys, Lieutenant F. H. Clayton, Ensign E. Broderip, Acting-Quartermaster, with H and K Companies and band.

Head-quarters arrived at Otahuhu from Wanganui on 22nd April, the other Companies rejoined Head-quarters on their being relieved at out-stations.

Head-quarters with four Companies marched from Otahuhu to Te Aramutu, upper Waikato.

The remainder of the Regiment being detached as follows :—One Company at ... Queen's Redoubt.
Ditto ... ... Ngaruawahia.
Ditto ... ... Whata Whata.
Ditto ... ... Te Rou.
Ditto ... ... Raglan.

Lieutenant Wyndham A. K. Thompson, who had been for some time Acting, was appointed Adjutant, from 1st March, 1866.

The Regiment received an order, on 7th October, to be in readiness for embarkation for England.

1866 The Regiment was inspected by Major General Chute, commanding troops in New Zealand, on the 8th December.

During the early part of 1867, the Regiment was concentrated at Auckland, preparatory to embarkation for England.

The Right Wing, under command of Brevet-Major James Stewart, embarked for England in the ship *Maori*, and sailed on the 30th March, consisting of:—

Rank and Names.		Officers.	N. C. Officers.	Drummers, Rank and File.	
Bt.-Major	James Stewart, in Command.				
Captain	Sir R. Douglas, Baronet.				
"	E. Gould Hasted.				
Lieutenant	W. de W. Waller.				
"	P. E. Powys, Acting Qr.-Master.	9	22	239	
Ensign	Robert Holmes.				
"	C. J. Matthews. Acting Adjutant.				
"	E. P. Benn.				
Asst.-Surg.	James Davis.				

Right Wing arrived at Liverpool on 31st July, 1867, and proceeded to Manchester by rail the same day.

Head-quarters and Left Wing, under command of Brevet-Lieutenant Colonel R. A. Logan, C.B., embarked for England on board the ship *Electric*, and sailed 12th April, 1867, consisting of:

Rank and Names.		Officers.	N. C. Officers.	Drummers, Rank and File.	Remarks.
Bt.-Lt.-Col.	R. A. Logan, C.B., Commanding.				
Bt.-Major	W. A. J. Shortt.				
"	H. R. Russell.				
Captain	Edward Mills.				
Lieutenant	H. D. C. Barton.				
"	H. M. Powell.				
"	Chas. Picot.	13	20	282	
"	Edwd. Broderip.				
Ensign	J. R. K. Tredennick				
Paymaster	Mark Matthews.				
Lieutenant	W. A. K. Thompson (Adjutant).				
Qr.-Master	Thos. Martindale.				
Surgeon	G. B. Popplewell.				

1867

FIFTY-SEVENTH REGIMENT.

Notes on the Homeward Voyage from New Zealand, abridged from a Local Newspaper, August, 1867:—

The Fifty-seventh Regiment paraded on the 12th April for the last time in the Albert Barracks, Auckland, and was inspected by Major-General Trevor Chute, commanding the Forces, and immediately embarked, on board the *Electric* (1,106 tons register), R. Leathwaite, Master.

The living cargo was found to consist of 13 Officers, 331 Non-commissioned Officers and Soldiers of the Fifty-seventh and various Corps serving in New Zealand, 5 Officers' wives, and 69 children, making a total, including the crew, of 510 souls, under the command of Lieutenant-Colonel Logan, C.B.

The vessel had a very good run to latitude 56° south, longitude 80° west, which brought her into the neighbourhood of Cape Horn, where, for ten days, a succession of gales, right aft, washed the decks, and obliged the hatches to be constantly battened down.

Some idea may be formed of the force of the wind by the ship's log, which ran off on three successive days, viz.: 26th, 27th, and 28th April, 285, 349, and 302 knots respectively. The glass fell on the 30th April lower than ever before noticed by the Captain; but the hurricane passed clear of the ship, brightening the weather, and enabling the vessel to clear "Cape Horn" without difficulty. The weather continued fine until the 24th May, when a gale began, and, gradually increasing, surpassed in violence anything before encountered. At 7 p.m., when the ship was still running, it being too hazardous to lay to, part of the bulwarks were wrenched away, sending the men at the wheel flying across the deck. The ship was taken aback, and could not be

1867 properly hove to until after half-an-hour of imminent danger, during which time she made from four to five miles *sternway*. At 10.15 p.m. a tremendous sea came over the poop, smashing the bulwarks, washing away the binnacle, and again sending flying the men at the wheel. Both poop ladders were washed away, as were also the after skylights. The glass of the centre hatch was broken, and the deck presented an extraordinary scene of confusion. The Boatswain was thrown down the after skylight, bringing with him the lamp, swinging tray, and everything stowed thereon. A hencoop, filled with poultry, was forced down the forward skylight, and down every opening poured volumes of water, extinguishing the lights, and filling the saloon and cabins with water.

The Boatswain and three of the crew were disabled, Lieutenant Barton, Fifty-seventh Regiment, was carried off his legs by the rush of water, but escaped with a dislocated elbow, and face terribly cut. Paymaster Matthews received a severe contusion, and several of the soldiers were more or less hurt.

Every sail was split, except the lower maintopsail, and had not the *Electric* proved herself a very staunch seaboat, she must, when taken aback in such a tremendous sea, have gone down stern foremost. Towards midnight the hurricane somewhat abated, but the cabins were half full of water, and beds and bedding were completely saturated.

The morning's light showed that the damage done was more serious than anticipated, but the weather cleared, and "all hands" were employed in restoring order.

On the following Monday another gale, freshening into a "perfect hurricane," again swept over the unfortunate ship, which was thrown on its beam ends, from which perilous position it was righted by cutting

1867 away the foresail. The crew had become so completely exhausted by this succession of storms, that one watch refused to go aloft to furl sail, whereby the topgallant mast and starboard cathead were sprung, and much damage done. Repairs were hardly concluded when another gale was encountered (29th May,) which compelled the Captain to lay to for 14 hours, during which time two foretopsails, lower maintopsail, and mizen-topsail were torn to ribbons and lost.

On the 2nd June, the fourth gale in nine days was experienced, again freshening to a hurricane, and again compelling the vessel to be hove to for many hours, during which more sails were destroyed, and the men at the wheel were several times washed away. Such a succession of disasters caused so much damage that repairs became necessary, and obliged the Captain to put into Ascension.

Sighted the island on 14th June, and not knowing the anchorage, ran in over the reef, without touching.

A pleasant eight days was passed on the island, and every attention was paid by the "Authorities," and by H.M. Ships *Flora* and *Espoir*, which happened to be at Ascension.

Having completed all necessary repairs, on Sunday, 23rd June, weighed anchor and sailed for England, and arrived at Plymouth on 28th July after a perilous voyage of 15,850 miles.

From Plymouth the vessel proceeded to Liverpool, where the Regiment landed on the 6th August and was despatched at once by rail to Manchester, there to be stationed "until further orders."

On the 7th August, Colonel Warre, C.B., who had returned to England in advance of the Regiment, resumed the command, from leave of absence.

1867 The establishment was reduced to 56 privates per Company, on reduction to home service.

Ensign Edward Seely Vidal joined on appointment on 9th October, 1867, and on the 6th November Quartermaster Sergeant Charles Vallassey Leech was appointed Quartermaster *vice* Martindale, deceased.

Major-General Sir John Garvock, K.C.B., made the usual inspection of the Regiment on the 30th October.

During the autumn of 1867 serious disturbances broke out in Manchester arising from the Fenian proclivities of the Irish population. The Troops were frequently held in readiness to assist the civil power and were augmented by the addition of the 72nd Highlanders and a half-battery of Artillery.

At the execution of the murderers of Police-Sergeant Brett, dense masses of people filled the streets and threatened to rescue the prisoners. A strong force of Cavalry, Artillery, and Infantry, under the immediate command of Colonel Warre, C.B. (acting under the orders of Major-General Sir John Garvock, K.C.B., Commanding the Northern District), guarded the precincts of the gaol and preserved order.

On the 28th November, 1867, while the Regiment was stationed at Salford Barracks, Manchester, the old Colours, which had been borne at the head of the Regiment during the last fifteen years of its eventful career, were replaced with the new Regulation Colours of a much smaller and more convenient pattern.

The new Colours were presented to the Regiment by Mrs. Warre, in the presence of Major-General Sir John Garvock, K.C.B., a brilliant Staff, and a numerous gathering of Officers, and gentlemen, with their families, from the surrounding country. The old Colours were trooped, and paraded in front of the Regiment, which was drawn up in line to salute and receive the Major-

QUEEN'S COLOUR.

REGIMENTAL COLOUR.

1867 General Commanding the District; after which the Regiment formed three sides of a square, the open space being occupied by the new Colours, crossed on a pile of drums, under the guard of the flank Companies of the Regiment. Ensigns Garnett and Collins were in attendance to receive the new Colours. As soon as the new Colours were consecrated by the Reverend P. C. Nicholson, Chaplain to the Garrison, Mrs. Warre presented them to the Ensigns and said:—

"The Officers have kindly requested me to present " these new Colours to the Regiment. I need not say " that I am deeply gratified by this request: I thank " them from my heart. They know that for twelve " years past the honour and welfare of the Fifty-seventh " have been inexpressibly dear to me. My hopes and " my prayers have always been with it. In giving these " new Colours to the care of Ensigns Garnett and " Collins, I entreat them to consider them as a sacred " charge, and to remember that these Colours represent " the honour and glory of the Regiment, and that those " to whom they are entrusted should prove themselves, " at all times, worthy of the trust. God bless the new " Colours and the Fifty-seventh Regiment."

Major-General Sir John Garvock then addressed the Regiment. He said they had "just received new Colours " from the wife of the Commanding Officer, and he could " readily understand the pleasurable feeling with which " Mrs. Warre had presented them to the Regiment." He, on his part, as the General Officer Commanding the District in which the Regiment was now serving, " was " anxious to express his full assurance that those new " Colours were well and worthily bestowed, that the " young Soldiers of the Regiment would emulate the " deeds of their predecessors, and that whenever those " emblems of the past glories of the Fifty-seventh should

1867 "chance to be unfurled before an enemy, those whose "duty it would be to guard, defend, and follow them, "would sustain the reputation of their country and their "Corps, would uphold the honour of their Sovereign, "and prove themselves worthy of the Service to which "they belonged."

Sir John Garvock then alluded to the past services of the Regiment, and felt sure that "all would be glad to "hear him speak, in the presence of so many strangers, "of the distinguished services of the 'Old Die Hards.'" The Major-General concluded a very spirited address by reminding the Fifty-seventh that "it, or rather what "remained of it, formed part of those 1,500 men out of "6,000 unconquerable British Soldiers, who stood "triumphant on that fatal hill at Albuhera, on the 16th "May, 1811."

He trusted that success might follow the Fifty-seventh wherever it went, and that "God, who looked down upon "warlike deeds, when they were performed in the "execution of duty, and to his honor and glory, with the "same favour with which He regarded the actions of "those whom He called to more peaceful pursuits, "might conduct the "Old Die Hards" to honor and "success in any quarter of the world to which they "might be sent to serve their Queen and their Country."

Colonel Warre, C.B., returned thanks on behalf of the Regiment to Sir John Garvock, for his presence on that occasion, and for the flattering terms in which he had spoken of the Regiment.

The Regiment then reformed line and received the new Colours with presented arms. After which it marched past with the new Colours flying and the ceremony was brought to a conclusion.

NOTE.—The old Colours which had been presented to the Regiment by the late Viscount Hardinge, when Colonel of the Regiment and

1867 The Officers of the Regiment gave a Ball in their Mess Room in the evening in honour of the event.

Lieutenant-Colonel E. Bowen, from half-pay, late Sixty-ninth Foot, appointed to be Lieutenant-Colonel of the Regiment *vice* Brevet-Colonel Henry James Warre, C.B., who retires upon half-pay, *Gazette*, 7th December, 1867.

The following Regimental Order was issued by Colonel Warre, on his retirement on half-pay.

"The Field Marshal Commanding-in-Chief having "approved of the retirement of Colonel Warre, C.B., "upon half-pay, he relinquishes with very great regret "the command of the Fifty-seventh Regiment which he "has had the honour to hold for upwards of twelve years, "and he desires to offer his most cordial acknowledge-"ments to the Officers, Non-Commissioned Officers and "men for the manner in which they have supported the "credit of the Regiment in the Field, and in Garrison, "during a period of unusual difficulty. The arduous "nature of the duties in which the Regiment has been "employed during its term of Foreign Service—in the "Crimea, in India, and in New Zealand—are too well "known to require repetition; on all occasions the conduct "of all ranks has elicited the warmest commendations "from the General Officers under whom the Regiment "was immediately serving and from His Royal Highness "The Field Marshal Commanding-in-Chief."

"In taking leave of the Regiment, Colonel Warre "trusts that he may hereafter be able to prove the deep "interest he must ever feel in the welfare of all, and he

Commander-in-Chief of the Forces, were, at the special request of the then Colonel-Lieutenant-General Charles Fox, entrusted to his charge, and at his death in 1873 they were removed to St. Paul's Cathedral, where they are now suspended over a Mural Marble Tablet erected to the memory of the Officers and men who fell in action, during the fifteen years that the Colours were carried at the head of the Regiment.

1867 "entreats Officers and soldiers to show, under the new "Colors which have lately been presented to the Regi- "ment, the same fortitude in the field, and the same "respect for discipline in their quarters, which have "already gained for them such high and well deserved "encomiums. Farewell."

1868 Ensign Arthur Neil appointed to the Regiment from the Eighty-seventh Foot, *Gazette* of the 22nd January.

Lieutenant Moutray Vance Hornidge appointed Instructor of Musketry, *Gazette* of 11th February.

The Regiment (strength as under) moved from Manchester to Aldershot on the 1st April, 1868, under the command of Lieutenant-Colonel Bowen.

Officers.	Sergeants.	Drummers.	Rank and File.
31	49	20	601

On the 7th May, the Regiment was inspected by Major-General Henry Kenny, commanding First Brigade, Aldershot.

Assistant-Surgeon Wilton Everett appointed to the Regiment *vice* Davis, exchanged to Thirty-ninth Foot.

The usual Autumn Inspection was made in October by Major-General Henry Kenny, Commanding First Brigade at Aldershot. The Major-General expressed himself highly pleased with the appearance of the men, the steadiness with which they performed their drill, and the cleanliness and good order of the barrack rooms.

Ensign John Woodhouse Ackland appointed to the Regiment, *Gazette* of the 12th December, 1868.

1869 Ensign Henry Thomas Hughes Hallett appointed to the Regiment, *Gazette*, 13th January, 1869; and on the 27th February, Ensign John Phillips appointed to the Regiment.

1869 The Regiment (strength as under) moved from Aldershot to Devonport on the 22nd March, 1869, viz.:—

Officers.	Sergeants.	Drummers.	Rank and File.
27	42	21	524

Ensign Asheton Biddulph appointed to the Regiment.

The establishment of the Regiment reduced to 520 privates, all other ranks to remain the same.

The Regiment was inspected by Major-General Sir Charles W. D. Staveley, K.C.B., Commanding Western District, on the 7th May, and on the 30th September.

Ensign George Chardin Denton appointed to the Regiment 29th October.

The Late War in New Zealand.

On the 3rd July, 1868, on the Order of the day for going into Committee of Supply, Viscount Enfield called attention to the services of the Forces employed in New Zealand during the last war.

The total number of Troops engaged was 9,000 of the Line and 300 Naval Brigade. Of these 688 had been killed or wounded; 18 Officers were killed and 56 wounded, of whom 15 had subsequently died. Out of the Naval Brigade 6 Officers and 14 men were killed, 8 Officers and 32 men wounded.

The Troops went through all the vicissitudes and hardships of a well-fought campaign. Viscount Fnfield would ask the Secretary of State whether any decoration was to be granted for such services.

The motion was seconded by Colonel North, who said that the men composing the Force in New Zealand went through greater fatigues with less excitement than the troops who had generally been engaged in foreign wars.

Lord Eustace Cecil remarked that we (England) had not been in the habit of rewarding our Troops in the way they had a right to expect.

In the absence of the Secretary of State for War, Mr. Disraeli admitted the hardships and promised that the subject should receive attention.

1870 On the 27th March, 1870, 383 medals for the war in New Zealand were distributed to the Officers and men who had served in New Zealand.

In June following, Her Majesty was most graciously pleased to approve of the word 'New Zealand' being borne on the Colours of the Fifty-seventh Regiment and of the Regiments who had served in New Zealand during the native wars 1845, '46, '47, 1860 and '61, and 1863, '64, '65, '66.

The following Regiments are distinguished by the words New Zealand being borne on their colours, viz.:—

Twelfth, Fourteenth, Eighteenth (Royal Irish), Fortieth, Forty-Third (Light Infantry), Fiftieth, Fifty-seventh, Fifty-eighth, Sixty-fifth, Sixty-Eighth (Light Infantry), Seventieth, Ninety-Sixth, and Ninety-Ninth.

Under authority dated War Office, 19th May, 1870, the establishment of the Regiment was reduced to 10 Companies, having 27 Combatant and 6 Staff-Officers and 568 Non-Commissioned Officers and rank and file. Total 601.

The usual inspections were made by Major-General Sir C. W. D., Staveley, K.C.B., Commanding the South-Western District.

The following appointment having appeared in the *London Gazette* of the 2nd August, was published for the information of the Regiment.

Quartermaster Joseph Whittaker, from Fifty-sixth foot, to be Quartermaster *vice* Leech.

Her Majesty has approved of the following augmen-

1870 tations to the establishment of the undermentioned Corps:—

Fifty-seventh Regiment:—Corporals, 40; Privates, 760; rank and file, 800.

Ensign John Woodhouse Ackland to be Lieutenant *vice* Brodirip, 5th September.

Ensign John Bonhote appointed to the Regiment, 8th September.

Ensign Thomas John De Burgh appointed to the Regiment, 8th September.

The Commanding Officer, with the deepest regret, announced to the Regiment the death of Captain Henry Miller Powell, who, it appears, was struck by lightning on the 26th October, while absent on leave.

The following promotion having appeared in the *London Gazette* of the 4th November, 1870, is published for information:—

Lieutenant W. A. K. Thompson to be Captain *vice* Powell, deceased.

Ensign H. J. H. Hallett to be Lieutenant *vice* Thompson, promoted.

Her Majesty has been greatly pleased to approve of the following appointment, dated 12th November, 1870:—

Lieutenant James R. K. Tredennick to be Adjutant *vice* Thompson, promoted.

The Regiment received orders to move out of Devonport on 28th November, 1870. Head-quarters consisting of D and F Companies, were stationed at Fort Tregantle, Cornwall; remaining Companies were distributed as follows:—

Companies.	Stations.	Companies.	Stations.
B	Devonport	A	Stonehouse
C	Fort Staddon	H	Devonport
E	Ditto	I	Ditto
G	Bull Point	K	Maker

1870 The following promotion having appeared in the *London Gazette*, dated 14th December, 1870, was published for information:—

Ensign Asheton Biddulph to be Lieutenant by purchase *vice* Barton, who retires.

Aubrey Reginald Hamilton, Gent., to be Ensign by purchase *vice* Biddulph, promoted.

1871 Her Majesty approved of the following alterations in the establishment of the undermentioned Regiment from the 1st February, 1871:—

Fifty-seventh Foot:—40 Corporals, 810 privates—850 rank and file.

The following appointment having appeared in the *London Gazette*, dated 11th February, 1871, was published for information:—

Lieutenant Charles John Matthews to be Instructor of Musketry *vice* Lieutenant M. V. Hornidge, who resignes that appointment.

The following promotion having appeared in the *London Gazette* of the 21st March, was published for information:—

Lieutenant-Colonel R. A. Logan, C.B., having completed qualifying service in the rank of Lieutenant-Colonel, to be Colonel in the Army dated.

The following promotion having appeared in the *London Gazette*, dated 10th May, 1871, was published for information:—

Ensign G. C. Denton to be Lieutenant by purchase *vice* Hornidge, who retires.

The following promotion having appeared in the *London Gazette*, 31st May, 1871, was published for information:—

Ensign John Bonhote to be Lieutenant by purchase, *vice* Ackland, who retires.

Paymaster-Major Matthews died at his residence at

1871 Horrabridge on the 13th June, 1871.

On the 7th September, the Regiment received orders to proceed to Ireland, and on the 18th embarked at the Dockyard, Devonport, on board H.M. Steam Ship *Orontes*, disembarked at Queenstown on 21st and 22nd September, and proceeded to occupy Limerick and out-stations.

Ensign Alfred Allen Garstin appointed to the Regiment *vice* Penton, promoted Lieutenant, *London Gazette*, 22nd September.

The Regiment was inspected by Major-General E. A. Holdich, C.B., Commanding the Cork District, on the 17th October.

The Regiment was inspected by the Right Hon. Lord Sandhurst, Commander of the Forces in Ireland, on the following day.

Purchase of Commissions abolished by Royal Warrant.

The rank of Ensign abolished and that of Sub-Lieutenant instituted.

An exchange between Lieutenant Bonhote and Lieutenant Hayne, 84th Regiment, sanctioned by Horse
1872 Guards on the 2nd November, 1871.

Ensigns de Burgh, Hamilton and Garstin appointed Lieutenants, and Gentleman Cadet John Eyer Massy, from Royal Military College, to be Sub-Lieutenant, January, 1872.

Paymaster-Major W. F. Scott, who joined on 14th October, 1871, transferred to the 30th Foot, on the 1st February, 1872.

Lieutenant Garnett retired from the Service.

On the 29th February, Head-quarters moved to Kinsale, detaching parties to occupy the out-stations.

Scarlet tunics and kersey frocks issued to the rank and file of the Regiment for trial, and blue Tweed trousers were substituted for black cloth for winter wear, and blue tartan for black tartan for summer wear.

1872 The Regiment was inspected by Major-General Holdich, C.B., Commanding the Cork District, on the 24th April.

Lieutenant Colonel Bowen retired from the service, *London Gazette* of the 14th May, 1872.

Major and Brevet-Colonel R. A. Logan, C.B., promoted Lieutenant-Colonel and assumed command of the Regiment *vice* Bowen who retires.

Captain and Brevet-Major James Stewart to be Major *vice* Colonel Logan promoted.

Lieutenant Picot to be Captain *vice* Stewart promoted.

Captain F. H. Clayton retired from the service, *London Gazette* of 18th June.

The Regiment was inspected by Major-General E. A. Holdich, C.B., commanding Cork District, on the 16th July, 1872.

The exchange of Lieutenant John Bonhote with Lieutenant A. N. Hayne, Eighty-fourth Foot, was antedated to 27th October, 1871.

The Commissions as Lieutenants of T. J. de Burgh, A. K. Hamilton, and A. A. Garstin, being unsaleable and not carrying any purchase rights, were antedated to 28th October, 1871.

Lieutenant Edward Sealy Vidal retired from the Service, *London Gazette*, 16th July, 1872.

Lieutenant John Samuel Jeffares (from half-pay, late Ninth Foot) posted to the Regiment *vice* C. Picot, promoted Captain, *London Gazette*, 13th August, 1872.

Lieutenant and Adjutant J. R. K. Tredennick to be Captain *vice* F. H. Clayton retired, dated 19th June, 1872.

Lieutenant Joseph Graham Smith, 1st West India Regiment, to be Lieutenant *vice* E. S. Vidal retired, *London Gazette*, 20th August, 1872.

Lieutenant C. J. Matthews (Instructor of Musketry)

1872 appointed Adjutant *vice* Lieutenant and Adjutant J. R. K. Tredennick promoted Captain, *London Gazette*, 10th September, 1872.

Lieutenant Dudley Davison Batty (from half-pay, late Sixty-seventh Foot), posted to the Regiment *vice* J. R. K. Tredennick promoted, *London Gazette*, 10th September, 1872.

Lieutenant H. T. H. Hallett appointed Instructor of Musketry *vice* Lieutenant C. J. Matthews appointed Adjutant, dated 11th September, 1872, and Commission as Adjutant subsequently antedated to 20th August.

Lieutenant J. G. Smith promoted Captain in the Ninety-seventh Foot in recognition of his gallant services, when engaged against the Indians at Orange Walk, British Honduras, *London Gazette* of 3rd December.

1873 Augustus West Hill, Gentleman, to be Sub-Lieutenant, dated 1st January, 1873.

Lieutenant John Samuel Jeffares to be Captain on half-pay from the 15th January, 1873.

Sub-Lieutenant John William Eyre Massy to be Lieutenant, dated 30th December, 1871.

Lieutenant William Wade Brownjohn from half-pay Second Foot to be Lieutenant *vice* J. S. Jeffares promoted half-pay Captain, dated 12th February, 1873.

David Farhill St. Clair, Gentleman, to be Sub-Lieutenant in succession to J. G. Smith promoted in Ninety-seventh Foot, dated 26th February, 1873.

Captain Edward Gould Hasted retired from the Service receiving the value of his Commission, dated 15th March, 1873.

Quartermaster Joseph Whittaker retired upon half-pay, dated 15th March, 1873.

Captain A. H. Douglass, died on 25th March, 1873, of '*Enteric Fever*.'

1873 Lieutenant H. D. Bicknell to be Captain *vice* E. G. Hasted retired, dated 15th March, 1873.

The Head-quarters from Kinsale and Detachments from out-stations moved to the Curragh Camp early in April, 1873.

The Regiment was inspected by Major-General Robert Wardlaw, C.B., Commanding Curragh District, on the 10th April.

General Charles Richard Fox died on the 13th April, 1873. (*See Appendix.*)

Quartermaster-Sergeant Thomas Wood to be Quarter-master *vice* J. Whittaker, retired on half-pay, *London Gazette* of the 23rd April.

Lieutenant General Freeman Murray to be Colonel *vice* General Charles Richard Fox deceased, dated 14th April, 1873.

Major and Brevet-Lieutenant-Colonel Henry Butler having completed the qualifying services with the rank of Lieutenant Colonel to be Colonel, dated 16th January, 1873.

Captain and Brevet-Major Henry Rose Hickman Russell retired upon temporary half-pay, dated 30th April, 1873.

Lieutenant Gordon Dewar (from the Sixty-fourth Foot) to be Lieutenant *vice* W. W. Brown John, who exchanges, dated 30th April, 1873.

Lieutenant Charles John Matthews to be Captain *vice* A. K. Douglass deceased, dated 26th March, 1873.

On the 1st May, 1873, the Regiment received orders to hold the undermentioned detail in readiness to proceed to Woolwich, to form part of the 50th Brigade Depot:—

Captains.	Subalterns.	Sergeants.	Corporals.	Drummers.	Privates.
2	2	6	5	2	20

1873 Major and Brevet-Colonel Henry Butler retired upon half-pay, *Gazette*, dated 14th May, 1873.

Captain Frederick J. Schomberg to be Major in the Army from 5th July, 1872, such antedate not to carry back pay prior to the 14th May, 1873, *London Gazette* 23rd May, 1873.

The Depot Companies under Command of Captain and Brevet-Major W. A. J. Shortt, with Lieutenants A. Collins and G. E. Denton, proceeded to Kingston, and embarked on board H.M. ship '*Simoon*,' for Woolwich, on the 31st May, 1873.

General Right Honourable Wm. R. Lord Sandhurst, G.C.B., G.C.S.I., Commanding the Forces in Ireland, was pleased to express his gratification at the general appearance of the Fifty-seventh Depot, upon the occasion of their hurried embarkation on the 31st May, 1873.

Lieutenant Thomas John de Burgh to be Adjutant *vice* Lieutenant Charles John Matthews promoted, dated 26th March, 1873.

Captain and Brevet-Major William Edward Brown to be Major *vice* Brevet-Colonel Henry Butler retired on half-pay, dated 14th May, 1873.

Lieutenant Arthur Collins to be Captain *vice* Brevet-Major W. E. Brown, dated 14th May, 1873.

On the 4th July, 1873, the Regiment paraded with the Curragh District Troops for inspection by the Right Honourable W. R. Lord Sandhurst, G.C.B., Commanding the Forces in Ireland, who afterwards was pleased to express his high opinion of the admirable manner in which the Troops turned out for his Review.

Captain H. J. Morewood (from half-pay late Thirtieth Foot) to be Captain *vice* Brevet-Major H. R. Russell retired on temporary half-pay, dated 5th July, 1873.

Lieutenant Arthur Biddulph retired from the service,

1873 receiving the value of his Commission, dated 5th July, 1873.

The Regiment was inspected by Major-General Robert Wardlaw, C.B., Commanding Curragh District, on the 14th July.

Lieutenant C. F. W. Moir (from half-pay, late 3rd West India Regiment) to be Lieutenant *vice* Charles John Matthews promoted, dated 16th July, 1873.

Lieutenant-General Sir Thomas Steele, K.C.B., was pleased to express his entire satisfaction at the promptitude with which the Regiment, at Camp Curragh, assembled on the night of the 10th August, to quell the disturbance between the North Cork Rifles and the Queen's County Militia.

"The Regiment was under Arms, with its Officers, in the Militia Square, with the least possible delay."

"The Major-General wishes for no greater proof of good discipline and soldierlike qualifications."

Charles H. Morris, Gentleman, to be Sub-Lieutenant in succession to A. Biddulph retired, dated 9th August, 1873.

On the 6th September an Order was received to hold the Regiment in readiness for embarkation early in November for Ceylon.

An exchange between Lieutenant G. C. Denton at the 50th Brigade Depot, and Lieutenant D. D. Batty, was sanctioned at the Horse-Guards on 8th September.

On the 15th September the Regiment was inspected by Major-General Robert Wardlaw, C.B., Commanding Curragh District, preparatory to embarkation.

Captain and Brevet-Major Frederick S. Schomberg retired from the service, receiving the value of his Commission, *London Gazette* of the 24th September.

The embarkation of the Regiment for Ceylon postponed to 7th December, 1873.

1873 The Regiment has been permitted, by His Royal Highness the Field Marshal Commanding-in-Chief, to wear the word "*Albuhera*," with a laurel wreath round the number, as a badge on the forage caps, also on the collars of the men's tunics.

SEE APPENDIX FOR CORRESPONDENCE.

Lieutenant Henry Reginald Bate (from 13th Foot) to be Captain *vice* Brevet-Major Schomberg retired, dated 18th October, 1873.

Lieutenant R. S. Calvert (from the late Ceylon Rifle Regiment) to be Lieutenant *vice* H. D. Bicknell promoted, dated 18th October, 1873.

The promotion of Lieutenant H. R. Bate (from the 13th Foot) to be Captain *vice* Brevet-Major Schomberg retired, which was notified in the *Gazette* of 17th October, 1873, is cancelled.

Lieutenant J. G. White (from the Royal Elthorne or 5th Middlesex Militia) to be Lieutenant *vice* A. Collins promoted, dated 12th November, 1873.

Lieutenant N. J. R. Blake (from the Dublin County Militia) to be Lieutenant, dated 12th November, 1873.

Lieutenant C. D. B. Michel (from the 7th Royal Lancashire Militia) to be Lieutenant, dated 12th November, 1873.

Major E. K. Jones (from the 13th Foot) to be Major *vice* W. E. Brown who exchanges, dated 19th November, 1873.

The embarkation of the Regiment for Ceylon again postponed to 24th December, 1873.

Lieutenant H. D. Wade to be Captain *vice* Brevet-Major Schomberg retired, dated 24th September, 1873.

The Depot Companies were attached to the First Battalion of the Twelfth Regiment.

The Regiment proceeded by train to Cork, thence by

1873 river steamer to Queenstown, embarked on 23rd December, 1873, on board Her Majesty's Indian Troop ship *Malabar*, and sailed for Ceylon the following day (strength as below):—

Field Officers.	Captains.	Subalterns.	Staff.	Staff-Sergeants.	Sergeants.	Corporals.	Drummers.	Privates.	Officers' Wives.	Officers' Children.	Soldiers' Wives.	Soldiers' Children.	Female Servants.	General Total.
2	5	9	3	8	33	37	16	676	5	4	70	117	2	987

The following Officers embarked with the Regiment:—

Lieutenant-Colonel R. A. Logan, C.B. (Colonel).

Major J. Stewart	Lieutenant Moir
Captain Tredennick	„ Garstin
„ Bicknell	„ Massey
„ Matthews	„ White
„ Morewood	„ Blake
„ Wade	„ Michel
Lieut. Denton	Adjutant de Burgh
„ Hayne	Quartermaster Wood
„ Dewar	Surgeon-Major Popplewell

Major E. V. Jones joined and embarked on board Her Majesty's ship *Malabar* at Malta.

1874 The Regiment arrived and disembarked at Colombo, Ceylon, on the 31st January, 1874; there were no casualties during the voyage.

On the 1st February, 1874, a Detachment consisting of Major Stewart, Captain Bicknell, Lieutenants Dewar and Garstin, with 6 Sergeants, 9 Corporals, 2 Drummers, 148 Privates proceeded by rail to Kandy, there to be stationed.

Lieutenant Richard Woodruffe Graham, from the

1874 North Tipperary Militia, to be Lieutenant, dated 21st January, 1874.

Malcohn Thomas Lyde, Gentleman, to be Sub-Lieutenant, dated 21st January, 1874.

On the 22nd January the old Colours of the Fifty-seventh (West Middlesex) Regiment, were deposited in St. Paul's Cathedral, London, under an escort of Brevet-Major Shortt, Captain Thompson, Captain Picot, Colour-Sergeants Sullivan and Osborne, Sergeants R. Rowe, McKey and Martin, and Corporal Coleman.

The following correspondence on the subject passed between Colonel R. A. Logan, C.B., and the Very Reverend the Dean of St. Paul's.

CURRAGH CAMP,
7th November, 1873.

My Dear Sir,

As Commanding Officer of the Fifty-seventh (West Middlesex) Regiment, I venture to address you on the following subject.

The Regiment which I have the honour to command has served with distinction in the Peninsula, where it gained the well earned soubriquet of the 'Die Hards:' in the Crimea, in India and in New Zealand. The Regiment is about to embark for Ceylon, on a tour of Foreign Service, and I, in conjunction with the Officers of the Regiment, am most anxious that the old Colours of the Regiment (which have lately been in possession of the late General Fox) should be placed in the Cathedral with which you have the honour to be connected, and which we think as a County Regiment would be far the most suitable place for them to be deposited, should there be no objection. I may mention that it is the wish of the Officers, should their proposal meet with your sanction, that the Colours may be placed in a situation where it would be possible to erect tablets in memory of Officers

1873 and men who have died or may die in the Service of their Country. It is the wish of the Military Authorities, that the feeling of localization should be encouraged as much as possible, and I venture with great deference to suggest that the placing of the Colours of a not undistinguished Regiment in the venerable Cathedral of the Metropolis may have some effects in procuring worthy Soldiers for Her Majesty and the Country by cementing a connection with their Country, hitherto much neglected. The well and hardly earned reputation of the Regiment is sufficient guarantee that the honour of the Colours entrusted to your charge will never be tarnished. With great respect I ask for an early reply as the Regiment under my command embarks for Ceylon early in December.

I am, &c.,

(Signed) R. A. LOGAN, Colonel.

Lieutenant-Colonel Commanding Fifty-seventh Regiment.

THE DEANERY, ST. PAUL'S,

My Dear Sir, *November* 10*th*, 1873.

I shall have great pleasure in taking charge of the old Colours of your distinguished Regiment and giving them a place in St. Paul's, as far as possible I shall be be glad to meet your wish, and that they may be placed in a situation where tablets may be at a future time erected near them in memory of those belonging to the Regiment; but it is necessary to remember that the interior of the Cathedral is likely soon to be decorated with Mosaic green marble on an extensive scale, and therefore all future Monumental Tablets must be subordinate in character and place to the Architect's plans.

Yours faithfully,

(Signed) R. W. CHURCH.

Dean of St. Paul's.

1873 CURRAGH CAMP,

12th November, 1873.

Dear Sir,

Your kind letter reached me to-day; I assure you it is deeply appreciated by myself and the Officers of the Fifty-seventh Regiment. I will take immediate steps to make the necessary arrangements for the conveyance of our old and valued Colours to your keeping, and when matters are sufficiently forward you will hear from me again on the subject. I need not say that it is our desire to meet, in all respects, your view in preserving the design for the decoration you speak of as contemplated for the future embellishment of our noble Cathedral. Again thanking you for the kind way in which you have responded to the wishes of the Regiment, and which is to them the preservation of a sacred relic,

I am, &c.,

(Signed) R. A. LOGAN, Colonel.

Lieutenant-Colonel Commanding Fifty-seventh Regiment.

1874 Lieutenant Sydney Edwin Bellingham, from the Louth Regiment of Militia, to be Lieutenant, dated 24th January, 1874.

Lieutenant Dudley Davison Batty retires from the Service, receiving the value of his Commission, dated 4th February, 1874.

Sub-Lieutenant Charles Henry Morris transferred to Fourteenth Foot, dated 4th February, 1874.

The Regiment was inspected by Major-General Henry Renny, C.S.I., Commanding Forces in Ceylon.

Captain and Brevet-Major William Aldersey Shortt to be Brevet-Lieutenant-Colonel, dated 7th February, 1874.

Lieutenant David Edward Wood from the 1st Royal

1874 Lanark Militia, to be Sub-Lieutenant in succession to H. D. Wade promoted, dated 28th February, 1874.

Charles B. Childe Pemberton, Gentleman, to be Sub-Lieutenant in succession to D. D. Batty retired, dated 28th February, 1874.

William Henry Morris Bent, Gentleman, to be Sub-Lieutenant *vice* C. A. Morris transferred to the Fourteenth Foot, dated 25th February, 1874.

Her Majesty was pleased to approve of the following establishment for the Regiment for 1874-5:—

1 Colonel.
1 Lieutenant-Colonel.
2 Majors.
8 Captains.
18 Lieuts. and Sub-Lieuts.
1 Adjutant.
1 Quartermaster.
1 Sergeant-Major.
1 Quartermaster-Sergeant.
1 Bandmaster.
1 Drum-Major.
1 Paymaster-Sergeant.
1 Orderly Room Clerk.
8 Colour-Sergeants.
1 Sergeant-Pioneer.
1 Sergeant-Cook.
1 Sergeant-Instructor of Musketry.
32 Sergeants.
40 Corporals.
16 Drummers.
780 Privates

Total all ranks, 917.

Sub-Lieutenant William Henry Morris Bent transferred to Thirty-eighth Foot, dated 8th April, 1874.

Lieutenant Henry Thomas Hughes Hallett (I. of M.), joined Fiftieth Brigade Depot for duty.

Captain Wyndham Algernon Robert Thompson retired from the Service, receiving the value of his Commission, dated 15th April, 1874.

Captain A. Collins (left sick at Curragh Camp on the embarkation of the Regiment for Foreign Service), Lieutenants R. W. Graham and S. E. Bellingham joined the Service Companies, 26th April, 1874.

Lieutenant Richard Calvert joined the Service Companies on appointment, 14th March 1874.

1874 Lieutenant William F. Wyndowe from Adjutant Recruiting District, to be Captain, *vice* W. A. K. Thompson, retired, dated 13th May, 1874.

Captain William F. Windowe to have the honorary rank of Major on retiring on full pay, dated 17th June, 1874.

Lieutenant A. K. Hamilton joined the Service Companies on 18th July, from leave of absence.

The promotion of Lieutenant and Adjutant W. F. Windowe, from Recruiting District, to be Captain, which was notified in the *Gazette* of 19th June, 1874, to be post-dated from the 15th May, 1871, to the 20th June, 1874.

Captain Robert Knapp Barrow, from half-pay Twenty-seventh Foot, to be Captain *vice* Captain W. F. Windowe, retired upon full pay, dated 11th July, 1874.

Major James Stewart, Fifty-seventh Regiment, to be Brevet-Lieutenant-Colonel, dated 28th May, 1874.

Sub-Lieutenant Charles Baldwyn Wilde Pemberton transferred to the Sixtieth Foot, dated 12th August, 1874.

The Regiment was inspected by Major-General J. A. Street, C.B., Commanding the Forces in Ceylon, on the 18th September.

Lieutenant Arthur Neville Hayne to be Instructor of Musketry *vice* Lieutenant H. T. H. Hallett who has resigned that appointment, dated 1st November, 1873.

A Draft consisting of Captain Robert Knapp Barrow, with 155 privates, joined at Colombo, Ceylon, from England in ship *Quang-se*, on 2nd December, 1874.

Lieutenant Gordon Dewar appointed Asst.-Instructor of Musketry to the Regiment from the 10th December, 1874.

1875 Captain Charles John Matthews appointed Acting Aide-de-Camp to Major-General John Alfred Street, C.B.,

1875 Commanding the Forces in Ceylon *vice* Captain W. Grant 6th Regiment, invalided.

Captain Charles Mansfield Clarke joined from England per Steamship *Eldorado*, on the 23rd March, 1875.

Her Majesty was pleased to approve of the following establishment for the Regiment, from 1st April, 1875-6:—

1	Colonel.	1	Paymaster-Sergeant.
1	Lieutenant-Colonel.	1	Armourer-Sergeant.
2	Majors.	1	Orderly Room Clerk.
8	Captains.	8	Colour-Sergeant.
18	Lieuts. and Sub-Lieuts.	1	Sergeant-Pioneer.
1	Adjutant.	1	Sergeant-Cook.
1	Quartermaster.	1	Serg.-Inst. of Musketry.
1	Sergeant-Major.	32	Sergeants.
1	Quartermaster-Sergeant.	40	Corporals.
1	Bandmaster.	16	Drummers.
1	Drum-Major.	780	Privates.

Total all ranks, 918.

Lieutenant Cecil Boucher Duff Michel appointed Acting Private Secretary to His Excellency the Governor of Ceylon, 10th April, 1875.

The Regiment was armed with the Martini-Henry rifle.

A Detachment consisting of Captain Henry David Bicknell, Lieutenant Arthur Neville (for duty at the Depot), with 22 invalids and 17 men for discharge), embarked for England, *viâ* the Cape of Good Hope, in the ship *Oxford*, on the 23rd April, 1875.

Lieutenant Gordon Dewar appointed Acting Instructor of Musketry, and Lieutenant Alfred Allen Garstin appointed Assistant-Instructor of Musketry to the Regiment, both from the 23rd April, 1875.

Captain and Brevet-Lieutenant-Colonel W. A. J.

1875 Shortt retired from the Service, receiving the value of his Commission, dated 28th April, 1875.

Lieutenant Henry Thomas Hughes Hallett to be Captain *vice* Brevet-Lieutenant-Colonel, W. A. J. Shortt retired, dated 28th April, 1875.

Captain James Richard Knox Tredennick embarked for England for duty at the Fiftieth Brigade Depot, Warley, on the 26th May, 1875.

Lieutenant Gordon Dewar to be Instructor of Musketry *vice* Lieutenant A. N. Hayne, who resigns that appointment, dated 23rd April, 1875.

Sub-Lieutenant Augustus West Hill to be Lieutenant, dated 1st February, 1873.

Sub-Lieutenant Charles Maitland Pelham Burn transferred to the First Foot, in succession to Lieutenant G. B. Keith promoted, dated 28th August, 1875.

The undermentioned Sub-Lieutenants from the unattached list to be Sub-Lieutenants in the Fifty-seventh Foot, the antedate not to carry back pay :—

Charles Maitland Pelham Burn *vice* W. H. M. Bent transferred to Thirty-eighth Foot, dated 13th June, 1874;

Charles Wallace Warden *vice* C. M. P. Burn transferred to the First Foot, dated 13th June, 1874;

Ernest Vernon Bellew, *vice* C. B. Childe Pemberton, transferred to the Sixtieth Foot, dated 21st September, 1874.

On the 24th and 25th September, 1875, the Regiment was inspected by Major-General John Alfred Street, C.B., commanding the Forces in Ceylon.

Sub-Lieutenant Charles Wallace Warden joined the Service Companies on appointment on the 15th November, 1875.

A Draft, consisting of Captain Charles Picot, Sub-Lieutenant Ernest Vernon Bellew, with Bandmaster Godfrey, 1 drummer, and 85 privates (1 Officer's wife,

1875 10 soldiers' wives, and 14 soldiers' children) joined at Colombo, Ceylon, from England, in Steamship *Thames*, on the 30th December, 1875.

Lieutenant-General Sir Edward Alan Holdich, K.C.B., to be Colonel *vice* Lieutenant-General Freeman Murray, transferred to the Ninety-third Foot, dated 11th December, 1875.

1876 Captain Charles John Matthews confirmed in his appointment as Aide-de-Camp to Major-General John A. Street, C.B., commanding the Forces in Ceylon, dated 8th January, 1876.

Sub-Lieutenant David Edward Wood transferred to the Eighth Hussars, dated 19th January, 1876.

The under-mentioned Sub-Lieutenant, from the unattached list, to be Sub-Lieutenant in the Fifty-seventh, the ante-date not to carry back pay.

Alexander Towers Clark in succession to Lieutenant H. T. H. Hallett, promoted, dated 22nd May, 1875.

Captain H. T. Hughes Hallett having passed the competitive examination for admission to the Staff College, Sandhurst, joined on the 1st February, 1876, for a course of study of two years.

Captain James Richard Knox Tredennick appointed Adjutant of the Royal Elthorne or Fifth Middlesex Militia, to serve with the rank of Captain, dated 11th February, 1876.

Sub-Lieutenant David Farhill St. Clair resigned his commission, dated 26th February, 1876.

Lieutenant Augustus West Hill joined the Service Companies on 5th March, on completion of 2 years' service at the Depot.

Sub-Lieutenant Alexander Towers Clark joined the Service Companies on appointment, 10th April, 1876.

Captain E. F. Lord Gifford, V.C., joined the Service

1876 Companies in Ceylon on the 12th August, 1876, on restoration to full pay.

Major and Brevet-Lieutenant-Colonel James Stewart to be Lieutenant-Colonel *vice* Brevet-Colonel R. A. Logan, C.B., who retired upon half-pay, 26th July, 1876.

Lieutenant H. C. Hinxman, Tenth Foot, was promoted Captain Fifty-seventh Foot, on 26th August, 1876, for his gallant services when engaged in the attack on the Stockade at Paroa, in the Malay Peninsula, on the 7th December, 1875.

Sub-Lieutenant Charles Wallace Warden, to be Lieutenant, antedated 13th June, 1874.

Lieutenant George Charles Denton, appointed Adjutant *vice* De Burgh transferred to Fifth Dragoon Guards, 25th September, 1876.

The rank of Sub-Lieutenant on first appointment in the Army was abolished, and that of second Lieutenant substituted by Royal Warrant, dated 30th October, 1876.

Major Edward Kent Jones, promoted Brevet Lieutenant-Colonel, dated 21st November, 1876.

1877.

Lieutenant Aubrey Reginald Hamilton retired from the Army receiving the value of an Ensigncy, 17th January 1877.

Sub-Lieutenant Ernest Vernon Bellairs to be Lieutenant, dated 21st September, 1874.

Sub-Lieutenant Ernest James Lennox Berkeley to be Lieutenant *vice* D. E. Wood transferred to Eighth Hussars, dated 12th February, 1876.

Lieutenant M. J. Lyde, 1 Sergeant, 70 rank and file, joined the Service Companies at Colombo, Ceylon.

Captain Arthur Archibald Denne Weigall from Seventy-sixth Foot, to be Captain *vice* Barton who exchange 10th February, 1877.

Sub-Lieutenant Edward John Sharpe from Twenty-

1877 third Foot, to be Lieutenant *vice* Lieutenant R. Calvert, deceased.

Surgeon-Major George Bell Poppelwell, M.D., who has been in medical charge of the Regiment for two years, embarked on 28th February for England, his tour of Foreign Service having expired.

Captain Weigall and Lieutenant Sharpe joined the Service Companies at Colombo, 6th April.

Captain Henry Falkner Morewood for duty at Fiftieth Brigade Depot, with 5 Sergeants and 64 rank and file time-expired men, embarked for England on the 7th April, 1877.

The Regiment was supplied with the valise equipment in lieu of knapsack and pouch belt, ordered to be discontinued.

The establishment of the Regiment reduced by two Subalterns for 1877.

Major and Brevet-Lieutenant Colonel Edward Kent Jones, who had embarked for England on Medical Certificate, died on his passage home on the 5th July, 1877.

The Monument to the Fifty-seventh (West-Middlesex) Regiment in St. Paul's Cathedral, London.

1877 At noon on the 12th July, 1877, a Marble Tablet, erected by the Fifty-seventh Regiment to the memory of their Comrades, was unveiled in the presence of General Freeman Murray, Sir Edward Allen Holdich, K.C.B., Majors-General Warre, C.B., and Inglis, C.B., and several other Officers and soldiers who have served in the gallant "Die Hards."

The Chaplain General and Canons Farrer and Wigley took part in the ceremony, which, owing to the absence of the Regiment in Ceylon, was not numerously attended, and was very simple in its character. The time honored and tattered remnants of the Colours, presented to the Regiment by its late Colonel, Viscount Hardinge, G.C.B., when Commanding-in-Chief the Army, had already been suspended upon the walls of St. Paul's, over the monument that now records the gallant deeds they witnessed in the Crimea, India, and New Zealand, and in conjunction with the monuments to the Light Division of the Crimean Army and the Seventy-seventh (or East Middlesex) Regiment, form an interesting group of Military Memorials, occupying the three divisions of the same recess, on the Northern Aisle of the Cathedral.

The Tablet, on being uncovered, showed a chaste and striking group surrounding the Saviour, who is consoling the Wounded and the Sick, and comforting the Widows and Orphans of those who have been killed in the service of their Country.

Above are two Angels with wings outstretched holding scrolls on which are the words :—

Grave where is thy victory?
Death where is thy sting?

1877 Below is a verse from St. Matthew's Gospel:—

Blessed are they that mourn, for they shall be comforted.

The Colours and military emblems and trophies form the base of the Monument.

The work is carefully and artistically executed by Mr. James Forsyth, of Baker-street.

Major-General Inglis, C.B., whose name has been associated with the Regiment since the days of Albuhera, presented the Monument to the Cathedral, and thanked the Dean and Chapter, not only for allowing the Memorial of their fallen Comrades to be placed upon the walls of the Cathedral, but for the kind interest they have taken in grouping it with others with whom the Regiment is associated.

Major General Warre, C.B., who commanded the Regiment during the greater part of the eventful period the Monument is intended to represent, also greeted his former Comrades, and was glad to see that the deep interest they took in the Regiment, in which they had served so loyally, had induced so many to give up at least a portion of their daily avocations, to take part in the interesting ceremony.

Canon Wigley, on behalf of the Dean, accepted the charge of the Monument, and expressed his gratification that the subject selected was of so chaste and religious a character. He expatiated on the bond of union between the Church and the Army, and exhorted all present to be good Christians as well as brave and dutiful Soldiers. A short prayer concluded the simple and unostentatious ceremony. The Veterans, chiefly in plain clothes, but wearing their hard won medals, closed round the Memorial to take a nearer look at the names inscribed upon a "Brass," which gives melancholy proof that the Regiment, locally associated with the Metropolitan County, is worthy of this tribute to their dead in the great

1877 Metropolitan Church. The names are given below of the seventeen Officers killed in action or died of their wounds, nearly all being cut off in the prime of life.

Two hundred and fifty-five Non-commissioned Officers and Privates were also killed or died during their hard service within a space of little more than a dozen years.

It is only scant justice to the zeal and perseverance of Captain (now Major) Charles Mansfield Clarke, by whom the subscriptions were collected, to state that the whole of the expense, amounting to nearly seven hundred pounds, had been defrayed by the Fifty-seventh Regiment. Officers and soldiers of all ranks now serving, or who formerly served, in the Regiment have lent their willing aid to make the monument worthy of the position it now occupies on the hallowed walls of St. Paul's.

N.B.—The following is the list of Officers whose names are recorded on the "Brass:"—

Crimea.

Lieutenant-Colonel Thomas Shadforth.

Captain Edward Stanley.

Lieutenant James Collins Ashwin and sixty Non-Commissioned Officers and men killed in action.

Colonel (Brigadier General) Thomas Leigh Goldie, Captain James Franklyn Bland, Captain George Herman Norman, Lieutenant George Udney Hague, Ensign George Michell, and twenty-one Non-Commissioned Officers and men died of wounds.

Captain John Auchmuty, Lieutenant D'Arcy Curwen, and one hundred and eighty-eight Non-Commissioned Officers and men died of disease.

New Zealand.

Captain Thomas J. W. Lloyd, Lieutenant Thomas Tragett, Assistant-Surgeon William Astle Hope, and

1877 nineteen Non-Commissioned Officers and men killed in action.

Brevet-Lieutenant Colonel Jason Hassard and seven Non-Commissioned Officers and men died of wounds.

Surgeon William MacAndrew, Ensign John Thornton Down, V.C., Ensign Andrew Balfour Duncan, and sixty Non-Commissioned Officers and men died of disease.

APPENDIX.

1. Roll of Officers appointed on the formation of the Fifty-seventh Regiment.
2. Succession of Honorary Colonels with dates of Commissions. Summary of War Services, &c.
3. Succession of Lieutenant-Colonels Commanding the Regiment. Dates of Commissions and Summary of War Services, &c.
4. Return of Officers who served with the Regiment during the Crimean War. Dates of Arrival in Crimea, &c.
5. Return of Officers, and Non-Commissioned Officers and men, who were killed or wounded or invalided in the Crimea, from 1854 to 1856.
6. Return of Non-Commissioned Officers promoted to Commissions for Gallant Service, &c.
7. Return of Officers, Non-Commissioned Officers and Soldiers, on whom English and Foreign Orders and distinctions have been conferred for their Services in the Field.
8. Major Aubin's notes (Appendix A,) *vide* Records, February 1814.
9. Return of Depot for N.S. Wales (Appendix B.)
10. Correspondence relative to granting the word *Albuhera* and Badge on buttons and shoulder straps. New pattern uniforms.

1. Roll of Officers appointed to the Fifty-seventh Regiment of Foot on its Formation in 1755.

Rank.	Names.	Date of Appointment.
Colonel	...John Arabin ...	...27th Dec., 1775.
Lieut.-Colonel	Thomas Wilkinson	...21st Dec., 1755.
Major...	...Thomas Townshend	...1st Jan., 1755.
Captain	...Lord Boyde ...	...10th Mar., 1746.
„	...Joseph Harrison	...7th Oct., 1755.
	...Samuel Cramer ...	...26th Dec., 1755.
	...William Craiff ...	...27th Dec., 1755.
	...John Clifford ...	...28th Dec., 1755.
„	...Daniel Clements	...29th Dec., 1755.
„	...Patrick Preston...	...30th Dec., 1755.
Capt.-Lieut.	...Thomas Bunbury	...25th Dec., 1755.
Lieutenant	...Edward Dartequenave	...26th Dec., 1755.
„	...George Holliday	...27th Dec., 1755.
	...Thomas Bennett	...28th Dec., 1755.
	...William Pye ...	...30th Dec., 1755.
	...Daniel Corneille...	...31st Dec., 1755.
	...Michael Cuffe ...	...2nd Jan., 1756.
	...Duncombe Colchester	...3rd Jan., 1756.
„	...Edward Shaw ...	...4th Jan., 1756.
„	...William Siree ...	...19th Feb., 1756.
Ensign	...R. Hickman ...	...4th Oct., 1755.
„	...John Nicholls ...	...12th Nov., 1755.
	...William Tong ...	...27th Dec., 1755.
	...William Townshend	...29th Dec., 1755.
	...Sir William Moore, Bart.	1st Jan., 1756.
	... — Brewer	...3rd Jan., 1756.
„	...Richard Bradshaw	...5th Jan., 1756
„	...John Alderenon...	...26th Feb., 1756.
Chaplain	...Vacant.	

Rank.	Names.	Date of Appointment.
Adjutant	...Edward Shaw ...	...4th Jan., 1756.
Quartermaster	Daniel Corneille	...21st Jan., 1756.
Surgeon	...Hugh Rose ...	...26th Jan., 1756.
Agent...	...Mr. Calcraft, Channel Row, Westminster.	

SUCCESSION OF HONORARY COLONELS FIFTY-SEVENTH REGIMENT.

	NAMES.	ENSIGN OR SUB-LIEUTENANT.	CAPTAIN.	MAJOR.	LIEUTENANT-COLONEL.	HONORARY COLONEL.	RANK IN THE ARMY.	REMARKS.
1	John Arabin	... ...	... ...	... ...	... ...	26th December, 1755	Colonel	Died 1757.
2	Sir D. Cunyngham, Bart....	... ...	... ...	... ...	1746	22nd March, 1767	Lieut.-General	Died 1765.
3	Sir G. Irvine, K.C.B.... ...	... ...	... ...	... ...	1755	4th November, 1767	General	Removed to Cavalry.
4	John Campbell	... ...	... ...	1757	1st February, 1762	2nd November, 1780	General	8th Sept., 1806, removed to another Regiment, and died 1809.
5	The Lord Hutchison, K.C.B., K.G.	... ...	1776	1781	13th March, 1783	8th September, 1806	General	1811 appointed to the 18th Royal Irish.
6	Sir Hew Dalrymple, K.C.B.	3rd April, 1863	14th July, 1768	17th December, 1777	21st September, 1781	27th April, 1811	Lieut.-General	Died 1830. *See* Appendix.
7	Sir William Inglis, K.C.B.	11th October, 1779	11th July, 1785	1st September, 1795	1st January, 1800	16th April, 1830	Lieut.-General	Died 1835. Services, *see* Appendix.
8	Sir Frederick Adam, G.C.B.	4th November, 1795	30th August, 1799	9th July, 1803	28th August, 1804	4th December, 1835	General	Died 1843. *See* Appendix.
9	The Viscount Hardinge, G.C.B.	8th October, 1798	7th April, 1804	13th April, 1809	30th May, 1811	31st May, 1843	Field-Marshal	Died 1856. *See* Appendix.
10	Sir Frederick Love, K.C.B.	26th October, 1804	11th July, 1811	16th March, 1815	5th May, 1825	24th September, 1856	General	Removed to 43rd Light Infantry. *See* Appendix.
11	Charles R. Fox	29th June, 1815	9th August, 1820	6th November, 1824	14th August, 1827	5th September, 1865	General	Died 1873. *See* Appendix.
12	Freeman Murray	24th February, 1825	21st December, 1832	20th August, 1844	5th November, 1847	14th April, 1873	Lieut.-General	Removed to Ninety-third Highlanders.
13	Sir Ed. Allan Holdich, K.C.B.	2nd July, 1841	22nd February, 1850	2nd August, 1850	28th May, 1853	11th December, 1875	General	Still surviving. *See* Appendix.

Colonel John Campbell.—1780 to 1806.

It is difficult to trace the early career of many very distinguished Officers, whose names and services offer but little clue to their identity in their earlier life.

On the enrolment of the Sixty-third Regiment, in 1757, we find the name of Colonel John Campbell as Major, and he was transferred to several Regiments during the twelve following years, when, in 1773, he was appointed Lieutenant-Colonel of the Fifty-seventh Regiment, continuing to serve with the Regiment until 1779, when he was promoted Major-General, but in 1780 was restored to its ranks as Honorary-Colonel, in which position he continued until September 1806, having in 1787 been promoted Lieutenant, and in 1797 to the rank of General in the Army.

(Editor.)

General The Right Honourable Baron Hutchinson, G.C.B., and K.G., of Alexandria, afterwards Earl of Donoughmore.

This distinguished Officer was the second son of John Hely Hutchinson, Earl of Donoughmore, who was Secretary of State for Ireland; he entered the Army 1774, as Cornet in Eighteenth Dragoons, and obtained the Lieutenant-Colonelcy of the Seventy-seventh Regiment in 1783.

At the commencement of the war in France in 1783, he raised the Ninety-fourth Regiment, and was promoted to the rank of Major-General 3rd May 1796, having previously served in Flanders as Aide-de-Camp to Sir Ralph Abercromby. In 1799 was severely wounded while gallantly leading his Brigade at the Helder.

In 1801 Major-General Hutchinson was second in command to Sir Ralph Abercromby, in Egypt; at whose death, at the the Battle of Alexandria, he succeeded to the chief command, and having pursued the French troops to Cairo, forced them to capitulate, and to evacuate Egypt. For this gallant service the Major-General was made Knight of the Military Order of the Bath, and created Baron Hutchinson of Alexandria and of Knocklofty in Ireland, with pension of £2,000 a year. In 1806, Lord Hutchinson, K.B., was appointed Colonel of the Fifty-seventh Regiment, and in the same year was entrusted with an extraordinary mission to St. Petersburgh. He became a full General in 1813, having in 1811 been transferred from the Fifty-seventh Regiment to the Colonelcy of the Eighteenth Royal Irish Regiment. Lord Hutchinson was made a Knight Grand Cross of the Bath in 1822 and on the death of his brother in 1825, succeeded to the Earldom of Donoughmore, and was then created Knight of the Most Noble Order of the Garter. After a long and distinguished career this gallant Officer died in the seventy-fifth year of his age in 1832.

(Editor.)

General Sir Hew Dalrymple, Bart.,

Appointed Colonel Fifty-seventh Regiment, 27th April, 1811, and continued in command until his death, 16th April, 1830.

This Officer was distinguished for his diplomatic as well as for his military services.

Having commenced his military career in 1763, he became Lieutenant-Colonel in 1781, and as Colonel in the Guards, saw service with the Duke of York in the first campaign in Flanders, 1793.

On promotion in 1794, was employed as Major-General on the Staff at Chatham, and subsequently as Lieutenant-Governor of Guernsey, from whence he was transferred to the command of the Northern District of England, before he was appointed Governor and Commander-in-Chief of the Troops at Gibraltar in 1807.

In 1808, although at the time England and Spain were nominally at war, the "prudent firmness" of Sir Hew Dalrymple checked the attempts of adventurers to create confusion in the South of Spain; and, foreseeing the outbreak of the Spanish Insurrection, he allowed the Gibraltar merchants to supply the Spanish Troops with money, arms and ammunition, whereby the latter were enabled to defeat the French at Baylen.

When Castanoz determined to oppose the projects of Napoleon, Sir Hew encouraged the Spaniards, advised the capture of the French Squadron at Cadiz; and in exposing the attempt of Junot to draw the British troops into an attack on Lisbon, endeavoured to secure the occupation of Cadiz by a British Force.

The tact and judgment shown by Sir Hew, when Prince Leopold of Sicily—a pretender for the Regency of Spain—accompanied by his brother-in-law the Duke of Orleans, attempted to land at Gibraltar, met with the unqualified approval of the British Minister (Lord Castlereagh,) and led to appointment of Sir Hew Dalrymple to the Command of the Army in the Peninsula.

Sir Hew arrived in Portugal at the moment when, having gained his first decisive battle at Vimeira, Sir Arthur Wellesley was prevented from following up his success by the untimely arrival of Sir Harry Burrard, and the delay caused by the difference of opinion of the rival Commanders enabled Junot to convey his shattered forces into security beyond the defiles of the mountains of Torres Vedras.

Having superseded both the above Generals, Sir Hew Dalrymple found that it was too late to resume active operations without reinforcements; and as the arrival of Sir John Moore's Division was very uncertain, he completed the "Convention of Cintra," thereby obtaining, by the French evacuation of Portugal, a clear base for future operations, but much vituperation from the British public. The vacillating policy of the British Ministry produced serious contentions at home, and led to the arraignment before a Military Court of Enquiry of the three Generals, who, in as many weeks, had been appointed to the command of the British Forces in Portugal.

Divided counsels fortunately prevented further obloquy from being cast on the victims of popular clamour. Sir Hew Dalrymple and Sir Harry Burrard were relieved from the responsibilities of their commands, and Sir Arthur Wellesley returned to Portugal to continue that victorious career which eventually drove the French troops out of Spain, and foiled the ambitious projects of Napoleon.

Sir Hew Dalrymple died in 1830.

(EDITOR.)

Lieutenant-General Sir William Inglis, K.C.B.

Appointed Ensign, Fifty-seventh Regiment, in 1779; Lieutenant 1782; Captain-Lieutenant 1785; Captain 1788; Major by Brevet 1795; the same year 1st Major, Fifty-seventh, by augmentation; Lieutenant-Colonel by Brevet 1800; Lieutenant-Colonel, Fifty-seventh, 1804; Colonel by Brevet 1810; shortly afterwards appointed Colonel on the Staff by the Duke of Wellington; Brigadier-General 1813; Major-General the same year and appointed to the Staff in the Peninsula; Lieutenant-General 1825.

He joined the Fifty-seventh at New York 1781, returned to England with his Regiment 1791; embarked for Ostend 1793, and served in Flanders under the Duke of York. Towards the end of that year returned to England with the Fifty-seventh, joined the Force under Lord Moira, embarked again for Ostend, joined the Duke of York at Malines, served in Flanders and Holland till May, 1795, and was present at the siege of Nimeguen. Embarked at Bremether, and on arrival in England joined the force forming under Sir Ralph Abercrombie for the West Indies; arrived at Barbadoes 1796, having encountered the destructive gales experienced by Admiral Christian's fleet. Major Inglis commanded a detachment of the Fifty-Seventh at the siege and fall of Morne Fortune and consequent capture of the Island of St. Lucia, and also against the insurgents in Granada. He accompanied his Regiment to Trinidad 1797, and remained there until 1802. He was employed in 1803 raising the Second Battalion, Fifty-seventh Regiment.

Lieutenant-Colonel Inglis succeeded to the command of the First Battalion in 1805 and proceeded to Gibraltar.

In 1809 he embarked with his Regiment for Lisbon

to join the army of Sir A. Wellesley. The Fifty-seventh was posted to the Second Brigade (Major-General Richard Stewart), in the Second (General Hill's) Division, and joined it in Spanish Estremadura. Consequent on the illness of General Stewart, Colonel Inglis commanded the Brigade on the march to and at the Battle of Busaco and subsequent retreat to the lines before Lisbon.

On the 16th May, 1811, he commanded the Fifty-seventh Regiment at the Battle of Albuhera. It was then this Regiment obtained the appellation of the "Die Hards," from words spoken by their Colonel to his men while standing with ordered arms under a heavy fire. Colonel Inglis' horse was shot under him while forming up the Regiment, and near the close of the action, after succeeding General Hoghton in command of the Brigade, he was severely wounded by a grapeshot which kept him from the Army in 1812. The greater part of that year he was President of a General Court-Martial at Lisbon.

In May, 1813, he was appointed to command the First Brigade of the Seventh Division, composed of the Fifty-first and Sixty-eighth Light Infantry, First Battalion, Eighty-second Regiment, and the Chasseurs Britanniques, which he commanded in the battles and affairs in the Pyrenees and France, more particularly 30th July, 1813, Pampeluna (horse shot under him) 31st July; 31st August (when his Brigade suffered very severely and he had another horse shot); on the 10th November, Echalar, where he received a severe contusion on the foot from a musket-ball. In 1814 he was present at Peyrehorade, on the 23rd of February, at the battle of Orthes, when his horse was wounded.

This Officer served with and followed the fortunes of the Fifty-seventh Regiment in all climates and in every service to which it was ordered from his first joining it, in 1781, until he gave up the command after the Battle of Albuhera. During that long period he had only two years' leave of absence, viz. from 1785 to 1787.

Sir W. Inglis was included in the vote of thanks by Parliament for the Battles of the Pyrenees and Orthes. He received the following decorations: a Field-Officer's Medal for Albuhera, a General Officer's Medal and two Clasps for Albuhera, Pyrenees and Nivelle, and Cross for the former Battles and Orthes. He was created a Knight Commander of the Bath, appointed Lieutenant-Governor of Kinsale, subsequently Governor of Cork, and in April, 1830, Colonel of the Fifty-seventh Regiment. He died November 29th, 1835, and was interred in Canterbury Cathedral.

(W. Inglis, Junr.)

General the Right Hon. Sir Frederick Adam, G.C.B., G.C.M.G.

Entered the Army in 1795, served as a Volunteer in 1799 in Sir Ralph Abercromby's Expedition to the Helder, and promoted by the Duke of York to a Company in the Ninth Foot, from which he was transferred to the Coldstream Guards in 1799; was present with the Coldstream Guards in Egypt 1801.

In July, 1806, as Lieutenant-Colonel of the Twenty-first Regiment, he landed in Sicily, and served with his Regiment in 1809, in Calabria, whilst Sir John Stuart was employed against the islands in the Bay of Naples. Engaged near Mili, and checked the progress of a very superior force of Neapolitan troops until the arrival of reinforcements defeated the enemy. In 1811, on appointment as Aide-de-Camp to His Royal Highness the Prince Regent, Lieutenant-Colonel Adam returned to England, but went to Sicily in the same year, on appointment as Deputy-Adjutant-General to the force under Lord William Bentinck. In 1812, having obtained the Brevet Rank of Colonel, he joined the British troops on the east coast of Spain. In 1813 he was appointed to command the Brigade composed of British and Foreign troops which formed the advance guard, and withstood the attack of some 5,000 French troops at Biar until ordered to rejoin the main body at Castalla. Although wounded in the affair at Biar, Colonel Adam was engaged at Castalla when the British and Spanish Forces repulsed the French, with a loss of 3,000. He commanded the same Brigade at the Siege of Taragossa, and continuing to command the advance of the Army after Lord W. Bentinck took the command, was present when the French stormed and took Fort Ordall, on the 12th September, 1813; in consequence of two very severe wounds on the above occasion, Colonel Adam was obliged to return to England, and received the rank of Major-General on 4th June, 1814. Major-General Adam served in the campaign to Flanders, and at Waterloo commanded the Third British Infantry Brigade, consisting of the Fifty-second, Seventy-first, and Ninety-fifth Regiments, when he was again severely wounded. In addition to the War Medal, the Russian and Austrian Orders of St. Anne and Maria Theresa were presented to him for Waterloo, and in June, 1815, he was created K.C.B. Having subsequently served in the Mediterranean, Sir Frederick Adam was, in 1821, decorated with the Ionian Order of St. Michael and St. George; and in 1824, being appointed Lord High Commissioner of the Ionian Islands, was made Grand Cross of the same Order, and, *ex officio*, Grand Master. Sir Frederick Adam was sworn in a Privy Councillor in 1831, and the following year was appointed Governor of Madras, where he remained until 1835. In 1840 he was made G.C.B., and appointed Colonel of the Fifty-seventh Regiment on the 4th December, 1835, but was removed to his old Regiment, the Twenty-first Royal North British Fusiliers, in 1843. He died suddenly on the 17th August, 1853, whilst returning from Greenwich Hospital, where he had been on a visit to his brother, Admiral Sir Charles Adam, an equally distinguished Officer in the Sister Service.

(EDITOR.)

FIELD-MARSHAL THE VISCOUNT HARDINGE, G.C.B., COMMANDING-IN-CHIEF THE ARMY AND COLONEL FIFTY-SEVENTH REGIMENT (1843-56).

Having entered the Army in 1798, at a very early age, this distinguished Officer passed rapidly through the lower grades and served as Deputy-Quartermaster-General of the Portuguese Army, under the command of Lieutenant-General (afterwards Marshal Lord) Beresford, throughout the Peninsular War. Commencing his career in 1808 at Roleia, Colonel Hardinge was wounded at Vimeira. Nevertheless he was present during Sir John Moore's retreat and at the victory (dearly bought by Moore's death) at Corunna, at the passage of the Douro, when Soult was driven out of Oporto, and during the operations which led to the Battle of Busaco. Although not present at Talavera, Colonel Hardinge was employed during the retreat of the British Allied Forces within the lines of Torres Vedras, where, owing to the admirable forethought of Napoleon's future conqueror, the Army found rest and immunity from the attacks of Massena's far superior Forces. On the 16th of May, 1811, at the critical moment when disaster was imminent, Colonel Hardinge by his 'cool judgment' and 'decisive action' retrieved the fortunes of the day, and on the slopes of *Albuhera* converted a possible retreat into so splendid a victory that "its ultimate effects, perhaps, determined "the issue of the war." (*Vide* Alison's 'History of Europe,' vol. viii. p. 381).

Colonel Hardinge was present at the Siege of Badajoz, at the glorious Battle of Salamanca, and was severely wounded at Vittoria (1813). His wound did not keep him long from his duty, for we find him actively employed wherever the Portuguese Army was engaged during the crossing of the Pyrenees, at the Passage of the Rivers

Nive and Nivelle, and at the Battle of Orthes, for all of which arduous services, besides earning a reputation for "*cool judgment*" and distinguished bravery, Colonel Hardinge received the Gold War Cross with five clasps.

When hostilities recommenced in 1815, Colonel Hardinge was entrusted by the Duke of Wellington with the important office of Commissioner at the Prussian Headquarters, and was so severely wounded on the 16th June at the Action at Ligny, that he lost his left hand, and was deprived of the glory of completing the short campaign at Waterloo.

Having obtained these well-merited honours for his gallant services, Major-General Sir Henry Hardinge, K.C.B., continued, during the long peace which followed the return of the English army from France (1818) to hold high military and political appointments. Having entered Parliament in 1823, he became Secretary at War in 1829 under the administration of the Duke of Wellington, and again in 1841 under that of Sir Robert Peel. In 1843, Sir Henry Hardinge was appointed Colonel of the Fifty-seventh Regiment, which had contributed at Albuhera to secure his great renown. In 1846 he was sent to replace Lord Ellenborough as Governor-General of India, when the unsettled state of the North-West Provinces created considerable alarm. On the rising of the Sikhs in 1845, Sir Henry Hardinge proceeded by forced marches to the scene of action, and waiving his military rank, acted as second in command under Sir Hugh (afterwards Viscount) Gough, with the Army that defeated the Sikh forces in the decisive Battles of Moodkee and Ferozeshah (1845) and Sobraon (1846).

For these battles Sir H. Hardinge obtained the medal and two clasps, and for his brilliant and disinterested military and political services in India was created Viscount Hardinge of Lahore.

In 1852, Viscount Hardinge was appointed Master-General of Ordnance in Lord Derby's Government, and in the same year succeeded the Duke of Wellington as Commander-in-Chief of the British Army.

Lord Hardinge continued to hold this high and responsible office during the Crimean War, 1854–56, and was created a Field Marshal of the Army on the successful termination of the Siege of Sebastopol in 1855.

The strain upon mind and body during this eventful period told upon a constitution partially enfeebled by his long and active military career; so that, in the deep feeling words of the late Prince Consort (see 'Life,' vol. iii.):—

"The Queen early in July, 1856, had the great pain "of seeing Lord Hardinge struck by paralysis during "an Audience with Her Majesty," at which he was submitting the Report of the Royal Commissioners, exonerating the Military Officers, he had appointed, from charges of neglect brought against them by the Civil Commissioners sent to the Crimea to ascertain the causes which had led to the breakdown of the Commissariat, and had produced so much mortality and sickness in the Army in the East.

Lord Hardinge survived the attack about two months, but the Country and the Army were deprived of his services. He died on the 24th September, 1856, regretted by all, and by none more than the gallant Regiment that had contributed to win his early fame.

(Editor.)

Lieut.-General Sir James Frederick Love, K.C.B., K.H., appointed to 57th Regiment, 24th Sept., 1856.

There were few more distinguished Light Infantry Officers than Sir Frederick Love, who was appointed to the 52nd Light Infantry in 1804, and served with it in the Expedition to Sweden under Sir John Moore, and afterwards throughout the War in the Peninsula, including the Battle of Corunna, the Storming of Ciudad Rodrigo, and all the actions and affairs in which the Light Division took part up to 1812.

During the Campaign in Holland, under Lord Lynedoch, he was present at the Attack on Merzen, and the Bombardment of Antwerp.

Having proceeded to America, he was present at the attack on New Orleans, where he was slightly wounded, and had two horses shot under him.

In the Campaign of 1815, Sir Frederick Love received four severe wounds at the Battle of Waterloo, when the 52nd Light Infantry charged the Imperial Guard. He received the Peninsular War Medal with four clasps for Corunna, Busaco, Fuentes d'Onor, and Ciudad Rodrigo. He also received the Waterloo Medal.

Colonel Love subsequently obtained the command of the 73rd Regiment, and was present in Canada in 1837-40 during the Insurrection, in which he took part, and was made C.B. On retiring from the command of his Regiment, and obtaining the promotion to the rank of Major-General, he was appointed Lieutenant-Governor and Commanding the troops in Jersey.

On the termination of this command, General Love was created K.C.B., and in 1865 was removed to the Colonelcy of the 43rd Light Infantry, with which his old Regiment, the 52nd, had always been brigaded during the Peninsular War.

(Editor.)

General Charles Richard Fox, appointed to Fifty-seventh, 5th September, 1865.

General Fox served in the Royal Navy from 1809 to 1813, and was present at the Siege of Cadiz in 1810 and at Tarragona in 1813, on board H.M. Ship *Malta*, Vice-Admiral Sir Benjamin Hallowell. He entered the Guards in 1815, and was present in France during the occupation of Paris, &c.

Although General Fox's Service in the Army was passed during a period of peace, when he had no opportunity of distinguishing himself on Active Service, his high attainments, and genial hospitality, made him universally respected, and he died in 1873 deeply regretted.

(Editor.)

General Sir Edward A. Holdich, K.C.B.

Joined the Eightieth Regiment as Ensign in the Colony of New South Wales in 1842, and in the autumn of 1844 proceeded thence with that Regiment to India.

Landing at Calcutta, the Regiment marched direct to Agra (early in 1845), and in the autumn of the same year marched to Umballah, and formed part of the Army of the Sutlej, then assembling on the frontier.

On the formation of the Army, Lieutenant Holdich was selected to act as Aide-de-Camp to Major-General Sir H. G. Smith, K.C.B., commanding the First Division of the Army of the Sutlej. In that capacity he served throughout the campaign, including the actions of Moodkee, Ferozeshah (wounded), Budiwal, Aliwal, and Sobraon, where he was severely wounded, and compelled to proceed to the Hills. (He received a Medal and three Clasps for this campaign).

In July, 1846, he was appointed Aide-de-Camp to Major-General Sir H. G. Smith, commanding the Cawnpore Division, and accompanied that Officer to Cawnpore, and subsequently to England in 1847.

In the autumn of the same year, 1847, proceeded to the Cape of Good Hope, as First Aide-de-Camp to Lieutenant-General Sir H. G. Smith, Bart., G.C.B., Governor and Commander-in-Chief of that colony, arriving at the Cape Frontier at the close of the Kaffir War, 1846-48. Accompanied Sir H. Smith on the Expedition across the Orange River against the Rebel Boers, and was present at the action and defeat of the Boers at Boen-Platz, on the 28th of August, 1848.

On promotion to a Company in the 88th Regiment, in 1858, he received the Brevet-Rank of Major, for previous services on the Sutlej and in South Africa.

On the breaking out of the Kaffir War, December,

1850, Major Holdich proceeded, on the 1st January, 1851, with the first reinforcements sent up to join Sir H. Smith, then on the frontier, and served throughout the War, being present at several skirmishes and engagements, until Sir H. Smith's recall (and relief by Lieutenant-General Sir G. Cathcart), when he accompanied him to England, 1852. Received Medal and promoted to rank of Lieutenant-Colonel, for services in the Kaffir War.

In the autumn of the same year, 1852, embarked for India to join the 80th Regiment, then on service in Burmah. Arriving at Rangoon early in 1853, was placed in command of a detachment of convalescents and recruits, en route to join the 88th Regiment, and with this detachment took part in an expedition in the Donabud District, under Major-Genoral Sir John Cheape, against the Rebel Chief Nagattom, which resulted (after several days' marching and skirmishing through dense jungle, the troops being without tents, and suffering severely from cholera) in the complete defeat of the Rebel and capture of his stronghold, on March 19th, 1853. On this occasion Major Holdich commanded the advance party, and at the final attack of the Stockade a Wing of Infantry of different Corps. Afterwards joined the Head-quarters of the Regiment at Prome, and returned to Calcutta at the end of 1853.

Received Medal and Clasp for Burmah, and created a C..B.

Returning to England early in 1854, again joined the Staff of Major-General Sir Henry Smith, then commanding at Plymouth, and subsequently the Northern District at Manchester.

In the summer of 1856, the Eightieth Regiment being ordered to the Cape of Good Hope (when another Kaffir outbreak was apprehended, Lieutenant-Colonel

Holdich resigned the Staff, and embarked with the Regiment at Liverpool, landing at Algoa Bay; marched with the Regiment to Fort Beaufort. Being offered an appointment on the Staff of Major-General Sir James Jackson, K.C.B., then commanding at the Cape, joined that Officer as Aide-de-Camp.

In 1857, the Eightieth Regiment being ordered to India (on the outbreak of the Sepoy Mutiny), resigned the Staff, and rejoined the Regiment, embarking with it at Algoa Bay, arriving at Calcutta in January, 1858. The Regiment was sent up by detachments to Allalabad, and subsequently to Cawnpore and Futtegher; during this time frequently employed in command of parties in pursuit of rebels and on escorts.

In May, 1858, having been promoted to a majority in the Twentieth Regiment and posted to the First Battalion then serving in India, was selected to proceed to Calcutta to raise a Depot Battalion from the recruits, arrived there from England; and with this Battalion to hold the command at Berhampore, in the District of Morshadabad, a much disaffected District, two disarmed native regiments being in the Cantonments.

In May, 1856, joined the 20th Regiment, then stationed at Gondole in Oude and forming part of a Frontier Brigade under Brigadier Horsford, who about this time was compelled to resign the command on account of ill-health, and Lieutenant-Colonel Holdich was appointed Brigadier to succeed him. In the autumn of 1859, the Troops composing the Brigade, together with the Brigade from the Gorruckpore District (in all about 10,000 men), the whole under Brigadier Holdich, were moved up to the immediate borders of Nepaul, and in co-operation with troops from Nepaul, under Sir Jung Bahadoor, swept the Terai where it was known that the Nana and a large body of rebels had taken refuge. This operation resulted in the capture of many noted leaders (among others the Commander-in-Chief of the Nana's Army, Jarval a Parsee, who was sent to Cawnpore and hanged there), and a large body of Sepoys, the last remnant of any organized body of mutineers.

For this service received the thanks of Government and Commander-in-Chief, and upon the breaking up of the Brigade was appointed by Lord Clyde Deputy-Adjutant-General to Her Majesty's Troops in India, and in 1861 to the Brigade of Rohilcund in the North-West Provinces of India.

At the expiration of five years in this Command returned to England, and was promoted Major-General 3rd September, 1867.

Commanded the Cork District (Ireland) from June 1st, 1871, to 1st April, 1874, when transferred to the Dublin District, and vacated Command (on promotion), 1st April, 1876.

Promoted Lieutenant-General, 28th April, 1873.

Created K.C.B., 24th May, 1875.

Promoted General, 1st October, 1877.

SUCCESSION OF LIEUTENANT-COLONELS COMMANDING.

NAMES.	Ensign.	Lieutenant.	Captain.	Major.	Lieut.-Col.	Colonel.	Army Rank.	REMARKS.
McLeroth	... ...	... ...	... ...	... ...	... ...	1871	... ...	Succeeded from Mjr. Sold out in 1782.
Brownlow	... ...	... ...	... ...	... ...	... ...	1872	... ...	From Major till 1791.
Hay M'Dowall ...	4th Aug. 1774	1st Sept. 1776	20th Sept. 1779	24th March, 1784	6th April, 1795	21st Aug. 1795	Mjr.-General 18th June, 1798 Lieut.-General 30th Oct. 1805	
Balfour	9th Oct. 1775	1778	6th Sept. 1780	24th March, 1794	1st Sept. 1795	25th Sept. 1803	Major-General 25th July, 1810	Promoted 1808.
Gledstanes	22nd Feb. 1771	28th April, 1774	22nd Sept. 1783	1st March, 1794	1st Sept. 1795	25th Sept. 1803	Major-General, 25th July, 1810	First to 2nd Batt. & in 1808 to 1st Batt.
Thos. Picton (afterwards Sir Thos., K.C.B.)	Sept. 1771	1776	1778	1st March, 1794	16th Nov. 1794	1st Jan. 1800	Mjr.-General 25th April, 1808 Lieut.-General 4th June, 1813 Killed in action 1815	
William Inglis (afterwards Sir W., K.C.B.)	11th Oct. 1779	3rd May, 1782	11th July, 1785	1st Sept. 1795	1st Jan. 1800	25th July, 1810	Major-General 4th June, 1813	Succeeded Colonel Balfour.
Macdonald	... ...	19th May, 1783	31st Aug. 1791	1st Jan. 1798	11th March, 1802	4th June, 1811	Removed from the Service 1814	To 2nd Batt. *vice* Gledstaner to 1st Battalion, 1811.
Spring	30th April, 1780	23rd April, 1793	6th May, 1795	1st Sept. 1804	30th May, 1811	4th June, 1813	Sold out 1819	Commanded 2nd Bt. after to 1st Batt. *vice* Arbuthnot.
Thos. Arbuthnot, (afterwards Sir Thos., K.C.B.) ...	23rd Nov. 1794	1st May, 1796	25th June, 1798	7th April, 1808	24th May, 1810	4th June, 1813	Lieut.-Colonel 57th Foot 24th March, 1814 Major-General 27th May, 1825 Lieut.-General 28th June, 1838 Died 26th January, 1849	*Vice* Macdonald, invalided.
O. Carey	26th Feb. 1801	5th June, 1801	27th Aug. 1804	2nd Nov. 1809	30th Sept. 1811	27th May, 1825	Major-General 10th Jan. 1837 Died 13th March, 1844	*Vice* Spring, sold out.

Henry Shadforth ...	23rd May, 1797	26th Aug. 1799	21st March, 1800	25th Feb. 1804	4th June, 1811	27th May, 1825	Major-General 10th Jan. 1837 Lieut.-General 9th Nov. 1846 General 20th June, 1854 Died 30th March, 1866	
H. R. Hartley... ...	8th Oct. 1812	2nd Sept. 1813	29th Nov. 1821	8th Nov. 1827	12th April, 1831	9th Nov. 1846	Mjr.-General 20th June, 1854 Died 7th August, 1854	
J. Allan	31st Dec. 1794	18th March, 1795	10th Sept. 1799	20th July, 1809	4th June, 1814 Lt.-Col. 57th Ft.	10th Jan. 1837 20th March, 1828	Major-General 9th Nov. 1846 Died 17th Feb. 1858	
G. E. Jones, K.H....	16th June, 1806	8th April, 1807	8th Oct. 1812	22nd July, 1830	8th Nov. 1833 Lt.-Col. 57th Ft.	9th Nov. 1846 17th July, 1835	Died 13th February 1849	*Vice* Hartley.
H. Shakespeare Phillips...	8th Jan. 1824	12th May, 1825	14th Feb. 1828	31st Aug. 1838	31st March, 1843 Lt.-Col. 57th Ft.	... ... 6th Aug. 1847	Died 21st November, 1849	*Vice* Jones.
Thos. Leigh Goldie.	13th Jan. 1825	9th Dec. 1825	24th Nov. 1828	22nd Dec. 1838	20th March, 1840 Lt.-Col. 57th Ft.	11th Nov. 1851 1st Aug. 1848	Died of wounds 6th November, 1854	*Vice* Phillips.
T. S. Powell, C.B....	13th May, 1826	31st May, 1831	13th Nov. 1825 57th Foot	23rd July, 1839 20th Sept. 1848	11th Nov. 1851	... ...	... ...	
Ths. Shadforth ...	8th April, 1825	10th Oct. 1826	12th April, 1831	29th March, 1844	20th June, 1854 Lt.-Col. 57th Ft.	... ... 7th Nov. 1854	Killed at Sebastopol 18th June, 1855	*Vice* Goldie, died of wounds 6th Nov.
Henry J. Warre, C.B.	3rd Feb. 1837	1st June, 1841	8th Jan. 1847	7th Nov. 1854	9th March, 1855 Col. H.P.	9th March, 1858 6th Dec. 1867	Brigadier-General 26th February, 1870 Mjr.-General 6th March, 1868	*Vice* Shadforth, killed at Sebastopol 18th June, 1855.
J. Alfred Street ...	29th Nov. 1839	5th Oct. 1841	7th Jan. 1848	12th Dec. 1854	19th June, 1855	11th Aug. 1858	Major-General 6th March, 1868	On augmentation, 2nd Lieut.-Colonel.
William Inglis, C.B.	7th Feb. 1840	31st Dec. 1841	26th Oct. 1849	12th Dec. 1854 Lt..-Col. 57th Ft.	2nd Nov. 1855 21st May, 1858	8th Aug. 1861	Major-General 6th March, 1868	On augmentation, transferred to 9th Foot.
E. Bowen	1st June, 1841	2nd Sept. 1845	29th June, 1849	12th March, 1861 Lt.-Col. 57th Ft.	1st April, 1866 7th Dec. 1867	... ...	Retired 24th April, 1872	*Vice* Warre, retired.
R. A. Logan, C.B....	26th Oct. 1841	3rd March, 1843	7th March, 1851	19th June, 1855 Lt.-Col.	22nd Feb. 1863 24th April, 1872	17th Feb. 1871	... ...	*Vice* Bowen, retired 24th April, 1872.
James Stewart ...	20th Jan. 1846	6th Nov. 1848	12th Oct. 1852	28th Oct. 1864	28th May, 1874 Lt.-Col. 57th Ft.	26th July, 1876	... ...	*Vice* Logan, retired.

COLONEL THOMAS SIDNEY POWELL, C.B.

Served throughout the Campaign in Affghanistan in 1838-39 as Aide-de-Camp and Interpreter to General Lord Keane. (Medal).

Having been transferred to the Fifty-seventh Regiment in 1848 as Major, he accompanied the Regiment to Corfu and thence to the Crimea, landing at the Katcha River, 24th September, 1854, just too late to take part in the passage of the River Alma. On the appointment of Colonel Goldie to the command of the First Brigade, Major Powell succeeded to the temporary command, and was present in command during the flank march round the head of the Harbour, and when the Regiment took up its ground for encampment on the heights before Sebastopol.

Being Field Officer of the day in the trenches on the 5th November, Major Powell was not present at Inkerman, but his conduct was specially mentioned in Lord Raglan's Dispatch; and on the 11th November he obtained the substantive rank of Lieutenant-Colonel. The arrival of Lieutenant-Colonel Thomas Shadforth on the 8th November deprived Major Powell of the command; and having been granted a substantive Lieutenant-Colonelcy, he was removed from the Regiment in order to take charge of the Invalids and Troops at Smyrna. (Medal and Clasps).

Lieutenant-Colonel Powell was, in 1855, appointed to the Fifty-third Foot, and continued in command of that Regiment in India when the Mutiny took place, and he was killed in Action while gallantly leading his Regiment in 1857. (Medal and C.B.)

(EDITOR.)

LIEUTENANT-COLONEL SHADFORTH,

Having served with the Fifty-seventh Regiment in Australia and India, remained in command of the Depot in England during the period the Fifty-seventh Regiment was stationed at Corfu.

Joined the Fifty-seventh at Camp before Sebastopol on the 8th November, 1855, and continued in command during the severe winter of 1854-55, taking his regular tour of duty in the trenches.

Was present in command on the 18th June, 1855, at the unsuccessful attack on the Redan, when at the head of his Regiment he charged across the Glacis, and was killed in action while gallantly endeavouring to carry out the orders of Brigadier-General Sir John Campbell, Baronet, who was also killed on this occasion.

Of the 19 Officers and 400 Non-Commissioned Officers and men who composed the attacking party on the right flank of the Redan on the 18th June, 9 Officers and 110 Non-Commissioned Officers and men were in a few minutes placed hors-de-combat.

Colonel Shadforth would have been recommended for the Companion of the Bath (C.B.) had he survived, and was entitled to Medal and Clasp for Sebastopol.

By the gracious consideration of Her Majesty, the Queen's apartments at Hampton Court Palace were assigned to Mrs. Shadforth on account of her husband's gallant conduct in the Crimea.

(EDITOR.)

LIEUTENANT-GENERAL HENRY J. WARRE, C.B.,

Whilst serving as Aide-de-Camp to the Commander of the Forces in Canada, 1839-43, was selected, with Lieutenant Vavasour, R.E., for "special duty," to report upon the River and Lake communication, with a view to the transport of Troops from Montreal to Red River Settlement, 2,300 miles. Recommended the Sea Route by Hudson's Bay and Lake Winipeg, by which the 6th Royal Regiment was conveyed to Fort Garry (1846) in the Hudson's Bay Company's Territory.

In order to carry out the Orders of Government, proceeded overland from Fort Garry across the Rocky Mountains to Fort Colvile, on the Columbia River (about 1,800 miles on horseback), from thence down the Columbia River to Fort Vancouver (about 700 miles in boats).

During the winter of 1845-46, visited and reported upon Vancouver's Island and Puget's Sound to lat. 49° north, and to the borders of California 42° south.

On return to England, 1846, received the thanks of the then Secretary of State for the Colonies (Earl Grey) for Report and Services during this arduous special duty.

In 1847-49, served on the Staff in England as Aide-de-Camp, and from 1849 to 1852 as Brigade-Major in the Northern District. Received the commendations of the General Officers in command, especially on the occasions of Her Majesty's visits to Liverpool, Fleetwood, York, and Castle Howard, when the military arrangements devolved on the Brigade-Major.

In the early part of 1853 joined the Fifty-seventh Regiment, on its proceeding on Foreign Service to Corfu, and being invalided in 1854, rejoined the Fifty-seventh in March, 1855, at Camp before Sebastopol. When, on the 18th June, 1855, Lieutenant-Colonel Shadforth was killed in action at the attack on the Great Redan, succeeded to the command of the Fifty-seventh Regiment, and continued in command during the remainder of the siege; at the assault and evacuation of Sebastopol on the 8th September; with the expedition to, bombardment and surrender of, Fort Kinburn, at the mouth of the Dnieper River (October 1855), until the conclusion of peace with Russia in 1856.

Mentioned in Dispatches, C.B., and Medal, &c. Continued in command of the 57th Regiment at Malta, 1856-57, and in May, 1858, conducted it through Egypt by the then incomplete railway to Suez, and by steamer to Bombay.

During 1858-59, commanded a Field Force (Infantry and Cavalry) and a line of Posts on the Taptee River, in conjunction with part of the Central Indian Field Force, under Lieutenant-General Sir Hugh Rose, K.C.B., to prevent the incursions of Rebel Natives into Khandiesch.

In 1859-60 he was appointed Brigadier in command of the Brigade at Mhow, under Major-General Sir John Michel, K.C.B., Commanding Malwa Division, and received the thanks of Lieutenant-General Sir H. Somerset, Commanding the Forces in India, for the "zeal and activity with which Colonel Warre performed the several duties of his command."

On the reduction of the Brigade at Mhow in 1860, having rejoined the Fifty-seventh Regiment at Poona, was nominated Acting Military Secretary to the Commander-in-Chief in India, and accompanied Sir Hugh Rose from Calcutta on his tour of inspection through Bengal and Oude.

When at Lucknow resigned the appointment of Military Secretary, to rejoin the Fifty-seventh, which had been ordered from Bombay on Active Service to New Zealand.

Having proceeded to New Zealand *via* Melbourne and Sydney, joined the Fifty-seventh Regiment shortly after its arrival at Taranaki, in February, 1861, was appointed (temporarily) Colonel on the Staff in command of the troops in Auckland, and Deputy-Governor of the Province during the absence of the Governor (Colonel Gore Browne, C.B.,) at the seat of war.

On the cessation of hostilities, April, 1861, rejoined the Fifty-seventh at New Plymouth, and continued as Senior Officer in command of the Regular and Militia Forces in the Province of Taranaki under *Martial Law*.

On the recommencement of hostilities in 1863, was present in command of the Fifty-seventh Regiment at the attack (under Lieutenant-General Cameron, C.B.,) of the Rebel Maori Redoubt on the Katikara River, 4th June, 1863, (*see* dispatches) and after the departure of General Cameron, as Colonel on the Staff and Government Agent from June, 1863, to the cessation of hostilities in 1866.

During this period Colonel Warre was present and in command of numerous reconnoitring expeditions and skirmishes, and at the assault and capture of the rebel positions (Pahs) at Kaitake, Maitatawa, Te Area, Warea, Opunaki, and Te Kewa, clearing the coast of Rebel Natives from about 25 miles north, to about 50 miles south, of New Plymouth.

On every occasion the conduct of the Regulars and Militia, and the successful result of the several engagements with comparatively little loss to the troops employed, elicited the commendation of the Secretary of State for War, the Field Marshal Commanding-in-Chief, and the Governor and Commander of the Forces in New Zealand (*see* Dispatches). When, in 1865, Major-General Trevor Chute, who succeeded Sir Duncan Cameron, determined to open the whole line of Coast from Taranaki (New Plymouth) to Wanganui (150 miles) he entrusted the command of the column from New Plymouth to Colonel Warre, who subsequently relieved Major-General Chute's Force, which had penetrated through dense bush at the back of Mount Egmont, and was reduced to great straits from want of food.

Before leaving New Zealand Colonel Warre was presented with a General Officer's sword by Captain Mace and the Mounted Volunteers who had rendered such good services during the war.

About the same time, the ladies of Taranaki presented a beautiful inlaid table, made of New Zealand woods, to Mrs. Warre, as a token of their regard and appreciation of the kind manner in which she had sympathised with them in their sufferings during the war.

After 12 years' consecutive Foreign and Colonial Service, Colonel Warre obtained leave to precede his Regiment, which, on its return to England in 1867, was quartered at Manchester.

During the Fenian disturbances in that city, terminating in the murder of Police-Sergeant Brett, Colonel Warre was in command of the troops (Cavalry, Artillery and Infantry) who were present at the gaol, to prevent any breach of the peace at the time of the execution of the Police Sergeant's murderers.

Having, December 1867, retired upon half-pay after twelve years' consecutive command of the Fifty-seventh Regiment, Colonel Warre remained unemployed until 1870, when he was appointed Brigadier in command of the Infantry Brigade in Dublin from whence, 1st August, 1870, he was transferred to the command of the Curragh Brigade; and on the 1st July, 1871, again transferred to the command of the Belfast District including the whole of Ulster.

Serious riots having taken place during Major-General Warre's command in the North of Ireland, he was appointed Justice of the Peace, and the troops were largely augmented on several occasions when required in aid of Civil Power. His services met with the approval of the Irish Government and of the Commander of the Forces in Ireland. Severe illness obliged him to resign the command at Belfast on the 31st December, 1874.

Major-General Warre commanded a Brigade at Petersfield, in 1876, under the Mobilization Scheme; and on 1st October, 1877, was promoted to the rank of Lieutenant-General under the General Officers' Retirement Warrant.

CRIMEA.

1. Extract from Field-Marshal Lord Raglan's Dispatch relating to the assault on the Redan, 18th June, 1855:

> "The distinguished gallantry of the Fifty-seventh Regiment under Lieutenant-Colonel Thomas Shadforth, and, when he fell, under Lieutenant-Colonel Warre, was conspicuous."

2. The *London Gazette* of the 5th of July, 1855, appointed Lieutenant-Colonel Warre to be Companion of the Bath for services on the 18th June, 1855.

3. On the occasion of the assault and evacuation of Sebastopol by the Russians, on the 8th and 9th September, 1855, the conduct of the Fifty-seventh Regiment, which occupied the front trenches between the Redan and Malakoff, was also mentioned in General Simpson's Dispatches.

Major-General the Honourable Sir A. A. Spencer, K.C.B., in command of the Expeditionary Force to Odessa and Kinburn, also mentions in high terms of commendation the conduct of the troops generally and of the Fifty-seventh Regiment on the occasion of the landing at, and the surrender of, Fort Kinburn; also in

Brigade Orders on the breaking up of the 4th Division at the conclusion of peace in 1856.

Extract from Lieutenant-General Cameron's Dispatch of the 9th June, 1863, *addressed to the Governor of New Zealand, Sir G. Grey. After describing the action of the 4th June, on the Katikara River, against the Rebel Maories:—*

> "I cannot speak too highly of the conduct of all the Officers and men present in this engagement, or of the conspicuous gallantry displayed by the Fifty-seventh Regiment, on whom the brunt of the action fell. The movements of this Regiment were most ably directed by Colonel Warre, whose zeal and activity throughout the action I have had the pleasure of bringing under the favourable notice of the Secretary of State for War and the Field Marshal Commanding in Chief."

The conduct of the Fifty-seventh Regiment in New Zealand, on all occasions, elicited the marked commendations of Sir Duncan Cameron, K.C.B., commanding the Forces, and of His Excellency Sir George Grey, K.C.B., the Governor of New Zealand, as well as the Secretary of State for War, and of H.R.H. the Field-Marshal Commanding in Chief of the Army, as shown by the following extracts from dispatches:—

1. Action on the banks of the Kaitikara River, Tatairamaka.

"1. Horse Guards, 28*th August*, 1863.

> "The whole of the operations were admirably "performed by the troops. The conduct of the "Fifty-seventh Regiment, under Colonel Warre, "C.B., being particularly deserving of commendation.
>
> "(Signed) W. F. FORSTER,
>
> "*Military Secretary.*"

2. Sundry affairs in 1863-6.

"Horse Guards, 20*th February*, 1864.

"H.R.H. the Duke of Cambridge recommends "that the undermentioned distinctions and rewards "should be bestowed upon the Officers and men in "consideration of the gallant and important services "which they have performed under the distinguished "leader, whose name his H.R.H. is happy to "recommend for the distinction of K.C.B." Here follow the names of 10 Officers for promotion, and 2 for that of C.B., concluding:

"I have to add that Colonel Mould, C.B., Colonel "Warre, C.B., being already full Colonels and C.B.s, "H.R.H. does not consider that any further "advancement can be granted for their recent "services; but the testimony that has been rendered "to their excellent conduct will be duly recorded in "their favour.

"(Signed) W. F. FORSTER,

"*Lieutenant-General and Military Secretary.*"

3. Destruction of Rebel Stockades, &c.

"3. War Office, 27*th June*, 1874.

"The operations conducted by Colonel Warre, "C.B., were marked by ability and skill, and the "result of the attack on Kaitake was highly "satisfactory.

"DE GREY & RIPON."

4. Destruction of Rebel Stockades.

"4. War Department, 22*nd August*, 1864.

"You enclose reports from Colonel Warre of the "operations which he has carried on in the district "under his more immediate command. I have pursued these reports with much satisfaction.

"(Signed) DE GREY & RIPON."

5. Destruction and Occupation of Mataitawa Te Arei, &c.

War Office, *26th January*, 1865.

Acknowledges receipt of Despatch (No. 100) November, 1864, reporting that Mataitawa and Te Arei, two formidable positions occupied by the rebels in the neighbourhood of New Plymouth, had been taken possession of by the troops under Colonel Warre, C.B.

"In reply I am to express the satisfaction with "which Lord De Grey and Ripon has received this "information.

"(Signed) E. LUGARD.

"*Lieutenant-General.*"

6. Skirmishes, 28th July, 3rd August, 1865.

War Office, *26th October*, 1865.

Acknowledges receipt of Despatches containing reports from Colonel Warre, C.B., of skirmishes on the 28th July, and 3rd August, 1865.

"Earl De Grey desires me to signify to you his "approval of the conduct of the officers and men "who were employed in these affairs."

"(Signed) E. LUGARD.

"*Lieutenant-General.*"

7. Opunaki and White Cliffs, &c.

Colonel Warre was also commended in subsequent despatches connected with the operations which led to the occupation of Opunaki, 50 miles to the South, and of Pukearuhi, 35 miles North, of New Plymouth.

(EDITOR.)

LIEUTENANT-GENERAL J. A. STREET, C.B.

Having joined the Ninety-eighth Regiment in 1839, Lieutenant Street served as Adjutant under that excellent soldier the Late Field-Marshal Lord Clyde, when the latter was in command of the Ninety-eighth Regiment.

Was present during the expedition to the North of China during 1842. Medal.

At the attack and capture of Chin-Kiang-Foo, and at the landing of the British Troops before Nankin.

Exchanged into and was present with the Fifty-seventh on its embarkation for Corfu in 1853, and proceeded with the Fifty-seventh to the Crimea in September, 1854, when he was appointed Brigade-Major to the First Brigade, under the Command of Brigadier-General Thomas Leigh Goldie, of the Fourth Division, being too late to take part in the Battle of the Alma. He accompanied the First Brigade and the Allied Army on the march round the Harbour, and encamped with the Fourth Division on the heights above Sebastopol.

Was present at the Battles of Balaklava and Inkerman, the assault on the Redan on the 18th of June, and at the evacuation of Sebastopol on the 8th of September, 1855, and as the Second-Lieutenant-Colonel of the Fifty-seventh Regiment accompanied the expedition of the Allied Fleets to Odessa, and was present at the bombardment and surrender of Fort Kinburn on the Dnieper River in October, 1855. Medal and three Clasps; Brevets of Major and Lieutenant-Colonel; C.B.; Sardinian and Turkish Medals, and 4th Class of the Medjidie.

Subsequently was in command of the Brigade Depot at Colchester, and on his promotion to the rank of Major General was appointed to the command of the troops in Ceylon, where he is now serving.

(EDITOR.)

Services of Major-General Inglis, C.B.

Major-General William Inglis, C.B., eldest son of Lieutenant-General Sir William Inglis, K.C.B., Colonel Fifty-seventh Regiment, was given an Ensigncy in the Fourth Regiment, Feb. 7th, 1840, being promised by Lord Hill a transfer to the Fifty-seventh, which was made the following month. Promoted Lieutenant, 1841; Captain, 1849; Brevet-Major, 1854; Major, 1855; Brevet-Lieutenant-Colonel, 1855; Lieutenant-Colonel, 1858; Colonel, 1861; Major-General, March, 1868. (August, 1874.)

This Officer sailed with drafts for Madras in 1840, and served with the Fifty-seventh at Fort St. George and Trichinopoly until 1844; in England and Ireland until 1853, when he embarked with Head-quarters for Corfu.

In 1854, he proceeded with his Regiment to the Crimea, was present at the Battles of Balaklava and Inkerman; in the latter he succeeded to the command after Captain Stanley was killed. At the assault on the Redan, June 18th, he was second in command to Colonel Warre after Colonel Shadforth fell; also at the assault on the 8th of September and fall of Sebastopol, and accompanied the Regiment on the expedition to Kinburn.

Lieutenant-Colonel Inglis was ordered to Malta at the end of 1855, and commanded a Camp for Musketry Instruction at St. George's Bay until the arrival of the Regiment in June, 1856. In 1858, the Fifty-seventh was ordered to India *via* Egypt; Brevet-Lieutenant-Colonel Inglis was gazetted Second-Lieutenant-Colonel, and being in England, was placed in command of drafts on board the *Earl of Balcarres* for Bombay where he rejoined his Regiment. He commanded a mixed Force in co-operation with the Central India Field Force at Seerpoor and Dhoolia, and was in command of the Regiment at Ahmednuggur and Poona, Colonel Warre being appointed to a Brigade at Mhow.

Lieutenant-Colonel Inglis returned to England in 1860 on leave of absence. The Fifty-seventh was ordered to New Zealand in that year. Lieutenant-Colonel Inglis took a passage to rejoin; but the Secretary of State for War refused to sanction the employment of a Second-Lieutenant-Colonel as the Regiment was struck off the Indian establishment. H.R.H. the Duke of Cambridge was pleased to appoint Colonel Inglis to the command of the 1st Battalion, 9th Regiment, at Corfu, in January, 1861; Colonel Inglis exchanged to a Depot Battalion in 1863, and to half-pay in 1867.

Major-General Inglis obtained the Brevets of Major and Lieutenant-Colonel and was mentioned in Lord Raglan's Inkerman despatch. Companion of the Bath, Knight of the Legion of Honour, and fifth Class of the Medjidie. He has received the Crimean Medal with Clasps for Balaklava, Inkerman and Sebastopol, and the Turkish War Medal.

(W.I.)

Colonel Robert Abraham Logan, C.B.

Served with the Fifty-seventh Regiment during the latter part of the Russian War in the Crimea, and afterwards at Malta.

Was in command of the Detachment of 200 of the Fifty-seventh which was sent from Malta by the Overland Route through Egypt, to Aden, in 1857. The men of this Detachment being the first troops that had passed through Egypt, en route to India, during the Mutiny, were dressed as civilians. Commanded the Detachment of Fifty-seventh at Aden for about two years, during which time the troops were engaged at times in a desultory warfare with the neighbouring Arabs. Their conduct on all occasions elicited flattering commendations from Brigadier-General Coghlan, C.B., in command.

Embarked with the 57th at Bombay, and was in command of the Regiment in New Zealand, in the early part of 1861. Was present at the attack on the native positions on the Waitara River, under Lieutenant-General Sir Thomas Pratt, K.CB., and was mentioned in the General's Despatch, and thanked in General Orders.

Was in command of the support (4 Companies) at the attack on the Kaitikara River on the 4th June, 1863, mentioned in Lieutenant-General Sir Duncan Cameron's Despatches, and was subsequently made C.B. (Companion of the Bath.)

Was in command of the troops at Wanganui, and was present during the subsequent operations on the West Coast of New Zealand, under Major-General Trevor Chute (Medal). Is now Colonel in command of the Brigade Depot at Woolwich.

(Editor.)

LIEUTENANT-COLONEL JAMES STEWART.

Comes from a family of soldiers, his great-grandfather having held a Commission in the Earl of Crawford's Regiment, now the Forty-Second Highlanders (Black Watch) in 1739; his grandfather entered the Seventeenth Regiment in 1759, and commanded the Sixty-eighth Regiment in 1788, dying a General-Officer in the Army in 1813: his father began as an Ensign in the Sixty-eighth Regiment in 1794, and was Lieutenant-Colonel of the Forty-sixth Regiment in 1821.

Colonel Stewart commenced his military career in the Fifty-seventh Regiment in 1846, and having served through all the intermediate ranks, succeeded to the command of the Regiment while serving in Ceylon, on the 26th July, 1876. Was present with his Regiment in the Crimea from the 6th September, 1855, at the bombardment and evacuation of Sebastopol on the 8th September, and until the conclusion of peace in June, 1856.

In October, 1855, accompanied the Fifty-seventh Regiment, which formed part of the Expeditionary Force to Odessa and the mouth of the Dnieper River. Was present at the bombardment and surrender of Fort Kinburn. Accompanied the Regiment from Malta to India; and having joined the Depot in England, subsequently rejoined the Regiment, while serving in New Zealand against the Rebel Maories; was present during the latter part of Major-General Thomas Pratt's operations on the Waitara River in 1861, and afterwards during the operations on the West Coast, 1863 to 1866.

Lieutenant-Colonel Stewart received the Medal and Clasp for Sebastopol, the Turkish War Medal, and also the New Zealand War Medal.

NOTE.—Colonel Stewart returned from Ceylon to England invalided in the beginning of 1878, and died at Guernsey, on the 6th of May, 1878, deeply regretted.

Crimean Campaign.

Return of Officers who proceeded with the Fifty-seventh from Corfu, or who subsequently joined the Regiment in the Crimea, showing date of arrival, promotions, and casualties.

Date of Arrival.	Rank and Names.	Remarks showing Casualties, &c., &c.
23rd Sept., 1854...	Lieut.-Col., & Col. T. Leigh Goldie	..Staff-Brigadier-General 2nd Brigade, 4th Division, died of wounds, Inkerman, 5th Nov., 1854.
	Major & Brevet-Lieut.-Col. T. Sydney Powell	...Promoted Lt.-Colonel and C.B.
	Captain E. Stanley	...........Killed in Action, 5th November, 1854.
	Captain J. Auchmuty	.........Invalided.
	Captain J. A. Street	............Staff as Brigade-Major, Bvt.-Mjr., & Lt.-Col.
	Captain William Inglis	.........Brought Regiment out of Action, 5th Nov., 1854, Brvt.-Major and Brvt.-Lieut.-Colonel.
	Captain Bland	.................Killed in Action, 5th November, 1854.
,,	Lieutenant H. Butler	.........Promoted & Brvt.-Mjr.
,,	Lieutenant & Adjutant C. W. St. Clair	... Horse shot, 5th Nov., 1854; severely wounded 18th June, 1855, promoted Capt., and Brevet-Major.
	Lieutenant G. J. Forsyth	......Promoted Captain and Brevet-Major.
	Lieutenant Norman	............Died of wounds, 18th June, 1855.
	Lieutenant U. Hague	.........Died of wounds, 5th November, 1854.
	Lieutenant A. M. Earle	......Aide - de - Camp, and Brigade - Major, 2nd Brigade, 4th Division, wounded, promoted Captain and Brevet-Major.
	Lieutenant K. Hugesson	......
,,	Lieutenant C. Venables	......Severely wounded.
,,	Lieutenant H. Buller	.........Wounded.
8th Nov., 1854 ...	Lieut.-Col. Thos. Shadforth	...Killed in Action, 18th June, 1855, and C.B.
15th Nov., 1854 ...	Captain Jason Hassard	......Brevet-Major.
,,	Captain Percy Lea	............Brevet-Major, severely wounded, 18th June 1855.
	Lieutenant A. Copland	....

Date of Arrival.	Rank and Names.	Remarks showing Casualties, &c., &c.
15th Nov., 1854	Ensign Michell	Died of wounds, 28th June, 1855.
,,	Ensign A. Shortt	
,,	Ensign A. Slade	Wounded, 18th June, 1855.
4th Feb., 1855	Captain W. Brown	
,,	Lieutenant Ingham	
,,	Lieutenant Ashwin	Killed in Action, 18th June, 1855.
27th Mar., 1855	Lieut.-Colonel H. J. Warre	Succeeded to command, 18th June, 1855, and C.B.
19th May, 1855	Lieutenant Jesse Coope	
,,	Lieutenant G. R. Waugh	Adjutant.
2nd June, 1855	Lieutenant Henry Bird	
11th June, 1855	Lieutenant Macartney	
,,	Lieutenant Wilmot	
,,	Lieutenant F. Grace	
3rd Sept., 1855	Lieutenant C. G. Clarke	
6th Sept., 1855	Captain J. Stewart	
,,	Lieutenant F. S. Schomberg	
,,	Lieutenant Sir Robert Douglas, Bart.	
,,	Lieutenant Darcy Curwin	Died in Camp, 8th Oct., 1855.
7th Sept., 1855	Lieutenant H. H. Chanter	
9th Sept., 1855	Lieutenant B. C. Bayntun	
12th Sept., 1855	Lieutenant H. R. Russell	
22nd Sept., 1855	Lieutenant S. H. Powell	
24th Sept., 1855	Lieutenant E. G. Hasted	
28th Dec., 1855	Lieutenant H. D. M. Shute	Invalided and died on voyage to India, 1858.
28th Dec., 1855	Lieutenant Edward Mills	
13th Mar., 1856	Captain G. V. B. Ardbuckle	
,,	Captain J. W. I. Lloyd	
19th Mar., 1856	Lieutenant Edward Brutton	
23rd Sept., 1854	Paymaster M. Matthews	
,,	Quarter-master J. Balcombe.	
,,	Surgeon J. Dickson	
,,	Assistant-Surgeon Scott	
,,	Assistant-Surgeon Brady	
14th Nov., 1854	Assistant-Surgeon Phelps	Promoted Ensign for gallant conduct on the 18th June, 1855.
29th Aug., 1855	Surgeon MacAndrew	
20th Nov., 1855	Assist.-Surgeon M. G. Griffin	
8th Feb., 1856	Dispenser of Medicines M. North	

Return showing the Names of Officers, Non-Commissioned Officers and Men who were killed, wounded, and died in the Crimea, from September, 1854, *to May,* 1856.

Officers.

KILLED IN ACTION.			DIED OF WOUNDS.			WOUNDED.		
RANK & NAMES		DATE.	RANK & NAMES.		DATE.	RK. & NAMES.		DATE.
						Lt.	Buller	24 Oct., 1854
Capt.	Stanley	5 Nov., 1854	Col.-Br.-Gen.	Goldie	Nov 5, 1854	Capt.	Earle	2 Mar., 1854
								18 June, 1855
Lt.-Col.	Shadforth	18 June, 1855	Capt.	Bland	5 Nov., 1854	"	Venables	5 Nov., 1854
								18 June, 1854
Lieut.	Ashwin	19 June, 1855	Lieut.	Hague	5 Nov., 1854	"	Lea	13 Dec., 1854
								18 June, 1855
			Ens.	Mitchell	18 Mar., 1855	"	St. Clair	18 June, 1855
			Capt.	Norman	18 June, 1855	Lt.	Slade	18 June, 1855

Non-Commissioned Officers and Men.

KILLED IN ACTION.	DIED OF WOUNDS.	WOUNDED.
53	16	244

DIED OF SICKNESS.		INVALIDED HOME NON.-COM. OFF. & MEN.	
OFFICERS.	N.-C.O. & MEN.	WOUNDS.	SICKNESS.
Cpt. Auchmuty, 13 Nov., 1854 Lieut. Curwin, 7 Oct., 1855	81	4	8

Strength of the Fifty-seventh Regiment on landing in, and leaving the Crimea.

	F.O.	Capt.	Sub.	Staff	Total	Sergts.	Drs.	R.&F.	Total
Landed 23rd Sept., 1854	2	5	8	6	21	45	10	685	740
Left 28th May, 1856	2	7	15	5	29	49	13	689	751

Admitted into Hospital in the Crimea (not from wounds) { 70 Officers / 1649 Men

Sent to Scutari { Sick.........212 (including 29 ophthalmia cases) / Wounded 120

Return of Non-commissioned Officers who have been promoted to Commissions in the Army while serving in the Fifty-seventh Regiment:—

1. Sergeant-Major John McNamee.
2. Colour-Sergeant John Dane.
3. Quartermaster-Sergeant James Balcombe.
4. Colour-Sergeant Thomas Grace.
5. Sergeant-Major George Rowland Waugh.
6. Colour-Sergeant Richard G. Collins.
7. Sergeant-Major George Cumming.
8. Quartermaster-Sergeant Thomas J. Leech.
9. Quartermaster-Sergeant Thomas Woods.

N.B.—It is a noteworthy fact, highly creditable to the individuals, and highly honourable to the Regiment, that seven out of the nine named above are the sons of old soldiers: their services are given below.

Another very estimable Non-commissioned Officer (Quartermaster-Sergeant William Collings) received the Medal and Annuity of £20 for long service and exemplary conduct on the 30th September, 1863, while serving in New Zealand, in which country he settled, and, entering the Colonial Forces, became Hon. Major of the Taranaki Militia. He died in 1875, in that country, respected and regretted.

Services of Non-Commissioned Officers of the Fifty-seventh (West Middlesex Regiment), who have been awarded Commissions in the Army for their exemplary conduct in Quarters, or their distinguished conduct in the Field.

1. Sergeant-Major John McNamee was appointed Ensign in January, 1837, and Adjutant of the Fifty-seventh Regiment on the 11th September, 1841; was present with the Regiment in New South Wales, and died in 1846 in India, while serving as Lieutenant and Adjutant. A subscription was made by which a considerable sum was raised for the benefit of his orphans. A son obtained a Commission and served with distinction in the Twentieth Regiment, retiring on full-pay as a Captain on the 17th May, 1876.

2. Colour-Sergeant John Dane served with the Fifty-seventh Regiment in the Madras Presidency, and was with the Light Company when it formed part of the Force sent into Courg on the rising of the natives in that Territory. He was appointed Ensign (by purchase) in May, 1838, and Lieutenant in July, 1840. In 1862 Lieutenant Dane was serving in the Sixty-second Regiment.

3. Lieutenant-Colonel James Balcombe entered the Fifty-seventh Regiment in 1835 (being then under age), and for 17 years served, with exemplary conduct, through all the grades of Non-Commissioned Officer.

On the 7th November, 1851, was appointed Quartermaster on the death, at Kilkenny, of the then Quartermaster David Morrow.

Accompanied the Fifty-seventh Regiment as Quartermaster to Corfu (1853), and proceeded with the Regiment in September 1854 to the Crimea. Served throughout the whole of the Crimean Campaign, and with the

Expedition to Kinburn (1855). Was present on all occasions, and his zealous attention to his very onerous duties, especially in bringing up rations and supplies during the very severe winter of 1854, gained him the esteem of Officers and men. Received the Crimean War Medal and Clasps for Balaklava, Inkerman and Sebastopol, also the Turkish War Medal.

On the termination of the war with Russia, Quartermaster Balcombe accompanied the Fifty-seventh Regiment to Malta (1856), and from thence through Egypt to Bombay, where he remained until October, 1859, when his exemplary conduct was recognized by his promotion to a Company unattached, and the date of his Commission was subsequently antedated, on the recommendation of his Commanding Officer, to the 1st April, 1857. Captain Balcombe's promotion and retirement from the Fifty-seventh Regiment (although a serious loss), was recognised by the Officers who presented him with a substantial mark of their esteem—a piece of plate. On the 3rd February, 1860, Captain Balcombe was appointed Adjutant of the Royal South Down Militia, in which Regiment he continued to serve until December, 1876, when, having been promoted Major in 1875, he retired with the honorary rank of Lieutenant-Colonel, receiving from Colonel Forde and the Officers of the South Down Regiment a similar mark of their esteem and appreciation of his zealous attention to his duties, to that offered by the Officers on his leaving the Fifty-seventh Regiment.

Lieutenant-Colonel J. Balcombe is now Secretary to the Clontarf Township, County of Dublin, which we trust enables him comfortably to provide for himself and family during the remainder of his active and honourable career.

4. Major Thomas Grace is the son of an old "Die Hard" who, having joined the Fifty-seventh in 1807, served throughout the Peninsular War, and was present at the Battle of Albuhera.

Major Grace joined the Regiment at Cannanore, Madras Presidency, in August, 1834, and returned with the Regiment to England in 1846, earning his promotion by a continued course of excellent conduct.

In 1853, Sergeant Grace accompanied the Regiment to the Crimea, and was present during the flank march, at the Battles of Balaklava and Inkerman (promoted Ensign), at the assault and capture of the Quarries, and as Lieutenant was in command of the leading Company at the attack on the Great Redan on the 18th June, 1855; was also present at the final assault and evacuation of Sebastopol on the 8th September, 1855. Having been selected for promotion to the rank of Ensign after the Victory at Inkerman, Ensign Grace was promoted Lieutenant, 2nd March, 1855, and accompanied the Regiment on the expedition to, and bombardment of, Kinburn.

On the return of the Expeditionary Force to the Crimea, Lieutenant Grace, on the recommendation of his Commanding Officer (Lieutenant-Colonel Warre, C.B.), and in consequence of his excellent conduct and constant attention to his duties—not having been a day absent from duty during the whole campaign—was appointed to the Land Transport Corps, with which Corps he remained until the termination of the war.

Lieutenant Grace then rejoined the Fifty-seventh, and subsequently was promoted to be Captain unattached for his excellent conduct while serving in the Land Transport Corps.

Captain Grace received the Medal, with Clasps, for Balaklava, Inkerman, and Sebastopol, also the Turkish

War Medal. He was also strongly recommended for the Reward for Good Conduct and Long Service, for which he was noted, as a special case, but failed to obtain on account of his retirement on full pay.

Captain Thomas Grace was appointed to the Ninth Regiment, and served in the Ionian Islands; subsequently transferred to the Third West India Regiment, and served in the West Indies and on the West Coast of Africa from May, 1863, to July, 1870, when, by the disbandment of the Third West India Regiment and reduction of the Army, he was compelled to retire on full pay, with the honorary rank as Major, after an honourable service of thirty-six years, twenty-six of which were passed abroad in India and the Colonies.

5. Lieutenant-Colonel George Rowland Waugh entered the Fifty-seventh Regiment in 1833, served for upwards of twenty years in India, and at home, as a Non-Commissioned Officer, during which time his conduct was exemplary. In 1854, under the Royal Warrant, was presented with the Medal for Good Conduct, and a gratuity of fifteen pounds.

Having been transferred to a Depot Battalion, he was, on the 12th February, 1855, brought back into the Fifty-seventh Regiment, as Adjutant, with the rank of Ensign. On the 19th June, 1855, he obtained his promotion to the rank of Lieutenant and, on the 16th January, 1866, to that of Captain. On the reduction of two Companies (1866) Captain Waugh was transferred to the Ninety-ninth Regiment, and in November, 1866, exchanged into the Seventy-third (Perthshire) Regiment, and proceeded with it to Hong Kong from whence, in 1869, the Regiment was sent to Ceylon.

Being, in 1869, offered a Majority on half-pay, Major Waugh returned to England, and on the 28th January,

1871, retired on full pay, with the honorary rank of Lieutenant-Colonel.

Served with the Fifty-seventh Regiment in the Crimea (Medal and Clasp), was present at the assault on the Redan, 18th June, 1855, and evacuation of Sebastopol, 8th September, also with the expedition to, and surrender of, Fort Kinburn on the Dnieper River (Turkish War Medal), in India, and during the Native War in New Zealand (Medal).

6. Ensign R. G. Collins, after a service of only six and a-half years, during which he became Orderly Room Clerk, with the rank of Colour-Sergeant, obtained his Commission as Ensign in January, 1856, on the recommendation of his Commanding Officer, Ensign Collins being the third Officer on whom Commissions had been conferred during the Crimean War through which Mr. Collins served, having been promoted Colour-Sergeant on the 6th November, 1854, for the care with he removed Colonel (Brigadier-General) Thos. Leigh Goldie from the field of Inkerman, after the latter had been mortally wounded.

In January, 1856, Mr. Collins was appointed to a Commission as Cornet in the Land Transport Corps, and served for some months with that Corps, but on the reduction of the Army, at the close of the Crimean War, he was placed on half-pay, and subsequently joined the Devonshire Constabulary in which he is now serving, having risen to be third Senior Officer in the County Police.

Mr. Collins sold out of the Third West India Regiment in 1860.

Medal and Clasps for Sebastopol.

(Editor.)

Return of Officers, Non-Commissioned Officers and Private Soldiers on whom various English and Foreign Orders have been conferred for distinguished conduct and gallantry in the Field before the enemy.

VICTORIA CROSS.

1. On the 23rd June, 1855, Private (1971) Charles McCorrie was recommended for the Victoria Cross for having taken up and thrown over the parapet a live shell, which exploded harmlessly outside the work.

The shell fell into the trench in which McCorrie and his comrades were at work; and but for the heroic conduct of this brave soldier, he and several of his comrades would in all probability have been killed or wounded.

Charles McCorrie having served throughout the Campaign in the Crimea, died at Malta on the 9th April, 1857, before he had obtained the coveted honour, the reward of his act of self-devotion.

2. Colour-Sergeant George Gardiner, Fifty-seventh Regiment. Acts of bravery on the 22nd March and 18th June, 1855, in the Crimea. For distinguished coolness and gallantry on the occasion of a Sortie, when he was Orderly-Sergeant to the Field Officer of the day (Left Attack) in having rallied the covering parties which had been driven from the trenches by the Russians. By his act of coolness upon this occasion the Russians was driven out of the trenches and the Sortie was repulsed.

Also for unflinching and devoted courage in the attack on the Redan on the 18th June, 1855, in having remained and encouraged others to remain in the holes made by the explosion of shells, from whence by making parapets of the dead bodies of their comrades, they kept up a continued fire until their ammunition, and that of their dead comrades, was exhausted, thus clearing the parapet of the Redan of the enemy.

This was done under a fire in which nearly half the Officers and a third of the rank and file of the storming party of the Regiment was placed hors-de-combat.

Strength of storming party 4 Field Officers, 5 Captains, 8 Subalterns, 2 Staff, and 400 rank and file.

Casualties—(killed and wounded) 1 Field Officer, 2 Captains, 5 Subalterns, 1 Staff, and 110 rank and file.

3 & 4. On the 2nd October, 1863, when engaged with the rebel natives at Poutoko, Taranaki, New Zealand, for conspicuous bravery and gallant conduct in rescuing a wounded comrade—

Ensign John Thornton Down,
Drummer Dudley Stagpoole,

responded to the call of the Officer commanding the Company for Volunteers to bring in the wounded man, who was lying at the edge of the bush, upon an open piece of cultivated land, exposed to a heavy fire at short range.

The above-named rushed to the front, and brought back the wounded man, in spite of the rebel Maories, who were concealed in the trees, and fired from behind the fallen trunks of trees within a very short distance.

The Medal for Distinguished Conduct in the Field had already been conferred on Drummer Stagpole for the energy and courage he displayed on the 25th September, 1863, at the skirmish near Kaipa-ko-pa-ko, in having twice brought in wounded men, although he himself was wounded in the head.

Legion of Honour.

The Legion of Honour and French War Medal was conferred by the Emperor of the French, on the recommendation of Lieutenant-Colonel Warre, C.B., Commanding Fifty-seventh Regiment, upon the following Officers and Rank and File:—

On the 2nd August, 1856, the Legion of Honour was conferred on—

Captain and Brevet-Major Henry Butler.
Captain and Brevet-Major G. J. Forsyth.
Captain and Brevet-Major A. M. Earle.
Sergeant-Major George Cumming.
Colour-Sergeant William Griffith.
Private James Burgess.

French War Medal.

On the 8th and 28th May, the French Military War Medal was conferred on—

Colour-Sergeant John McCardle.
Colour-Sergeant John Coughlan.
Colour-Sergeant J. F. Andrews.
Colour-Sergeant John Jones.
Corporal Thomas Connell.
Lance-Corporal William Kinnarney.
Lance-Corporal John Murray.
Private Thomas Anderson.

Sardinian War Medal.

Lieutenant-Colonel J. A. Street.
Captain and Brevet-Major C. W. St. Clair.
Captain and Brevet-Major G. J. Forsyth.
Lieutenant A. F. A. Slade.
Drummer Michael Norton.
Private Jeremiah Healy.

Turkish Order of the Medjidie (5th Class).

Lieutenant-Colonel H. J. Warre, C.B.
Lieutenant-Colonel J. A. Street, C.B., (4th Class), Staff.
Major and Brevet-Lieutenant-Colonel W. Inglis.
Captain and Brevet-Major Percy Lea.

Captain and Brevet-Major Jason Hassard.
Captain and Brevet-Major A. M. Earle.
Captain W. E. Brown.
Captain Charles Venables.
Captain J. C. Ingham.
Lieutenant W. A. S. Shortt.
Lieutenant A. F. A. Slade.
Ensign J. S. Phelps.

Turkish War Medal.

Six hundred and sixty-seven Turkish Crimean Medals were also conferred on the Officers, Non-commissioned Officers, and soldiers of the Fifty-seventh Regiment present in the Crimea.

APPENDIX LETTER A.

Skirmishes of the 12th and 15th February, as supplied by Major Aubin's Notes.

The Division on the 14th February, 1814, fell in with the enemy, occupying a strong position on the heights near the town of Hilette and Espilette. Being vigorously attacked, he soon gave way, and retreated in the direction of Garis. On this occasion the Light Company had two men wounded. Major Cameron, of the Buffs, who commanded the Light Companies of the Brigade on this occasion, received an extraordinary wound: when in the act of giving a word of command, a ball entered his mouth, knocking out three of his teeth. The ball for some time could not be found, but was eventually extracted from the root of his tongue.

On the evening of the 15th the Division again fell in with the enemy, commanded by General Harispe, posted on some strong heights near the Town of Garis. After a very short halt to reconnoitre, the order was given "to take the Hill." Major-General Pringle's Brigade immediately advanced, and, in contiguous close columns, steadily ascended the hill, under the constant fire of the enemy, without returning a shot. On the summit being gained, the enemy retired until they reached the point where their principal force appeared to be concentrated: here they made an obstinate resistance against Major-General Pringle's Brigade. The other Brigades of the Division, not having been so soon put in motion, and having a greater distance to proceed to their points of attack, did not gain the heights for some time, but on their appearance the enemy was forced to retire, with the loss of several Officers and men taken prisoners. The following morning the Regiment (being almost in a state of nudity for want of clothing) was ordered to take charge of the above-mentioned prisoners, amounting to about 7 Officers and 200 men, and to proceed to St. Jean de Luz. Having received new clothing, the Regiment lost no time in rejoining the Division, which it effected at Orthes on the 27th February at the time that the Army was warmly engaged with the enemy. Upon reaching the eminence where Lord Hill stood, surrounded by his Staff, the Regiment halted, awaiting the orders of General Byng, to whom an Officer had been sent to announce the arrival of the Regiment on the Field.

Having rejoined the Brigade, it moved forward towards Toulouse, and on the 13th of March was partially engaged with the enemy near the Town of Ayre. On the 18th the Division fell in with the rear guard of the enemy. The right was warmly engaged during the greater part of the day. General Byng, whose Brigade formed the left, perceiving that the enemy had given way, bivouacked for the night at about 3 p.m., sending the Light Companies, under the command of Captain H. McLaine, to support a party of the Fourteenth Dragoons, and to guard the roads leading to the Village of Couchez, on the left of the Brigade. At about 4 p.m. some Cavalry came galloping down the road, and stated that a column of Infantry was advancing. Captain McLaine ordered the Light Companies to check the advance of the enemy. On the appearance of Infantry, the enemy halted, and after maintaining a brisk fire for a short time, retired to some distance for the night. On this occasion Lieutenant Aubin, who commanded the Light Company, was severely wounded.

APPENDIX LETTER B.

Return of Detachments of the Depot embarked for New South Wales on board Convict Ships.

Names of the Ships.	Officers' Names on Board each Ship.		Strength of Detachment.				Dates of Embarkation and Arrival.	
			Sergeants.	Corporals.	Drummers.	Privates.	Embarked.	Arrived.
Morley	Captain ... Ensign......	Hunt .... Alexander ...	2	3	1	44	27 Sept. 1827	8th March, 1828; except John Hill, Private, drowned on the passage, 29th Nov., 1827.
Asia	Lieutenant	Edwards.........	1	1	...	16	1 Sept. 1827	15th March, 1828.
Hooghly ...	Captain ...	Wilman		...	...	1	17 Oct. 1827	27th February, 1828.
Mariner ...	Captain ...	Jackson	1	1	...	23	18 Oct. 1827	15th March, 1828.
Borodina	Captain ... Ensign......	Aubin .... Aubin	1	3	...	44	6 Dec., 1827	17th July, 1828.
Mangles	Lt. & Adjt. Lieutenant	Hill .... Kidd............	1	2	...	...	9 Jan., 1828	3rd June, 1828.
Bussorah...	Lieutenant	Fraser, 26 Rgt.	1	...	...	24	... ...	1st September, 1828.
Merchant..	Captain ...	Daveny	...	...	...	1	... ...	14th September, 1828.
		Total Embarked...	7	10	1	153		

APPENDIX LETTER C.

Correspondence relative to granting permission for Fifty-seventh Regiment to wear the word "Albuhera" and Badge, &c.

CURRAGH CAMP, 1*st May*, 1873.

SIR,

I have the honour to request you will move His Royal Highness the Field-Marshal Commanding-in-Chief to obtain Her Majesty's permission for the Regiment under my command to wear the word "Albuhera," with a laurel wreath round the number as a badge on their forage caps and shoulder straps. I beg to enclose a copy of a letter showing that such permission was granted in the year 1816, and to add that this badge has been worn on the buttons ever since that time. I request this favour in consequence of the adoption of an universal button throughout the Service, which has deprived the Regiment of a decoration granted by Royal Warrant and of which the men have ever been justly proud.

The Military Secretary, Horse-Guards, London.

I have, &c.,
(Sd.) R. A. LOGAN, *Colonel, Lieutenant-Colonel Commg. 57th Regiment.*

Copy of a Letter from the Adjutant-General, Horse-Guards, to the Officer Commanding 57th Regiment.

SIR,

51 / 57th Foot / 883 C. 12964.

With reference to your letter of the 1st inst., addressed to the Military Secretary, requesting permission for the Regiment under your command to wear as a badge the word "Albuhera" surrounded by a laurel wreath, I am directed by H.R.H. the Field-Marshal Commanding-in-Chief to request that you will be so good as to forward for approval a pattern of the proposed badge.

You are also requested to state whether you allude to Glengarry caps or Officers' caps only. I am to add that any badge on the shoulder straps of Officers' patrol jackets must be above, and separate from the numeral, and that men are not allowed to wear badges on anything except their Glengarry caps and collars.

Horse-Guards, I have, &c.,
War Office, 23rd May, 1873. (Sd.) SOAME JENYNS.

Copy of a Letter from Colonel R. A. Logan, C.B., to Adjutant-General, Horse-Guards, London. No. 375/73 C. 12964.

CURRAGH CAMP, *24th June,* 1873.

SIR,

With reference to your letter 51/57th Foot/860 C. 12964. of the 23rd ultimo, I have the honour to forward a pattern of the proposed badge for the Officers' and men's forage caps and Glengarry caps, also for the shoulder straps of the Officers' patrol jackets of the Regiment under my command, and to request that you will be pleased to obtain the permission of His Royal Highness the Field-Marshal Commanding-in-Chief for their approval.

The Adjutant-General, Horse-Guards, London.

I have, &c.,
(Sd.) R. A. LOGAN, *Colonel,*
Lieutenant-Colonel Commg.
57th Regiment.

Copy of a Letter from the Adjutant-General, Horse-Guards, to Officer Commanding 57th Regiment C. 14573 50/57 Foot/864

HORSE-GUARDS,
WAR OFFICE, *5th July,* 1873.

SIR,

By desire of the Field-Marshal Commanding-in-Chief

I have the honour to acknowledge the receipt of your letter of the 24th ult., and to request that you will be pleased to state for the information of His Royal Highness what authority exists in the Records of the Regiment for its wearing the "laurel wreath."

The letter dated Horse-Guards, 3rd February, 1816, authorised the word "*Albuhera*" to be borne on the colours and appointments of the Fifty-seventh Foot, but no mention is made of the "laurel wreath," as stated in your letter of the 1st May last, although it was worn on the buttons of the Regiment.

The Officer Commanding 57th Regiment.

I have, etc.,
(Sd.) J. W. ARMSTRONG.
Deputy-Adjutant-General.

Copy of a Letter from Colonel R. A. Logan, C.B., to Adjutant-General, Horse-Guards, London, No. 416/73

CURRAGH CAMP, 8*th July*, 1873.

SIR,

In reply to your letter C. 14572 57/57th Foot/884 of 5th July, 1873, I have the honour to state for the information of the Field-Marshal Commanding-in-Chief that I am unable to find in the Records of the Regiment any special authority for its wearing the "laurel wreath" in addition to the word "Albuhera," but I am of opinion that such must have been granted, as the wreath has always been worn on the sealed-pattern button, and is considered an essential part of the decoration. We request sanction to wear it on our caps and shoulder straps, now that we no longer wear it on our buttons.

I have, &c.,
(Signed) R. A. LOGAN, *Colonel,*
Lieutenant-Colonel Commanding 57th Regiment.

The Adjutant-General, Horse-Guards, London.

Copy of a Letter from the Adjutant General, Horse Guards, to Officer Commanding 57th Regiment C. 15058

57
57th Foot
885

HORSE GUARDS,

WAR OFFICE, *4th August*, 1873.

SIR,

I have the honour, by direction of the Field-Marshal Commanding-in-Chief, to acknowledge the receipt of your letter of the 8th ultimo, and in enclosing the drawings of badges proposed to be worn on the forage caps and shoulder straps of the 57th Regiment, to request you will be pleased to furnish for His Royal Highness's inspection patterns of badges prepared in accordance with these drawings, which must be returned to the Adjutant-General.

I have, &c.,

(Signed) G. WOLSELEY,

(For Adjutant-General).

Officer Commanding 57th Regiment,
Curragh.

CURRAGH CAMP, *6th August*, 1873.

SIR,

With reference to Horse Guards Letter C. 15058
51
57th Foot
885
I have the honour to forward patterns of badges prepared in accordance with annexed drawings.

I have, &c.,

(Signed) R. A. LOGAN, *Colonel,*

Lieut.-Colonel Commanding 57th Regiment.

Adjutant-General, Horse Guards,
London.

Copy of a Letter from Colonel R. A. Logan, C.B., to Adjutant-General, Horse Guards, $\frac{\text{No. 569}}{73}$

CURRAGH CAMP, 9*th September*, 1873.

Sir,

With reference to Horse Guards letter C. 15058 $\frac{57}{\frac{\text{57th Foot}}{885}}$ I have the honour to request you will inform me whether the pattern badges (forwarded on the 6th August, 1873), to be worn on the forage caps and shoulder straps of the Regiment under my command have yet been approved of, as the Regiment is under orders to proceed to Ceylon early in November. I am desirous of obtaining this information previous to embarkation in order to enable me to make arrangements for the supply of badges both to Officers and men.

The Adjutant-General, Horse-Guards.

I have, etc.,
(Sd.) R. A. LOGAN, *Colonel,*
Lieutenant-Colonel Commg.
57*th Regiment.*

Copy of a Letter from Adjutant-General, Horse-Guards, to Officer Commanding 57*th Regiment* $\frac{57}{\frac{\text{57th Foot}}{887}}$ C. 1873.

HORSE-GUARDS,
WAR OFFICE, 15*th September*, 1873.

Sir,

In reply to your letter of the 9th inst., relative to the pattern badges for forage caps and shoulder straps proposed to be worn in the Regiment under your command, I have to inform you that no decision can be arrived at on the subject until the return of H.R.H. the Field Marshal Commanding-in-Chief.

I have, etc.,
(Sd.) SOAME JENYNS, *A.A.G.*

Officer, Commanding 57*th Regiment,*
Curragh.

Copy of a Letter from Adjutant-General, Horse-Guards, to Officer Commanding 57*th Regiment* $\frac{51}{\frac{\text{57th Foot}}{887}}$

HORSE-GUARDS,
WAR OFFICE, 3*rd October*, 1873.

SIR,

I am directed by the Field Marshal Commanding-in-Chief, to acknowledge the receipt of your letter of the 9th ultimo, and to acquaint you that H.R.H. approves of the badges forwarded therewith, and which are now returned, being worn on the forage caps and shoulder straps of the Regiment under your command, the dark blue on the forage caps, that in scarlet on the shoulder straps of the Officers above the numeral.

I am to request that you will be pleased to forward one of each of these badges, to be deposited in the Officers' pattern room, at the Horse-Guards, War Office.

The Officer Commanding Fifty-seventh Regiment, Curragh.

I have, etc.,
(Sd.) J. W. ARMSTRONG,
Deputy-Adjutant-General.

Copy of a Letter from Colonel R. A. Logan, C.B., to Adjutant-General, Horse Guards, No. 243.

SIR,

CURRAGH CAMP, 28*th October*, 1873.

Adverting to former correspondence on the subject of badges to be worn by the Regiment under my command, I have the honour to request you will be good enough to inform me whether it is to be understood that a similar ornament (only of brass), to that authorised to be worn on the shoulder straps of the Officers, may be worn on the collar of the men's tunics and kersey frocks.

The Adjutant-General, Horse-Guards.

I have, etc.,
(Sd.) R. A. LOGAN, *Colonel,*
Lieutenant-Colonel Commg.
Fifty-seventh Regiment.

Copy of a Letter from the Adjutant-General, Horse-Guards, to Officer Commanding 57th Regiment, 51/57th Foot/893 C. 3525.

HORSE GUARDS,

WAR OFFICE,

SIR, *22nd September*, 1873.

I am directed by H.R.H. the Field-Marshal Commanding-in-Chief to acknowledge the receipt of your letter of the 28th ult., and to acquaint you that the badge authorised to be worn on the shoulder-straps of the Officers of the Regiment under your command may be worn (only made of brass) on the collars of the men's tunics and kersey frocks.

I am to add that four of the badges should be sent to the Director of Clothing, Pimlico, for approval and sealing, three to be retained in the pattern room, and the fourth to be returned to you for the guidance of future supplies. The cost to the public must not exceed 4½d. a pair.

I have, etc.,

(Sd.) F. S. VACHER, *Deputy-Adjutant,*
(For Adjutant-General.)

The Officer
Commanding 57th Regiment,
Curragh.

Death of Lieutenant-Colonel J. Stewart.—Succession of Lieutenant-Colonel Charles Mansfield Clarke.

Lieutenant-Colonel J. Stewart was invalided from Ceylon, and died in Jersey, after his return to England, on the 6th May, 1878.

Since the body of this work was in type, Major Charles Mansfield Clarke succeeded to the command of the Regiment, *vice* Lieutenant-Colonel James Stewart, deceased.

Lieutenant-Colonel Charles Mansfield Clarke was appointed Ensign in 1856, Lieutenant in 1859, Captain in 1867, Major in 1876 and Lieutenant-Colonel May 7th, 1878. He served in the 57th Regiment with the column under Colonel Warre on the Taptee River in co-operation with the Central India Field Force in 1858; served also in the New Zealand War of 1861, and was present at the operations before Te Arei. Also during the war in 1863-66 was present as Adjutant of the 57th Regiment at the action of Watikara (mentioned in despatches), and as D.A.Q.M.G. from June, 1863, to March, 1866, in the province of Taranaki, including the action near Potoho, capture of the Maori positions at Almahu, Kaitake, Mataibawa, and Te Arei; operations at Warea and Te Parea, and various minor affairs. (Repeatedly mentioned in despatches.)

Captain Charles Picot, appointed Major, January 23rd, 1878.

Captain Jas. R. K. Tredennick, appointed Major, May 7th, 1878.

APPENDIX OF CORRESPONDENCE.

Copy of a letter from Lieutenant-General Inglis to the Marquis of Londonderry.

BRIGHTON, *2nd May*, 1828.

MY LORD,

It is with great regret I observe in your History of the Peninsular War, that your Lordship mentions that the 57th Regiment lost their colours at the Battle of Albuhera, and in the same paragraph, that many prisoners were made by the enemy.

My being in command of the 57th Regiment on that day will be a sufficient apology for my addressing you on this subject, which your Lordship will admit my feelings as a soldier are naturally most deeply interested in. I take the liberty to annex a copy of the paragraph alluded to, with one or two remarks.

I have the honor to be,

My Lord,

Your most obedient servant,

(Signed) WM. INGLIS,

Lieutenant-General.

Lieutenant-General the Marquis of Londonderry, &c. &c.

(COPY). PAGE 535. QUARTO EDITION.

At this moment we had lost a whole Brigade of Artillery, a large number of prisoners, and eight stand of colours belonging to the Buffs, the 66th, the 48th, and the 57th Regiment.

REMARKS.

The 57th Regiment brought into the field on the 16th of May, 1811, at the Battle of Albuhera, 579 rank and file, out of which number 415 were killed and wounded; the remaining 164 were marched off the field by Lieutenant-Adjutant Maine, who was only the fourteenth officer in rank at the commencement of the action, the colours are in my possession, and not one man was missing.

WM. INGLIS,
Lieutenant-General.

Copy of a letter from the Marquis of Londonderry to Lieutenant-General Inglis.

HOLDERNESS HOUSE, *May 9th*, 1828.

SIR,

On my arrival from Paris, yesterday, I received your letter of the 2nd instant, I much regret that there should have been any inaccuracy on my part in my allusion to the 57th Regiment, my information as to the events of the Battle of Albuhera was collected hastily at the moment, and I was not a personal observer in the field.

The passage you allude to, mentions at one moment we lost a whole Brigade of Artillery, a large number of prisoners belonging to several different corps, but there is no specification of any number of prisoners, particularly to the 57th Regiment, and out of 415 killed and wounded, it is not surprising if amongst these, prisoners were stated to exist; with regard to the colours, some were at one moment taken, as I am informed; but your own knowledge clearly proves the standards of the 57th were not taken, and if there is a second edition I shall be very glad to rectify an error by construction, which, however, permit me to say, I consider as reflecting not in the smallest degree upon the corps who so gallantly and gloriously triumphed at the conclusion of that memorable battle, and I hope you will permit me to add, from the various opportunities which I had of remarking the 57th, they do not possess many more sincere admirers than myself.

I have the honor to be,
&c. &c. &c.,
(Signed) V. L.

Lieutenant-General,
SIR WM. INGLIS, K.C.B.

Second Letter from General Inglis to Lord Londonderry.

BRIGHTON, 18*th July*, 1828.

MY LORD,

I am extremely sorry to observe in the second edition of your Lordship's narrative of the Peninsular War it still appears that the 57th Regiment lost their colours at the Battle of Albuhera on the 16th May, 1811, and that it likewise appears in the Naval and Military Magazine as an abstract from your Lordship's history.

I beg to refer your Lordship to my former Letter on this subject, with your Lordship's reply, dated 9th May, 1828. Considering the high authority of your Lordship, holding the first official situation in that Army at the perod, I trust you will allow me to express myself, feeling it an imperious duty to defend the honour of my old friends as their commander, besides my very long service with them, having entered the Service as Ensign in the 57th Regiment in the year 1779.

I have the honour to be,
My Lord,
Your Lordship's most obedient humble Servant,
(Signed) W. INGLIS.

Lieutenant-General the Most Noble
The Marquis of Londonderry, &c., &c.

Answer to second letter from General Inglis.

July 21*st*, 1828.

Sir,

I am honoured with your second letter, in date the 18th July, relative to the error in my book as to the 57th Regiment.

In the next edition your letters to me and my answers will appear in the Appendix, and I am entirely ready to admit your more accurate knowledge and information made relative to the Corps commanded by yourself.

I have the honour to be,

Your obedient,

(Signed) Vane Londonderry.

W. Mitchell & Co., Printers, 39, Charing Cross.

CPSIA information can be obtained
at www.ICGtesting.com
Printed in the USA
LVOW13*1415141117
556253LV00011B/255/P

9 780265 901519